D0632769

THE MALE MIND AT WORK

THE MALE MIND AT WORK

DEBORAH J. SWISS

a woman's guide to working with men

PERSEUS PUBLISHING
Cambridge, Massachusetts

A CIP record for this book is available from the Library of Congress
ISBN 0-7382-0327-0

Perseus Publishing is a member of the Perseus Books Group.

Find us on the World Wide Web at http://www.perseuspublishing.com

Text design by Jeff Williams
Set in 11-point Palatino by Perseus Publishing Services

First printing, July 2000
1 2 3 4 5 6 7 8 9 10—03 02 01 00

To Audrey Block, Kathy Puccia, and Judy Walker

CONTENTS

Acknowledgments

My friends and family provided inspiration throughout every phase of this project. My children, Alex and Alison Rice-Swiss, hold the most special place in my heart and make me very proud. As parents and grandparents, Ed and Peg Swiss have always offered extraordinary support that I truly treasure.

Patti Hunt Dirlam, Terri Goldberg, Cynthia Johnson, and Judy and Harry Warren are friends I cherish. Kay Coughlin, my dear friend and neighbor, always extends kind words and good cheer along with her superb proofreading skills. Leslie Brody offered valuable comments that were particularly helpful to the early phases of manuscript development. I also thank the superb staff at Cary Memorial Library for their assistance.

My literary agent Mike Snell, with whom I celebrate ten years of work and friendship, deserves special praise for his brilliant editing, excellent advice, and good humor from book development to final draft. Jacqueline Murphy, my editor at Perseus Publishing, is, without question, the best editor on the planet. Marco Pavia gracefully moved the book through its final production phases. Cherie Potts and Pat Steffens once again provided first-rate transcription skills. And I thank the men I interviewed for giving so generously of their time.

This book is dedicated to three extraordinary women and exceptional friends who cheer me on in everything I do: Audrey Block, Kathy Puccia, and Judy Walker.

Introduction

QUESTION: What career advice will you pass on to your son?
ANSWER: "The system is built for you. So go in there and kick butt."
QUESTION: What will you say to your daughter about her career?
ANSWER: "Hey, you're coming into someone else's stadium. You'll have to play by a different set of rules."

— *John Lucas, 33, Marketing Director,* **Fortune 500 Company**

This single comment, more than any other, encapsulates the reasons I wrote this book. While I do not agree with John's perspective, it provides an eye-opening peek into the male mind at work. Why would a young, highly educated man feel this way, viewing his daughter's career so differently from his son's?

The degree of comfort, confidence, and control we bring to the workplace strongly affects our success and depends on our self-perception, our view of where we fit or don't fit in the culture, and the type of reinforcement we receive growing up and later from peers and superiors. In many environments, gender plays a role, defining how we evaluate and react to everyday business situations. The terrain often looks quite different for women because the system to which John refers is designed to support and reflect a male code of work.

For over a year, I conducted in-depth interviews with 52 successful men about how they think and act in the workplace. These men work in businesses ranging from start-ups to law firms, from wholesale apparel to high tech, and in positions from middle to top-level management. All hold college degrees and many hold advanced degrees. With the option of remaining anonymous, the men I interviewed responded openly and honestly to the questions women most want answered, questions I heard from the women I interviewed for my two earlier books, *Women and the Work/Family Dilemma* and *Women Breaking Through.*

For instance:

- Do men really view work through a different gender lens?
- Why don't men take things so personally on the job?
- Are men more confident or do they just put on a good front?
- What do men really think about working with women? What stands in the way of effective alliances between women and men at work?
- What traits do they admire about the female mind at work, and why?

Five among the 52 men I interviewed serve as CEOs, in companies ranging in size from $20 million to $1 billion. The men vary in age from 29 to 64, with the majority in their thirties and forties. They work in Fortune 500 companies, high-tech firms, brokerage companies, banks, consulting, academia, and entrepreneurial settings. My sample includes interviews with a father and son, and two men, self-identified as gay, who share their unique vantage point on issues that perpetuate the gender gap.

My interviews uncovered a broad spectrum of opinions about women in the workplace. For example, a 39-year-old CEO of a $1 billion company described his own slow and arduous journey toward fully welcoming women at the top. In the end, he believes his newfound awareness has enhanced his own leadership and effectiveness for his shareholders. Other men voiced concern about what they see as political correctness carried to extremes, causing them great discomfort over working too closely with women and an abiding fear of false accusations of discrimination. At the extreme end of the spectrum, a 34-year-old Wall Street vice president boldly admitted: "I'd rather there were not women working here."

As men spoke of the comfort they feel in their own careers, they often attributed their sense of security to the majority position bestowed on them in most business environments. Journalist Bruce Kohl, observing that men seldom think about the automatic power that maleness accords them in many settings, commented: "It's as if men perceive that you could drop a boulder into a pond and it's not going to have any impact as long as they're getting done what needs to be done."

Even so, a man's supremely confident stance sometimes masks insecurity. Behind the bravado and the swagger of confidence, men often suffer the same doubts and vulnerabilities to which women will more readily admit. What men show to the outside world, however, differs dramatically. The brave face provides yet another layer of protective gear men wear to guard themselves against revealing emotions of insecurity, self-doubt, or fear. As attorney Barry Walker puts it: "The male psyche will do everything in its power to prevent a man from admitting he has been wounded."

Of course, such emotional distance also offers certain advantages in the workplace. For starters, it enables men to suppress any inclination toward unwarranted self-blame by maintaining an attitude that focuses on their accomplishments rather than their mistakes. Men, for instance, readily conclude that a mistake is just a mistake, something that can offer valuable lessons for future growth. And, in many cases, men decide that a jerk is just a jerk, feeling no overriding urge to "fix" a difficult person or to change their own behavior to appease him or her.

Men also demonstrated self-deprecating humor as they identified their own frailties. "Guys are much more like dogs," asserted one investment partner. "With a dog, you raise your voice and say 'No!' and the dog will look at you and get it." Men of all ages expressed admiration for unique perspectives offered by the female mind at work. One man, age 45, working in a predominantly male field, admitted: "Most of the women I work with are smarter and more qualified than the men at this level. They had to be just to get here!" Some men even voiced a strong preference for working for a female boss. Ray Ingalls, a 29-year-old business manager says, "I generally prefer working with women rather than men. I'd rather have relationships that are based not on competitiveness but on working in a combined effort toward the same goal."

What surprised me most was the honesty with which men answered my questions. Because I wanted to hear truthful answers, not the answers a man might voice publicly, I offered each man the option of anonymity. Some men granted permission to use their names and others requested a pseudonym, but all talked openly about their careers and their companies, their professional challenges and successes, and their generally unspoken vulnerabilities.

Some voiced opinions I found offensive, such as when they focused on issues of a woman's appearance or of holding women to a higher standard than the men in the office. Others described exemplary management styles, inspiring for both men and women and profitable for any organization. Not only do their responses begin to unravel the mysteries of the male mind at work, but they provide vital knowledge women can use to open windows of opportunity for themselves.

What really goes on behind the gamesmanship that often permeates the way men transact business?

Should a woman even listen to a male boss who recommends that she incorporate "swagger in her step"?

Why do some men prefer to work for a woman?

What leadership secrets enable men to welcome and support top-notch talent, regardless of gender?

What does it take to revise the unwritten rules of work?

How do men define life balance and success?

As men answered these questions, they shattered some myths about what really goes on in the male mind while confirming for women realities about gender differences that may never change. *The Male Mind at Work* does not suggest that women should turn into men, or vice versa. Rather than engage in a debate about who is better at business, this book explores the male mind in an effort to create the sort of understanding that can promote a woman's success. Firsthand accounts, gleaned from more than 1,100 pages of interview transcripts, offer surprising revelations about the achievements and missteps of men, providing powerful inside information that will heighten a woman's confidence in leveraging her own unique strengths.

Insights into how and why men practice and perpetuate the unwritten rules of work offer women a deeper understanding of how to interpret the workplace cues that men relay so naturally to one another, among a group that has formed bonds both subtle and secure, unspoken and intractable. This information generates strategies women can put to immediate use, including ways to react when superiors pass on their ideas, what it takes to win recognition for their talent, and ways to counteract dangerous stereotypes and misconceptions about women at work.

A Look Through the Male Lens

Of course, not all men think and act alike; nor do all women. We all know hard-hitting and aggressive women and gentle and acquiescent men. Each of us carries some measure of conventional masculine and feminine traits. Yet men and women often approach a broad range of career issues differently: conveying competence; facing competition; participating on a team and building business alliances; saying no and setting limits; dealing with difficult people and difficult situations; managing and motivating others.

I do not share the opinions voiced by many of the men I interviewed, but I learned from every one of them, as they revealed surprising disclosures about what makes the male mind tick. The stories these successful businessmen told me in their own words provide fresh and useful insights for women who feel frustrated, or unnecessarily challenged, by men who seem to speak a different language and play by a different set of rules.

By looking through the male lens on work, a woman can gain valuable truths about the male psyche so that she can rise above gender politics, compete with confidence, and succeed on her own terms.

1

The Confidence Game

Adding Swagger to Your Step

"Women need to swagger," announced Eric Stephens, a vice president in the biotech industry. When I heard these words, I tried to put aside the first image that sprang to mind: a tough-looking woman striding into the conference-room doors with six-guns strapped to her hips. Shouldering aside a couple of men, she slaps the dust off her chaps and mutters: "Let's get down to business." No, Eric meant something quite different.

During a performance review with a woman he ranked as a star among his 150-person staff, he voiced only one criticism: "Jean, you need to swagger. You need to be more self-confident because you're better than you think you are." Using a specific example, Eric pointed to Jean's recent presentation capping off six months of sensitive negotiations and a signed business contract. "It was very earnest, but there was absolutely no swagger. There are times when swagger is called for." In Eric's view, a swagger expresses confidence, self-esteem, steadfast faith in yourself, a position that inspires others to take you seriously.

In Eric's mind, by adopting what he deems a weaker posture, Jean failed to project significant confidence to convince her audience that she fully controlled the situation. Eric's viewpoint boils down to packaging, rather than substance. "She is incredibly well-qualified, has excellent business judgment, works very hard, and is very competitive," Eric insists. "She is typically better informed and better prepared than most people. But she needs to do a better job of making that information known to everybody. She gave a presentation today in which she took the senior management of the company through an excellent summary of a major business development deal—very sensitive negotiations that she handled extremely well. The only thing missing was that she didn't broadcast more of a sense of assurance." Eric says the predominantly male group did not fully grasp Jean's exceptional competence simply because she did not transmit self-assurance in a way they would understand.

Eric's advice for Jean says a lot about how men evaluate business associates. If women dominated the management team, would they measure confidence and competence the same way? Eric's observation that Jean is better than she thinks she is opens up an interesting line of inquiry. When it comes to judging a person's ability, how significantly does style weigh into the equation?

When a man enters a business meeting, he usually encounters a majority who basically look and act the same way he does. A woman, on the other hand, often enters an environment where the majority look and act differently. The men measure both the man and the woman with the same yardstick. The more swagger they see, the more respect they feel. For men, swagger can include bragging and touting accomplishments in order to form bonds with other men, while for women, such showing off may get in the way of establishing interpersonal connections with other women. Eric's judgment about Jean echoed a theme I heard from many men. In their eyes, women do not always clothe their solid substance with a style men applaud and understand. In fact, some men went a step further when musing about women and the confidence factor, bluntly asserting: "Women need more self-esteem."

Joe Leghorn, an attorney who has mentored many women and men, obsbrves: "I think a fair number of women have self-confidence issues. I encourage them to believe in themselves, reminding them that men tend to bluff their way through anything." Mark Kramer, a college professor, says: "I see more confidence in men than I do in women." For some men, believing in yourself matters as much as the quality of your decision. In Mark's view: "It's OK to be wrong. I'd rather you be confident and wrong. At least you're taking a stand." Several men readily admitted that they believe a man can get away with more mistakes than a woman can, partly, it seems, because a mistake does not take the swagger out of a man's stride as much as it does a woman's. Why? Largely because, as men told me, women are often held to a higher performance standard.

Without a doubt, bluffing your way through a situation can serve a man well. A career counselor once described the phenomenon beautifully. Men, she said, feel perfectly comfortable applying for a job for which they possess only 50 percent of the requisite skills. Women, she said, only feel comfortable if they possess 70 percent of the necessary skills. In the course of conducting interviews for this book, I ran across one man in the midst of a job hunt. His strategy? Go for the jobs that he most wants, even if he lacks some of the stated requirements. "I'll go ahead and apply for the job. When the time comes, I'll grab a book on the subject and figure out what I don't know." That's another example of swagger: marching confidently into the bullring without a sharp sword. And why wouldn't men swagger, when their behavior is reinforced by unwritten rules that reflect the male code?

Work culture certainly plays a leading role in defining which communication styles will draw the most attention. Eric and Jean work in what he calls a "verbal food fight" culture. "There is a high noise level, and in order to play in that," he explains, "you have to be a little rough-and-tumble." Swagger helps. "You don't have to have the answers, but you have to be ready to dish it out. That qualifies you to be part of the crowd."

A supremely secure woman, however, may feel no need to flaunt her talent, adopting instead a less aggressive posture. Even as young girls, many women learn to act modestly about touting their abilities and accomplishments. A good girl just lets her talent speak for itself.

Concerning the typically male style of projecting assurance, Leslie Brody, associate professor of psychology at Boston University, cites twenty years of research that has consistently found that girls and boys view their accomplishments differently: "Boys—from elementary school through high school—rate themselves as more confident even when their actual performance scores on a test are the same as the girls'." Other studies, Leslie says, have examined how men and women rate the effect of boasting. "The women all felt that other women would dislike them and judge them as being smug." In marked contrast, Leslie observes, "The men didn't have any of these feelings and, in fact, they felt that the people they were boasting to would like them more. Men have no trouble saying 'I did this' and being proud of it." Of course, men expect other men to do likewise.

If a woman understands why men act the way they do, she can use that knowledge to diffuse the effect of objectionable workplace behaviors dictated by the male code. For example, once a woman acknowledges that men welcome verbal dueling among colleagues, she need not feel challenged by behaviors she might normally deem ridiculous.

Ever since Eric conveyed his learn-to-swagger advice to Jean, she has adopted a new perspective on the verbal games at work. Eric now observes: "Jean is much more comfortable challenging people when they come back to her with faulty arguments." While her level of inner confidence may have always been high, Jean now sees more clearly what it takes to reach her primarily male audience. With Eric's blunt feedback, Jean developed a style to showcase her talent, more effectively asserting herself among the noisy boys.

Noisy Boys

One eleven-year-old girl with an affinity for math described what she observed in her sixth-grade class: "The boys are jumping up and down raising both hands. And then they start yelling out the answers—which usually aren't even right. It's *really* annoying."

Bill Winn, a psychologist, suggests that from childhood on, girls confront the challenge of making themselves heard above "the noisy boys in the classroom who are encouraged to verbalize and assert their opinions, rightly or wrongly." This challenge, he says, follows many women into the workplace: "To the extent that this behavior continues in the office or board room, it may be seen as immodest, uncharacteristic, or unfeminine for a woman to assert herself—so she's hit by a kind of double whammy." If she remains quiet, no one hears her. If she imitates the boys and becomes too noisy, others may dismiss her as too pushy.

Many women feel like outsiders in the world where men practice their age-old rituals for proving their power. As I observed a young boy, probably seven or eight years old, heading toward a baseball field full of boys, I could not help but speculate how he might behave years later in a business suit. With arms swinging widely, chest puffed out, head held high, the boy jumped right into the game with a look that did not question, for even a second, his right to belong. In marked contrast, I have often seen young girls move cautiously, taking care not to disrupt the group and invite their disapproval. In a male-dominated setting such politeness sometimes becomes a liability, but just how far should a woman go in the direction of assertiveness?

Regardless of our degree of self-assurance, most of us let signals from our peers boost or erode our confidence. The words "rough-and-tumble" that Eric used to describe his workplace also fit one of the male cultural stereotypes. Even at a young age, boys compete with each other both as a way to bond with one another and as a way to establish relative positions in the boy hierarchy. Girls, on the other hand, try to equalize the status of all group members. As psychologist William Pollack observes in his book *Real Boys: Rescuing Our Sons from the Myths of Boyhood,* "Boys tend to engage in active, competitive games. Girls, on the other hand, tend to play cooperatively in smaller groups." For boys, he says, "taunting, boasting, and jousting with one another is part of the fun."

Pat Heim, a gender consultant, describes scenarios like this as "verbal chest beating." Men, she says, engage in this behavior as a means of establishing their position among other men. "The misconception comes when women label this as inappropriate behavior, not realizing that if you live in a hierarchy, you'd better do some chest beating or you end up at the bottom of the pyramid. And that's not a comfortable place for a man to be."

A hierarchical male culture emerges early on when young boys play together and forge friendships. Samuel Shem and Janet Surrey, authors of *We Have to Talk: Healing Dialogues Between Women and Men,* observe that young boys focus on their power over, rather than connection to, others. "Groups fall into little patriarchies and hierarchies, with up-down, power-over rules and orders." Women, on the other hand, often rely on what Deborah Tannen, author of *You Just Don't Understand,* terms "onedownmanship" to develop and solidify their relationships. By avoiding a game of oneupmanship, by evening out rather than asserting power, a woman establishes what Tannen describes as a symmetrical connection.

According to the male code, when men talk to one another, they expect interruption—in fact, they welcome and even value it. In contrast, suggests Tannen, interruption for a woman may signal impoliteness or a lack of control, stifling collegiality. Ironically, in a man's view, interruption equals control. In staff meetings, Ray Ingalls, a business manager, sees a consistent pattern of men ignoring or talking over the few women in the room. "Women are easily overlooked if they don't speak out," he observes. "If women don't offer their opinion, no one is going to ask them, but men will ask other men." To make herself heard, suggests Ray, a woman must overcome her resistance to interrupting and speak out forcefully, symbolically beating her chest, if necessary.

Many men never outgrow the habit of using noisy interactions to test each other's mettle. As Eric explains: "You have to be willing to go toe-to-toe and get very argumentative." Half the time, he says, the other person does not want to express a strong conviction as much as he wants to see what you're made of.

At the beginning of our conversation, Eric told me that he rates the women in his department as top performers: "The women have star quality. The guys are only working on it." Why, then, did he urge Jean to develop some swagger? To level the playing field. As Eric knows, less qualified men can project more confidence than more highly qualified women.

The Mask of Invulnerability

Do boys generally receive more early reinforcement about the value and power of confident behavior? According to psychologist Leslie Brody, they do, partly because they have enjoyed a position of gender superiority since the first time they played with girls on the playground. When I asked Leslie to comment on whether men actually possess more confidence than women or whether they simply act that way, she responded: "Both are true. Men probably *are* more confident than women, and they also are better at masking any fears or doubts they may have."

Early in their lives, little boys become fully schooled in what it means to command power and status. Leslie explains: "Girls learn very early on to believe that they *are* viewed as lower status and less powerful. That undermines confidence." In part, this happens through the physical dominance that boys usually exert in their play.

From about adolescence on, a girl may experience varying levels of belief in herself and her abilities. In contrast to this experience, Barry Walker, an attorney, says: "I can't remember a time in my life when I wasn't fundamentally secure about what I was doing." Barry also admits: "Walking into new circumstances with new people, with new duties and responsibilities, you always have some level of doubt. But then your natural being comes out and you have enough faith in your mental acuity or your articulateness or your leadership skills to overcome the angst that is created by a challenging environment."

By the time men enter the workplace, the "I must carry myself confidently" strategy has become second nature. Many men point to their junior high years as the pivotal point when confidence began to play a crucial role in their behavior. Eric comments, "In junior high, boys get schooled in affecting more self-confidence than the girls, even if you don't have it." To win the boys' game, at work and at play, you need confidence, whether based on substance or not.

Confidence spawns a sense of control, both over self and circumstances. Even when it comes fairly late in a man's development, it serves as a dominant factor in social interactions. Paul Meyers, a thirty-two-year-old CEO, described his experience of lacking confidence in middle school, then acquiring it later in life, as something that drives him today: "I was absolutely not confident growing up. I was a fat teenager who had the crap beaten out of me in middle school." He does, however, take great pride in the fact that he has managed to achieve overwhelming success in his career.

Paul believes that at some level men suffer fears about success and achievement, even if they don't show it. The differences in how they handle fear, he thinks, result from cultural expectations about behavior. "By the time boys hit middle school, we figure out that if you show your true feelings, somebody is going to beat the hell out of you—or torment you psychologically."

As someone responsible for a $50 million company, Paul now appreciates the usefulness of masking feelings of fear and self-doubt. When, for instance, he was engineering a major business deal, Paul needed to engage in some behind-the-scenes maneuvering or risk losing the contract. Throughout the process, despite a certain amount of anxiety, he strove to convey confidence to all concerned, especially his employees: "Part of my goal was to keep the troops in line, and in that effort, it becomes incredibly important not to panic and show fear," he says. "No matter how panicked the sales group got, I kept saying: 'OK, we're going to work through this. I am going to help you take care of it.'"

When telling this story, Paul likens himself to a pilot winging his plane through extreme turbulence: "You figure you're going to crash and the pilot may have wet his pants, but he sits there and calmly says: 'Don't worry. This is normal.' The pilot may be going berserk, but if he's cool, it takes some of the pressure off and you're cool." That mask of invulnerability represents a critical leadership skill, says Paul. "No matter how scared I am, or how much I think there is no way in hell we're going to pull this one off, I can't let my people feel that."

One business owner and former marine described that leadership skill in terms of a battlefield experience: "You can never let the enemy detect fear. If you doubt yourself for even one second, you could lose your life." In other words, skills, without confidence, mean nothing.

In answer to the question "Do men feel more secure or do they just act that way?" Barry Walker responded immediately: "We *appear* to be less woundable. We're great actors. Absolutely wonderful actors. We are no more secure than a woman of equal position. We just make it appear that we are. And part of the time we convince ourselves that we are."

For boys, the appearance of control also determines whether they succeed socially during their first interactions with members of the opposite sex. Paul remembers: "The guys who had the most success with women were the guys who had confidence." From an early age, he equated confidence with power: "There is something about confidence that is palpable in people. It sometimes gets mistaken as charisma, but there is a level of confidence that must be anthropological in nature."

Eric, recalling this defining period in his own life, talks of the adolescent days when nothing mattered more than peer approval. A quest for acceptance fueled his intense drive to act cool, confident, and in control, even when he felt exactly the opposite. For him, bragging provided both power and protection. As William Pollack, the psychologist, points out, bragging amounts to little more than "a façade of confidence and bravado that boys erect to hide what they perceive as a shameful sense of vulnerability."

Although external bravado may signal more internal vulnerability, standing your ground and steadfastly holding your own becomes an early measure of manhood. "Men have been taught to act more secure because you have to carry 'attitude' when you're playing sports or hanging out with a bunch of guys," Eric says. "If you sit there betraying your insecurity, there is a pack impulse that takes over."

Eric recalls a boy, desperate for approval, who overtly showed his vulnerability to the in-crowd. "Let's see how far we can get him to twist himself," became the group's refrain whenever this boy tried to join them. "After this happened three or four times, people had totally lost respect for him." In this context, a mask of invulnerability might have shielded the boy from derision and prompted greater acceptance.

Insights like Eric's offer clues for women about how and why men so fervently hide any hint of insecurity. By understanding the mask of invulnerability, women can learn to look beneath it for true male feelings, and they can even borrow it to succeed in situations when that stance is required.

The Shield of Confidence

Would men bother with projecting a secure demeanor if doing so didn't get results? Jim Barnes, a senior vice president at a brokerage firm, answered that question succinctly when he said: "Confidence is a huge issue when there's $20 million on the table." Referring to potential clients who size him up carefully when it comes to turning over their money to him, he says: "We listen to them, but we are also very definitive in making recommendations with great confidence. We don't want them walking out the door wondering 'Geez, is what they're recommending OK? I'm not sure they think so.'"

Whenever Dean Mechlowitz, a sales manager, walks into a meeting, with his boss or a client, he somehow always projects an aura of authority with few words and no noisy bravado. Having watched Dean in action, I asked him directly: "Do you ever doubt yourself?" He immediately responded: "No." Then he added with a knowing smile: "Never."

After Dean described his career history, I asked him, "At any point in your work life, have you said to yourself 'I can't do this', or 'I'm not sure I can do this'?" Again, he answered with a definitive "No." Throughout our conversation, Dean displayed a level of self-assurance that summarily dismisses fear, sponsors boldness, and reinforces the strong positions he dares to take.

Early in our interview, Dean alerted me that we might be interrupted by a call about a big telecommunications deal. When the phone rang, I could not help but note how he responded to the potential customer: "I hear what you're saying, but here's what we're able to do from our end. Call me back at three and we'll talk again." He sounded so confident, I might have bought swampland in Florida from him.

Conventional wisdom dictates that wooing an important customer requires a certain amount of deference. Instead, Dean always takes the upper hand in any business negotiation. Someone observing Dean for the first time might consider him unbelievably arrogant. But when you see Dean at his desk before 7:30 each morning and often after 7:30 in the evening, you realize he strives for *both* style and substance.

Dean has worked hard for his confidence. An engineer by training with a patented product on his resume, he has carved out his own lucrative niche in the telecom industry. Recruited for his current job by a man for whom he had worked at another company, Dean feels fully comfortable in his environment. He and his boss know and respect each other, and they each know what to expect from the other.

Does Dean's unwavering personal conviction come from deep inside, or does it represent a well-rehearsed act put on for the sake of customer approval, a powerful negotiation tool designed to close the deal? As a well-trained salesman, Dean knows full well that a customer's inclination to buy depends as much on belief in the salesperson as it does on faith in the product. Perhaps he has simply learned never to reveal even a hint of weakness or uncertainty. Or, maybe Dean truly suffers no self-doubt.

After talking with dozens of self-assured men, I came to see the phenomenon as a double-sided coin. One side of the coin displays an ability to dismiss certain emotions, while the other depicts careful training in the "big wheel" boy code. As Pollack suggests in *Real Boys*: "This is the imperative men and boys feel to achieve status, dominance, and power. Or understood another way, the 'big wheel' refers to the way in which boys and men are taught to avoid shame at all costs, to wear the mask of coolness, to act as though everything is going all right, as though everything is under control, even if it isn't."

Men routinely send themselves inspirational messages that perpetually refuel their professional ego and allow them to respond with polished assurance even when they do not feel close to being 100 percent certain. For many of the men I interviewed, all it takes is about 60-to-70 percent certainty to convince themselves that they know what they are doing.

Unshakable belief in yourself also gives you something to fall back on when the going gets rough, enabling you to circumvent emotions that might otherwise devolve into feelings of vulnerability. Marty Bennett, a twenty-nine-year-old sales representative, says: "Nothing really scares me except maybe being out of work for a year. But, you know, that doesn't even scare me because I know that if anything were to happen with my job, I could find another one quickly."

By figuring out what his customers want to see, Marty minimizes the chance that he will be anything other than successful. He steadfastly refuses to surrender to what he sees as a weak state of mind: "You have to be somewhat cocky because you know a customer can smell fear. And you can't let them think that they're taking any kind of a risk when they buy from you."

Men may experience fear but they will try hard not to show it because they wish to appear invulnerable, heroic, wearing what William Pollack calls the mask of masculinity. A life that centers on action rather than emotion encourages a man to ask: What's the worst that can happen? And if it does, how can I fix it? Even under the most dire circumstances, a man will go to great lengths both to resist certain emotions and to reveal as little as possible if he does succumb to them.

Like Marty, Dean Mechlowitz cites, as an example, the ultimate loss of control professionally: "If you lose your job, yeah, you'll be stressed out until you find another one, but as soon as you find a new job, you'll blame other people for your losing your job and say that they didn't know what they're doing anyway."

If confidence, real or imagined, conquers fear, then a lack of confidence makes you vulnerable to fear, undermining both talent and hard work. Ben Adams, a customer service manager, described what he perceives as widely varying levels of self-assurance among the women who report to him. Those who appear less secure undercut their credibility, severely limiting career opportunities. Ben explains: "Women [who work for me] are always asking for reassurance to make sure they're doing the right thing. They tend to get burned out faster because they are afraid, at every turn, of making a mistake." As their boss, Ben assumes the role of a coach when he tells them: "You own this. Make the decision. If you make a mistake, we'll correct it and move on."

As the supervisor of forty-five people, many of them female, Ben encourages his subordinates to believe in themselves and their abilities. "Women in this day and age should not let fear get in their way," he says. "A lot of women surpass what men can do in many areas."

An unwavering belief in yourself opens doors that otherwise might remain shut. When Mike Snell, a literary agent, reflects upon the differences he perceives between male and female writers just starting out, he says: "Men have more confidence at the outset. They've gained more confidence through socialization experiences—sports, the military, for example. A young man feels more optimistic that he can make it up the mountain, when you're standing at the bottom looking at the snowy peak, than the woman alongside him." Mike quickly adds that this sort of confidence does not reflect intelligence or capabilities. Men may find it somewhat easier to break in, but the women who do make it are strong and resilient: "I'd say the average woman author is older than male peers, having taken longer to get to the point where she feels confident that she has the knowledge to write a book." The real differences, he believes, are psychological, internal, intuitive, and emotional.

Self-assurance wavers more for some than for others, but men, by and large, share the ability to suppress self-doubt, concentrating instead on presenting a winning attitude. Coupled with emotional distance, the two powerfully reinforce one another and provide the foundation for the male code at work.

Show Me the Confidence

It goes without saying that belief in yourself augments all of the elements likely to accelerate a career: closing a deal, taking a risk, exerting leadership, making a difficult decision, recovering from a mistake, and getting noticed in an organization. But according to the male code, you must not only *feel* confident, you must convince the world of the fact. Men will trust and confide in a colleague who projects an attitude that says "If you stick with me, we'll both get to the top." By doing so, they win an open-arms welcome into the organization's informal channels of communication and become privy to career-enhancing and confidence-building information.

Bill Winn, a psychologist and executive coach, talks about the contagious effect of belief in yourself. He likens it to the positive influence of an "I can carry the ball" attitude that a star player uses to pump up a team. As Bill observes: "The kind of robustness that comes from being confident and self-reliant can give others a sense that 'This person has a can-do attitude and can deliver the goods.'"

Dean Mechlowitz agrees: "You can do things quietly, but you need to take credit for your ideas. Otherwise, you don't get raises or promotions." I asked Dean "How do you do that without people finding you too pushy?" He responded with a chuckle: "That's not the issue. Your question is very telling. When you do something, it's not too pushy to tell your boss what you've done." Touting your accomplishments need not be as blatant as saying, "I just did something wonderful!" Choosing the right words can make the point without making you look foolish: "Here's what I found out about the product. These are the errors it's causing. And here's what I'm going to do about it." In other words, you present the fact that you did a great job as just another piece of information.

As a gender consultant, Pat Heim observes that skillful male self-promoters are extraordinarily graceful about bringing the topic of conversation around to their successes. "You think you're talking about the time of day or the weather, and then suddenly, he's saying 'Well, yes, since you brought it up, I was the first human being ever to do that . . . and I did it cheaper and faster than anybody ever thought possible.'" Pat's reaction is: "How did we get to this topic? I don't remember asking about this."

Making your successes known, without appearing arrogant, takes practice. Unlike the chest-beating stance, decidedly off-putting for most women, women can make their achievements known in subtle ways that also bring reward and recognition. As an example, Pat cites a remote employee who started sending her weekly e-mails on the status of her projects. "Smart woman," Pat says. "She used the weekly report as a way of discussing her successes under the guise of keeping me updated."

Jeff Klein, a high-tech manager, observes that men, in many cases, have mastered the ability to cover any lapses in self-assurance by the very words they use. A man might say "We're going to do this," expressing his opinion with positive, action-oriented phrasing. A woman will more likely say "I've been thinking about some of the things we might do," which to Jeff connotes "a possible lack of confidence about which way to go." Although a man's approach may come across as more decisive and hard-hitting, Jeff also believes: "Underneath it all, both sexes can be just as insecure. The man is just covering it up."

Greg Block, a director at the North American Commission for Envi-romental Cooperation, suggests that the context in which a man acts often allows him to project a more self-assured stance than a woman who feels equally secure. "In traditional work environments, men have to exude confidence all the time or they're eroding image. They set out to create that image as deal-maker or decision-maker. Men do this, in part, through their social demeanor—the backslapping, the talk about sports, their comfort level initiating jokes, the way they speak in public. It all sends the message 'I'm in control.'"

In Greg's view, everybody loves a hero and a hero maker. Having observed successful self-promoters in both the political arena and in the private sector, he comments: "What seems to work well for them is giving credit to a lot of people. They tell stories about other people and they make them heroes. The effective ones don't undersell themselves, but in acknowledging other people's successes, it's not always out of a genuine interest in them. It's often partly a promotional strategy with an implied connection that puts them in the category of the individual they're talking about." At the other extreme, Greg sees self-promoters who do it so badly they actually put their careers in jeopardy.

Too Much of a Good Thing

Any strength pushed too far can become a weakness. While unassertiveness courts one set of problems, over-assertiveness creates another. Leslie Brody calls the latter the "always certain, sometimes right" syndrome, a situation in which too much self-glorification undermines control and backfires, for both men and women.

As Frank Andryauskas, a partner in an Internet start-up, considers the work environment his daughters will enter, he thinks about the delicate balance between earned confidence and unfounded bravado. Talking about long-term success, he points to a recent lesson learned by one of his daughters: "Sarah lost her first swim race today. And I basically said: 'Thank goodness.' On the one hand, you need confidence to succeed. On the other hand, you also need the reality of knowing that there is always someone better. Sooner or later, particularly in the business world when you start getting into the billion-dollar organizations, there is always someone better." You should avoid the peril, he says, of defining your identity too much in terms of star quality. "Then you can crash very rapidly and your self-esteem can be shattered."

Jeff Klein, too, warns against overplaying the bravado hand. Grabbing too much of the spotlight can quickly undermine credibility. He cited a woman who seemed to forget about her teammates the minute she stepped in front of senior management. Instead of talking about her group's efforts, she would begin every presentation with "*I* decided to do this. *I* put this in place." To Jeff, this approach telegraphed phoniness: "She was a great self-promoter and that kind of turned me off about her. I was always suspicious of her real capabilities."

When Eric Stephens offered Jean his developmental advice, he took care to distinguish swagger from self-promotion, viewing the former as positive and the latter as negative. The difference essentially boils down to an issue of style and degree. Assertively and courageously stepping forward with your good idea brings the right kind of recognition. Too much talk about yourself produces the opposite effect. Like many of the men to whom I spoke, Eric cautions, "The more you self-promote, the more obvious it is." People perceive insecurity in those who toot their own horn too loudly. For a woman, the balance is even more tenuous in settings where gender alone is likely to invoke close and critical scrutiny.

Mark Kramer, a professor, recalls his annoyance at a colleague who, according to his perspective, felt the need to trot out her credentials in inappropriate forums. "We'd be discussing a playwright or a performance and Susan would somehow manage to work in something from her resume: 'Oh, I worked with so-and-so who knew so-and-so at that theater.'" This boasting, he thought, might stem from Susan's having been ignored or interrupted in other meetings: "Do women seem more defensive because it's *so* male-dominated in academics? Is it their attempt at equal footing—women wanting people to be aware that they've done just as much as any of the guys here?"

Did Mark overreact to Susan's self-promotion? Probably. Perhaps she simply hoped to connect with him more the way a man would, and he found that off-putting. Is Susan's intention to boast or simply to express the personal connection she feels to her professional networks?

Mark does qualify his remarks by saying that he does not think Susan is egotistical, but merely uncomfortable in her professional role. "It just feels like she has to prove something. And I wonder if that's really necessary." Since he considers Susan a friend, he wants to remind her that he already knows how good she is: "Sometimes I want to stop her and say 'Look, I know you are very intelligent. I know you've done a lot. I have too. I just don't want to talk about it all the time.'"

Men I interviewed also commented on women who take modesty to an extreme. Marty Bennett, who works for a pharmaceutical company, dislikes self-effacement more than self-promotion. As an example, he says: "I saw a woman given a compliment in front of a large group of people. She basically turned the comment down with a 'No, no. I really didn't do that much.' And she started acting very nervous, which made her look kind of silly." To explain this scenario, Leslie Brody, author of *Gender, Emotion, and the Family* suggests: "Women may inhibit expressions of pride in order to protect the feelings of others, especially other women, as well as to preserve their relationships with them."

Paul Meyers, a CEO with a strong ego, praises the power of self-assurance in one breath and cautions against excess in the next. As belief in himself has matured, so has his ability to read people and to inspire them. This, he says, has played a significant role in fostering loyalty among his employees. "People respond to confidence. The big danger—with an exclamation point—is in becoming over-confident. In our organization, I also encourage a humbleness that is critical to good business. If people say 'You did a good job,' I say, 'Well, we're going to try to do even better.'"

The Power of Positive Thinking

As Paul discovered, confidence breeds power and power breeds more confidence. As a man promotes his own status, his image expands in the eyes of others. When people treat him with more respect, he respects himself even more.

Barry Walker, an attorney who made two major career changes in his late fifties, discussed his initial trepidation about entering two new environments in four years. "But then I said to myself, 'I know I'm the smartest guy on the block!' Even if I'm not, I say that to myself because I am not going to be intimidated by new circumstances, or even a new career." This theme emerged repeatedly throughout my interviews: the messages we send ourselves shape our own expectations and ultimately how others perceive us. Women often tell me that they strive for perfection, crossing every *t* and dotting every *i*, in an effort to appear competent. Men generally rely on confidence and bravado to project an aura of success.

Calculated self-assurance, even when you don't feel supremely confident, can become a self-fulfilling prophecy. As long as you have built a baseline of competence and accomplishment, acting in control can foster the real thing. No one wants to associate with a blowhard who merely *thinks* he's great. But when you act assured and in control, provided you do not cross into arrogance, others begin to believe in you as well. Colleagues approach you for advice, key assignments cross your path, and your own confidence rockets to yet another level. Positive reinforcement refuels confidence.

The male code bolsters approving messages a man sends himself. However, men do not readily give women the type of support men give one another—the pat on the back, the nod, and, as one man told me, "even the occasional grunt." This phenomenon may explain why men perceive even successful women as less in control, less self-assured.

In fact, in heavily male environments, a woman may find her positive thinking challenged instead of reinforced by those around her. When she does, she can employ a trick men use to activate a confident persona. "The mind can do wonderful things when it's pressed," suggests Barry Walker. "You constantly remind yourself: 'I am terrific. I am not afraid of this. I'm going to do a damn great job.'"

Consider how the cycle of positive thinking builds upon itself. Men manufacture an aura of competence and self-assurance. This, says Barry, "allows men to create a shield of invulnerability on any subject, at any time." Confidence opens the door for feeling happier and more secure. This positive outlook promotes success. Success makes you more self-assured. It all fits together. And, Barry concludes, self-confidence enables "more men than women to enjoy the work they do." Although this conclusion took me somewhat by surprise, because I know many women who thrive on their work, I heard it over and over from men of all ages.

Mark Kramer, a man in his early thirties, says: "I think men seem to derive more pleasure from their work, whereas women sometimes seem to derive it in spite of their work." When I asked Mark to speculate on why he thinks women draw less enjoyment from their work, he answered: "I don't know, but perhaps women are more relationship oriented and derive more pleasure from that aspect of their life."

Perceptions about success, when filtered through the male lens, can cause serious misconceptions about what really goes on in a woman's mind. My own research on working women indicates that many women do, in fact, truly enjoy their work and derive ego gratification from a job well done, just the way a man does. When a woman verbalizes concern about her life outside of work, including role conflicts less often experienced by a man, she may appear less connected to her work than she really is. In their book, *In a Time of Fallen Heroes: The Re-creation of Masculinity,* William Betcher and William Pollack offer this explanation for why a man ties his identity more closely to his job: "Men have long used work to bolster their self-esteem and to make up for deficiencies in relationships." If so, this provides yet another incentive for a man to send himself positive messages explicitly designed to bolster his professional ego.

Jeff Klein, sixty, finds men more private at work than their female colleagues. "A lot of women wear their hearts on their sleeves, always expressing what's going on in their mind, in their life. Among men, you don't expose yourself because you'll appear weak." As a result, he says, men mistakenly view women as more vulnerable than they actually are.

Ironically, women may see men inaccurately, too. Despite the bravado dictated by the male code, Barry Walker admits that men frequently feel insecure: "No matter how confident the most secure among us is, we are all, at root, very thin-skinned, very sensitive, very paranoid." A fearless image, he suggests, can be a powerfully effective tool, and he advises women to "Cultivate it with a passion!" How does Barry accomplish this? "Force of will. You make yourself something that you are probably not, by saying to yourself: 'I must be this. This is the role I must play if I want to succeed.'"

Macho Man

While women may not suffer from a confidence deficiency, we may think differently about the image we want to project, rejecting the bold and fearless stance recommended by Barry Walker. As a way of explaining these differences, Leslie Brody in *Gender, Emotion and the Family* stresses display rules—social norms that regulate who can express emotion, what emotions they can express, and in what context. "The limitations on the kinds of emotions women are allowed to express make it hard for them to change the status quo and become more powerful," Brody says. "If men are discouraged from expressing vulnerability and warmth, they will be less likely to exhibit weakness leading to their own defeat, thus making them more likely to succeed in a competitive role. However, they will also be less likely to be successful at caretaking and intimate relationships. In other words, the expression of particular emotions leads to carrying out particular social functions more easily."

When I asked Bill Haber, thirty-one, to talk a little more about his instinctive affinity for confidence, he replied: "It's about being macho. That's what being a *man* is. There are expressions that men use when women aren't around about how much balls you've got in business. It's just a measure of courage." What does a natural reliance on confidence do for men? Besides establishing and fortifying their position in the hierarchy at work, it reinforces the comfort they already feel in their own skins.

Clearly, women can't simply tell themselves: Thou shalt be confident. The male code of confidence is complicated and has been reinforced by the cultural norms in many workplaces for decades. It includes many unwritten rules that govern a highly competitive, every-man-for-himself world. Not surprisingly, when I asked men to describe a woman they admire in business, many chose phrases like "tough as nails," "fearless," and "completely unflappable."

Bruce Kohl, a journalist, believes that most men do not appreciate the many benefits that their majority position bestows on them. "In traditional workplace cultures, men have been given the power, and they have harnessed it, and over-harnessed it, and sort of gone crazy with it. This leads them to think: 'It's all about me. I can do what I want.' There's really a 'me, me, me' culture for many men."

Management consultant Pat Heim suggests that such an egocentric culture demands that men strive to appear in control, even when quite the opposite is true. A woman, she believes, can more freely commiserate with another woman about her insecurities. For example, a woman will admit: "Here I am in the middle of this assignment and I don't know what I'm doing. I'm really afraid I'm going to screw this up." Her female colleague knows just how to respond: "I'm sure you can do this. You've been successful in the past. I'm behind you." Men, Pat says, cannot engage in conversations like this. "They are perceived as wimps if they do. So a man really does not have the option to say: 'I'm afraid I'm going to fail.'"

During a presentation, for example, a man may disguise unfamiliarity with the content by simply conveying an expert's image. In contrast, attorney Joe Leghorn has witnessed female lawyers "who because of temperament, background, and training tend to defer to men." This particularly frustrates him when he knows the woman possesses stronger credentials than a male counterpart: "The woman might have a better idea and a better approach, but simply because a guy challenges her and says something different, she'll go along with him." He strongly advises female colleagues: "You've got to break out of this mold."

An article in *The Wall Street Journal* entitled "Men and Women Fall Back into Kids' Roles at Corporate Meetings" suggests that women sometimes feel the need to apologize for their work for no good reason and too much apologizing makes even the best performer seem incompetent. The article describes how quickly one woman undermined her credibility with painfully honest admissions of tiny imperfections in her work: "She said she was sorry several times. Then she went on to give a flawless presentation with perfect slides. The man who followed her launched right into his presentation with no apologies whatsoever—and his slides weren't nearly as well put together."

In addition, the article suggests, men make a statement about power with their physical presence, standing up to walk around a room, spreading their papers across a conference-room table, or stretching out in their chairs. To fortify this stance of control, men less often ask questions in a meeting, just as they resist asking directions on the road. While women are more likely admit when they don't know the answer, men swiftly make one up when they don't.

Schooled by past experience—having been talked over, ignored, or challenged in a way that her male colleagues have not been—a woman may justifiably worry about perfection on all fronts. Frozen out from traditions built on the male code, she may see only one option: Go the extra mile. Ensure credibility and acceptance by doing everything right. But in some respects, this strategy can backfire if she focuses on too many details and misses the big picture.

When I interviewed Gary Pierce, a partner in a major consulting firm, he confessed that he often takes a leap of faith when scrutinized by a client. "I trust my instincts, which are right about 80 percent of the time." When I asked what happens when he returns to his office, crunches the numbers, and discovers flaws in his bold answer, he replied: "I call the client and simply say, 'Look, I have some new information here. This is the number you should be using.'" Immediately, his client compliments him for staying on top of the problem. So Gary looks like even more of a hero. "These clients are paying me for my expertise," he says, "so if I don't act like I know what I'm doing, I've lost them." In other words, as Gary sees it, making it up, within reason, can be a better option than wavering on a recommendation.

Gary's story once again exemplifies how the male mind directs a win-win scenario despite facts that suggest the opposite.

"Women Don't Know How Good They Are"

What enables a man to fabricate a winning scenario out of little more than sheer nerve? Why do many women feel so uncomfortable doing the same?

David Kohl, a Dallas insurance vice president, offers this insight: "Women don't know how good they are." In David's view, women send men this message when they appear to question their self worth, doubting themselves on issues they really needn't second-guess. For example, David has observed women who, after making a decision, will immediately begin to ask: Did I make the right decision? Was there a better course of action? Although David agrees that weighing alternatives makes good sense, questioning self-worth does not. As he sees it, "questioning their self-worth, which leads to indecision, comes across as a weakness."

To explain why, from a man's point of view, a woman appears tentative on the job, Bill Haber observes: "I've never met a man who wonders if his gender is affecting his business effectiveness, but I think that's something women sometimes feel. I think women can be just as effective as men if they don't have any insecurities. But I have to admit—men have caused a lot of those insecurities."

"Women," says one senior executive, "tend to be more hesitant than men when it comes to being decisive." This is a sentiment I heard again and again as men described an area in which they believe they excel.

Sound decision-making, of course, requires more than simply believing in yourself. For men, comfort with power, support from their peers, and control over their environment all help. "We men like to be in charge," asserts David Kohl. "So we give off the perception that we're very, very controlled and decisive." Pride propels men into the man-in-charge mode. Men have developed a knack, David says, for navigating self-doubt. "By not getting too close to people, we're able to make decisions and not feel them as much."

Decisiveness, like beauty, is in the eyes of the beholder. Scanned through the male lens, a good decision is a swift decision. Seen through the female lens, the best decision is a thoroughly considered one about which everyone can agree. That takes time, and to many men it may look indecisive.

Frank Andryauskas has had first-hand experience with the ways different styles are regarded. He told me he once had to repackage his style of communication, dropping "feminine" traits for "masculine" ones. It happened during intensive psychological testing required for senior management at Staples, the office supply store where he previously worked. His evaluation read: "Frank is a very collaborative personality. He may not be able to survive with the strong egos on the management team." Frank offers advice for anyone who shares his distaste for a macho, competitive style. To make himself heard among very aggressive personalities, Frank says laughingly: "I learned to simply say things with incredible firmness, with a tone of 'This is the absolute truth. Anyone who doubts this self-evident truth has to be an idiot.'"

What if someone dismisses Frank's proposal because he did not present it forcefully enough? He reverts to Plan B. When his colleagues' body language signals disinterest or they turn to someone else to start another conversation, Frank realizes: "They heard it, but it didn't register." To get back on track, "I literally call them to task by saying, 'Now does everyone understand what I just said? Because I want to make sure we have total agreement on this. *And* here's what I'm going to do.'" From this point on, in the absence of any contradiction, Frank equates silence with approval.

Like Frank, many women assume, at least initially, that intelligence, skills, experience, and drive will win in the workplace. In cultures that reverberate with bravado, however, personal conviction will always draw more notice than a strictly content-driven approach.

The status of outsider in a still male-defined workplace may cause even the most supremely confident woman to question, at some level, her right to belong and participate. Even men, who in most organizations enjoy a comfortable majority position, worry about achieving success. Yet, as a man peers through the male lens, he may see a woman as professionally vulnerable when she is, in fact, quite secure. By virtue of their socialization and acculturation, men have been well-trained in how to wear the mask of confidence. The mask gives a man permission to do what might seem foreign to a woman: walk with swagger in his step even when he feels as if he's walking on eggshells.

Code Breakers

According to the male code, you project confidence, whether you feel it or not, because that projection defines your character in the eyes of others. As Paul Meyers, the CEO of a $50 million company, said, "People smell fear. There are many times when I've been scared out of my wits in front of my board, but I would never, ever show it."

A woman may possess plenty of self-esteem, yet fail to project it in a way that a man will understand. We certainly don't need to swagger the way men do, but we do need to recognize how it influences the male mind at work. In cultures built on the male code, the confidence we project will make the strongest initial impression. As we learn to decipher the male code, we will uncover both new strategies to use at work and new ways to sharpen our own skills, without losing a sense of who we are and who we want to be professionally.

A man may actually feel less secure than the woman he criticizes, but he will likely not show it. To compensate for a lack of substance, he will rely on bravado. At the other extreme, a woman may follow too dutifully the theory that excellent results speak for themselves. Add second-guessing a decision to that and a potentially lethal combination forms that can undermine the respect she deserves.

Women and men may hear that same competent inner voice, yet process its message quite differently. While a man uses it as the propelling drive behind a forceful presence, a woman may keep it in the background lest she strike others as a forceful bitch.

On the job, women may worry more than men about the consequences of making a mistake, and for good reason. The double standard often evolves into a higher standard, particularly in companies where only a few women make it past middle management. Yet sometimes, with little more than belief in ourselves to back us, we need to risk making a mistake in order to grasp the next rung of success.

How can a woman win the confidence game without selling out?

Code Breaker #1

Act self-assured even when you're not. Walk into a room as if you own it. Never let them see you sweat.

As I closed my interview with Glenn Sears, an executive in a Silicon Valley high tech firm, he said: "I know your subject for this study is men, but there's a senior woman at this company you *must* speak to. I've learned a lot from her and she's highly respected, not just as a manager, but as a leader." Although I had not intended to interview women for this particular project, Glenn's words convinced me that I should interview Connie Moore. And I'm glad I did.

The story of Connie Moore, a vice president in the Silicon Valley high-tech firm, demonstrates how a woman can use self-assurance to reinforce her proven business skills. Connie fortifies belief in herself with a simple, yet potent, strategy: Keep the focus on the job. What does it take to do the work? What skills are needed? What skills do I possess? Isn't that why I was hired in the first place? How do I apply those skills to ultimately make a profit for the stockholders?

As she asks herself these basic questions, Connie conveys her business persona without excess worry about looking foolish or making an occasional mistake. When it comes to bravado, each person needs to answer the question "How much is too much?" Without resorting to the level of bravado that reverberates among many of her male colleagues, Connie makes herself heard among the noisy boys she works with every day.

Code Breaker #2

Avoid the perfectionist trap as a barrier to feeling in control.

While no one wants to make falling flat on your face a routine habit, Connie observes: "Women, in general, tend to over-prepare, and this is a trap I've fallen into, where I want to be absolutely perfect before I'm willing to take a step." Connie has, however, followed a wise mentor's advice: "Don't demand perfection. Better to get out there. Take the 60 percent certainty and allow yourself not to have all the information."

Code Breaker #3

Create your own shield of confidence by striking the right balance between absolute certainty and a reliable hunch about an action or decision.

A big payoff awaits those who muster the courage to take risks, suggests one CEO: "When you achieve success, it makes you more confident. And that leads you to an even greater level of success." Set your own level of confidence. For one person, that means acting more self-assured than she feels. For another, it may mean diving right into situations you welcome and dread at the same time.

For Connie, it meant addressing head-on what she saw as a weakness, speaking in front of huge audiences, a skill prerequisite to surviving and thriving within the top ranks of a highly competitive high-tech firm. To strengthen that skill? "I volunteered to speak at three major sites with about 250 people at each location. Then I enrolled myself in a Dale Carnegie strategic presentations course and got them to coach me specifically for these presentations." How did Connie fare? "The seminars were a wild success," she says with a smile, "and I got to the point where I really enjoyed getting up and giving speeches."

Code Breaker #4

Never underestimate your own business instincts.

Sandra Benton, an engineer, places a lot of stock in attitude and believing in herself. "You have to remember that no one's saying you're a bad person because your idea is wrong. It's more like 'OK, let's start with this idea and see how we can build on it.'" While this approach may not always eliminate heated debate or dissenting opinions, it does lay the groundwork for what happens afterwards. "When it's over, it's over and you move on to the next issue," Sandra says, with a shrug. "No big deal." Having worked almost exclusively with men, Sandra has learned to take personal offense out of most of the equation. "You have to be able to engage in a constructive disagreement or debate over the right answer without taking it personally. You're just hashing out ideas and maybe what you end up with in the end is not completely your idea, but you've pulled together the best from everyone's ideas."

For Sandra, learning to assert her business vision means marshaling facts to back you up in a meeting and to hold the attention of a group of intelligent people with strong egos. Getting yourself heard and recognized, she believes, accomplishes at least half the battle. "I've watched successful men do this. You can drill down on their ideas and, because they've done the successful background research and investigated different possibilities, you really hear what they are saying—whether you agree with them or not."

Code Breaker #5

You don't have to swagger like a man to command his attention.

As Connie Moore has grown more comfortable making executive presentations, she avoids words such as "I think maybe we should consider the possibility . . . ." Qualifying or apologetic statements, she emphasizes, steal your thunder before you've even begun. Find the balance: "Get out there strongly, but with a tone that invites comments and massaging of your ideas." Most importantly, share credit generously with those who deserve it.

Connie now wills herself *not* to enter a room with the fears that used to wear her down, fears that someone was going to ask her a question she would not have the answer to and she would "feel like an idiot." She has learned to enjoy legitimate questions, rather than feel under siege by them. How? No apologies. Keep it short and to the point. "Let me do some research. I'll send that information to you by e-mail this afternoon."

The power of personal conviction lies in its potential to reframe perspective. Even when men have every reason not to feel confident, they force themselves to don the mask. With first-hand experience, Connie observes: "If you build up inside you the confidence to do something once, you can enjoy the feeling of success—and not just success, but a feeling of excitement and invigoration of tackling something like a puzzle. This is a problem to be solved. This is actually fun!"

Code Breaker #6

Use confidence to gain control.

Self-assurance inspires others to believe in you as much as you believe in yourself. Connie puts this into practice as she constantly sends herself messages: positive, powerful, yet realistic: "I don't know everything, but I do know a lot. I'm passionate about this and I'll take an aggressive approach to get it done. I want this to be successful. And as a leader, by golly, I'm going to make it happen."

How do men make it happen? Many rely on the game face to reinforce messages of comfort, confidence, and control on the playing fields they have long dominated. A glimpse into the male mind at work reveals that attitude, more than anything else, instills a sense of control that is reinforced by subtle and not-so-subtle cues men relay to one another every day.

2

Nothing Personal:

Putting on the Game Face

When Ellen Briggs first walked through the front doors as a new recruit in a large international firm, she eagerly anticipated a challenging career in a company where the active recruitment of women seemed to signal real opportunity for professional reward. Then she received "the memo."

Early one morning as Ellen sorted through her inbox, she came across the following invitation printed on company letterhead: "Shoot your neighbor! Come join our annual paint-ball outing this Saturday at 1 P.M. sharp!" Scanning quickly through paragraphs effusive with the words "team-building" and "fun," she finally came to the concluding message printed above the RSVP: "Buy your own fatigue jumpsuit for only $50!"

On one hand, Ellen chuckled over the image of some of her teammates squeezing into zippered fatigues, a picture humorously at odds with their quietly conservative, button-down-collar, pin-striped-suit workday demeanor. On the other hand, Ellen thought, "What insanity." Then she visualized telling her husband: "Guess what? My boss expects me to spend a beautiful Saturday afternoon crawling around on a muddy field, armed with a gun loaded with paint."

If the event had been a one-time aberration, Ellen might have shrugged it off as a silly bonding experience among men. But then she discovered how much company business took place in settings that screamed "Men only!" And the warning seemed to get louder the closer women rose to top management. Time after time, senior executives reaffirmed their exclusively male traditions, from donning golf shirts bearing the company logo to taking clients on hunting trips to shoot ducks. Now an executive vice president at a competitor company, Ellen shakes her head and remarks: "The sad part of this story is, they *still* don't get it. Women are leaving the company in droves and the men don't have a clue why."

Men often find clarity in the simple elegance of sports imagery applied to business. Phrases such as "Monday-morning quarterback," "We dropped the ball on that one," or "That was a slam dunk!" echo in the hallways of many organizations. For women who do not speak or think in this language, the words carry little magic. For men, they serve as talismans as they put on their game face, an act that differentiates their world from the world of women. The game face serves both an offensive purpose ("Look at me, I'm tough.") and a defensive purpose ("I'm tough. You can't hurt me.").

On his playing field, a man must fearlessly compete, back the team at all costs, and avoid displaying emotions that might telegraph his insecurities. In return for his hard work and unquestioned loyalty, the team delivers important individual benefits. If I lose, I can blame the team. If I hit someone too hard, the coach will take the blame because he told me to do it. If I make an error, a teammate will show me how to do better the next time.

Behind the words and the symbolism lies the male ego safely protected under the cover of the game face. Anything that might somehow slow the flow of play—indecision, hesitation, fear, distraction—will not penetrate this protective gear. When a man puts on a game face, he removes negative emotions from the undertaking, insulates himself from self-blame, and fortifies his risk-taking ability. If he wins, great. If he loses, "It's only a game." Bill Haber, a sales director, explains the significance of this all-purpose game gear: "Business is an insensitive process. Being insensitive serves us well."

Bill's words answer the persistent question: Why don't men take things so personally on the job? Defining business as a sport defuses the explosive potential of an emotional bomb. Bill explains: "You can't worry about hurt feelings when you're in the game." He adds: "I may not like the guy. He may not like me, but for chrissakes pass the ball!"

When women say that "men speak in a different language," we often mean that quite literally. John Lucas, a marketing director, admits:

"We feel a blood lust about crushing the competition." Another manager observes: "Men can be sneaky too, but we call it competition." In describing the joy of the hunt, he said: "You set the traps for the competition even before they know they're competing with you. That's the fun part of my job."

Men believe that while a woman at work often worries about hurting feelings or stepping on toes, a man concentrates on tackling the opposition and running with the ball. As Brian O'Neil, thirty-six, vice president of an Internet company, explains: "When guys compete and girls compete, it's a different kind of competition. For women, it's a lot more personal. For guys, it's just like a football game. I might break your legs, but it's not personal." In his game, action overrules emotion.

Brian cites the many benefits of keeping things at work superficial. "When you let things get under your skin," he says, "you're in trouble. You start making decisions based on emotions rather than facts." Brian has trained himself to recognize when he's entering what he considers a dangerous emotional realm. "You start to second-guess yourself, wondering 'Was it me? What did I do?'" If he catches himself assuming the burden of guilt, Brian reminds himself: "No! No! This is a game. What are the rules? Oh yeah: 'Let's not get emotional about it. Play by the rules and keep your goal in mind.'"

By putting himself in control of his emotions, a man can let go of a bad day: Lost this one, but tomorrow it's a brand-new game. Women I've interviewed often observe that their husbands seem to carry home much less of the weight of the world than they do. As Bill Haber suggests: "We put on a game face at work. And that game face is a different person. How can we take things personally when we're not being ourselves?" It's as simple as that, yet not so simple. A man *is,* in fact, being himself when he wears a game face, protecting him from what he fears most: appearing vulnerable, emotional, self-doubting, or self-blaming.

William Betcher and William Pollack, authors of *In a Time of Fallen Heroes,* observe: "In belonging to the team, one belongs to the world of men." This men-at-work/men-at-play mentality serves two purposes. First, it establishes some emotional distance from women. Second, it provides a "nostalgic link to boyhood." As men connect through shared action, they feel little need to talk about it. Actions, not words, bond them together on the playing field and in the office. A man wins a game and moves on to the next. Even when he loses, he feels no need to look back.

Although Barry Walker, a Florida business consultant, thinks it overly simplistic to define everything male as goal-oriented and everything female as process-oriented, he acknowledges the truth behind the image of the goal-oriented male. Men's primary focus, suggests Barry, goes a long way toward explaining much of why they behave the way they do. "Sports has a lot to do with it. We really are goal-focused. The goal is to get the ball over the line, get the ball in the cup, get to home plate. Even sexual innuendo uses sports language: 'I got to first base. I got to second base. I hit a home run.'" That, summarizes Barry, "is the perfect example of a goal-oriented male."

The Testosterone Test

Hell-bent on scoring a goal, a man might trample the competition, or even teammates who obstruct his path. Strategy (winning the game) justifies tactics (moves that get him closer to the goal). Bill Haber points to the extreme example of Latrell Sprewell, the basketball player whose battle with his own coach escalated into a public attempt to strangle him during a practice. "The players on his team hate him. His coach hates him. Doesn't make a damn bit of difference because he *scores.*" The team simply traded the player to another team, where he continues to play. In the workplace, Bill suggests, this same attitude prevails: "We're all in it to win."

Yet a win-at-all-costs mentality sanctions behavior that, over the long term, may actually hurt the team. Consider the example of Tom Chase, CEO of a $1 billion enterprise. As he describes his senior management team, he says: "Usually we tear up the enemy. We're hunters, we're doing what we're supposed to do, and everything is great. But every once in a while, one of us gets in a feeding frenzy trying to get the job done." He admits that someone accurately described them as a school of sharks. "When one of our fellow sharks gets nicked and bleeds, we sort of mindlessly tear each other apart. We forget that what we're biting right now is the arm of our colleague." In other words, certain tactics can actually thwart strategy, moving you away from, rather than toward, your goal.

Many men, of course, have evolved beyond Neanderthal behavior. For instance, Eric Stephens, the executive in a biotech firm, describes the contrast between his knowledge-based company and more traditional corporate settings: "When our sales and marketing people travel to customer sites, they are forced to enter a world many would rather have left behind." Eric refers to these companies as the "Cro-Magnon world" where crude sexual jokes set the tone for interaction between men and women. Here, business success becomes a testosterone test. Do you have the balls to tackle this? How tough are you? Can you fly across the country all night, shine at a 7:00 A.M. meeting, and head back on the next red-eye, ready for battle?

A few years back, Eric was put to the testosterone test at a Wall Street firm. "The impression I was given was that it was a test of manhood," Eric now says with a chuckle. You passed the test if you could "take the hit," which in this case meant refusing to be crushed by punishing company traditions, and remaining macho enough to endure last-minute, number-crunching all-nighters, followed by a quick shower in the office, then off to face some tough-talking investment bankers whose questions would grow more grueling with each passing minute. After this comes a celebratory high five and a drink at the local bar.

As Eric sees it, fraternizing and athletic hazing presages what happens in macho work cultures today. Reluctantly, he describes "the corrosive type of bonding that happens when you are asked to lower your standards to be part of the larger group." This go-along-to-get-along attitude, he suggests, differs dramatically from positive teamwork, where individuals revise their standards for the sake of the team. "And it's very explicit," says Eric. "It's what you're supposed to do. To the extent you don't join in, you are going to be excluded. It's in the dynamic—whether you're singing off-color jokes on the bus or whether you get involved in a fight with the other team." Loyalty to the team, and even to the Neanderthal stragglers, becomes a badge of honor. Can you pass the testosterone test? "Are you with us or are you against us? We all have to know that you can take the heat." This, recalls Eric, reminds him of male adolescent behavior more than anything else.

For many men, coming of age on a sports team yields a host of positive and productive lessons for life and for work. Others, however, relish corrosive male bonding, those aggressive activities that may test manhood but may also create insensitive behavior. As Eric sees it, "Years later, men at work are still asking their group to take that test."

As much as Eric disdains corporate hazing, he also sees some value in a little healthy office horseplay. The women who fare best in a predominantly male environment, he suggests, "give themselves a chance to play with the men and are cool enough to take the heat." In Eric's view, the ability to hang tough in the heat of the game enabled one particular woman he knows to lead an all-male sales team successfully. "The sales group loves this woman because she has a high friction coefficient. She can take it, but she can also dish it out."

While some men rejoice when a woman passes the testosterone test, others feel threatened. As William Betcher and William Pollack suggest in *In a Time of Fallen Heroes*: "Sports emphatically differentiate a man from the world of woman. He reaffirms his manhood through the rituals he shares exclusively with men." When a woman enters the room, a man who practices exclusivity will, more often than not, treat her as a competitor rather than a teammate.

Crush the Competition

John Lucas, who works in a *Fortune* 500 company, describes a business strategy he believes many men share: "We want to crush the competition. We're motivated toward action because of our desire to crush them. Whatever they do, we can do it better." Among women, he believes: "They want to distill it down into less emotional terms. They think more in terms of: 'This is the right thing to do.' There is less of a blood lust, for lack of a better word."

A man's comfort with competition originates, in part, in his comfort with testosterone-driven aggression. The activities in which a young boy participates, suggest Margaret Hennig and Anne Jardim in *The Managerial Woman*, prepare him for what he will face in business: "He is expected to be aggressive and he is rewarded for it. . . . He is expected to run himself ragged at games, to be independent, to initiate. He is, in short, rewarded and confirmed for deflecting aggression into useful paths and he begins to acquire a sense of confidence in his own ability progressively to master his small environment."

An aggressive tone of voice and assertive body language fortify the male stance. Ray Ingalls, who works in high tech, describes an extreme example, which occurred in a meeting between two warring colleagues, Chuck and Tim. "They had such an antagonistic relationship that the meeting was going absolutely nowhere. In fact, tempers were really beginning to flare. At one point, Tim got up and Chuck physically blocked the door to prevent him from leaving. Tim was clearly physically intimidated by it and sat back down. And you know what? They actually did work something out as a result of Chuck asserting himself in this way. It was shocking behavior, but surprisingly it worked. All I could think was 'We've really devolved in some way.'"

Reward for successful aggression reinforces both confidence and emotional distance in the male mind. Clinical psychologist Leslie Brody suggests that men hide most emotions, except anger and competitiveness, as a necessary adaptation to the workplace. While aggression taken to extremes can hurt everyone in sight, less harmful doses of aggression can supply a positive source of drive and energy for men.

Hennig and Jardim observe that a woman often asks "How will we play?" or "What's the process?", while a man will often focus on the prize associated with crushing the competition. Hennig and Jardim write: "What lies behind this difference in response begins with small boys learning about teams, about being members of teams, about winning and losing. Their concept of strategy may at first be a very simple one: how you win may mean no more than getting the fat boys on your team so you can trample the skinny boys on the other."

As a man's team gains strength, so does his ego. The competitive male reinforces the confident male. Betcher and Pollack explain in their book why men willingly entrust to the team a piece of their identity: "While there are sports of individual achievement, men's connections to other men are nowhere so palpable and unashamedly acknowledged as in The Team. Through it a man experiences an intense sense of belonging, of community, even of love, that he may never find anywhere else."

As a man channels such intense emotions into his team, he also surrenders others. Men frequently remind themselves what a coach might have said to them at a young age: "You can't worry about hurt feelings when you're playing the game." Later in life, following the coach's rule allows them to repress, or ignore entirely, the interpersonal dilemmas a woman would likely take to heart on the job. Bill Haber explains why he thinks this way: "You can knock someone down and still be their friend. In what sport do you score a goal by being sensitive to the other player? None! In what sport do you score a goal by making sure everyone is communicating? None!"

Bill succinctly describes the game plan that his male colleagues carry into the office: "Pass the ball. Kick it. Damn, I missed! Kick it again! Score! Points!" First, they focus on immediate action with little or no discussion. Quick results follow as a man suppresses random emotions that might delay the win. How does this play out in the office? In a meeting, men can battle verbally, then walk out together, patting each other on the back, broad smiles on their faces.

If men don't let many things get under their skins, how do they resolve conflicts they cannot avoid? Brian O'Neil, thirty-six, sticking to the game analogy, explains: "Men will put on the boxing gloves and go at it: 'Let's take it outside. We'll see who draws blood first and then we'll call it done.'" The workplace version of "settling it outside" may take place on a bar stool after work: "You take the guy out for a beer to try to settle it. First of all, you have three to four drinks to get loose. Then you say, 'Hey, man, what's the deal here? Are we going to fight over this or are we going to settle it?'" In other words, get to the point. Clarify the agenda: "Let's get it on the mat and either we're going to fight it out or we're not."

Many men find "duking it out" therapeutic. Release of anger and aggression signifies the end of the game. If a woman links her professional relationship with a colleague to a personal connection, she may not so easily detach herself from a negative interaction that seems to contradict a friendship. For a man, confronting or challenging a colleague need not signal disrespect. In fact, it may communicate quite the opposite. A man can spar with a friend, strike him out, or knock him off his feet with an overhead smash at the net, but when the final gun sounds, they shake hands and head out for a beer.

The male code includes firm rules about when to challenge a team member and when to defer in the best interests of the group. John Lucas recalls an example from his experience at a *Fortune* 500 company when a woman new to his group demonstrated, as he saw it, absolutely no understanding of the team she had joined. After a grueling meeting and lengthy discussion, Beth persisted as the sole dissenting voice. As John describes it, "Beth decided to dig her heels in and hold up our decision." How did her behavior differ from John's? "I tended to acquiesce to the team, thinking 'I've only been at this for four years and the rest of the team has ten years' experience, so I'm with them.'"

After the meeting, John found himself fuming as he speculated about why Beth took such an adversarial stand: "On what basis is she disagreeing? She formulated her own opinion and was going to stick by it instead of being a team player. This struck me as really odd. She kept pushing back with her own opinion instead of joining the team and building consensus." In John's mind, Beth seemed focused more on personal victory than on a team win. Beth had violated a sacred creed: You should defeat a competitor, but never a teammate. In Beth's mind, she may have been trying to spark the team to an even bigger win through a fresh approach. In fact, operating under a different set of rules from the men seated around her, Beth may well have been following her own version of team player.

While John viewed Beth as a liability for the team, would he think the same about a man who took a similar position? Might he, instead, label him a hero? Was the group's consensus based on history or hidden agendas Beth knew nothing about? Assuming she did not ignore her group's motives in favor of a better move for the firm, but out of some sort of error in judgment, would John more quickly have forgiven a man in the same situation? Whatever the answers to these questions, Beth, in John's mind, challenged the team code that men have come to accept.

I Owe It to the Team

The male code relies on clearly understood rules and expectations. Nowhere do these rules come more forcefully into play than in the teams men love to form and join. Their own success often depends on their team's success, which explains John's strong reaction to what he saw as Beth's defiance of the team. This rule of "I owe it to the team" explains behavior that may appear illogical and even ridiculous to women, but for men supports and solidifies the team.

Brian O'Neil, the Internet company vice president, describes the critical role that belonging to a team plays in a man's life on the job: "The one thing most important to both guys and gals is positive recognition. For guys, the next most important thing is being part of the team." Women, he believes, tend to remain more isolated at work, in part because joining the team requires so much more than simply forging an alliance. "Guys need to be accepted as part of the team or they take it personally," Brian says. "When you exclude a guy, it starts to get ugly. He's going to react and start swinging." He does so because how highly he values himself depends on how highly the team values him.

In their book, Betcher and Pollack suggest that, according to the male code, belonging to the team affirms a man's masculinity, provided he obeys the clear rules that govern team members' behavior: "As with any group process, each individual's self-esteem becomes enhanced by a cohesive group in which individual goals are subordinated to the good of the whole." For a woman, her gender can blackball her from membership in certain exclusive groups, and it certainly raises the bar in terms of the effort it will take for her to gain acceptance.

Paul Meyers, a thirty-two-year-old CEO, places a strong emphasis on pumping up the various teams in his wholesale business, inspiring them to compete aggressively with what he calls macho tactics. He says he believes that "business is not about ego or macho, it's about making money." But when he talks to his employees about competition, he tells them that "nobody remembers number two" and "I don't like to lose." When conveying these messages, Paul sets a tone that says: "We're going to win. Those guys are really good, but we're going to be even better." Quite naturally, he assumes the role of coach: "prodding, encouraging, pushing, stretching." If the competition beats them, Paul, like a good coach who always looks ahead to the next game, tells his team: "Look, we got caught by a particular company last time, but we're not going to let them win again."

The unwritten rules women encounter in many male-oriented work cultures include explicit do's and don't's with respect to team loyalty. Greg Block, a director at the NAFTA Environmental Commission, recalls learning to speak in the organization's tone. "In many organizations, we try to be very careful to speak in the 'we,' removing ourselves from the cause and effect. One shouldn't highlight their individual role in the organizational image. It wouldn't be appropriate."

Not surprisingly, the term team player can mean one thing to a woman and something quite different to a man. Exploring this difference, management consultant Pat Heim describes how she encouraged team building among executives in a session targeted for just that purpose. "I put them into small groups and asked them to identify their roles and responsibilities as members of the executive team," Pat says. "The spokesperson for the first group was a man named Bill. And number one on that group's list was to 'be a team player.' So I asked Bill 'What does that mean?' Bill replied: 'It means to follow orders. Support unquestioningly and do what needs to be done even if I don't want to.'" In other words, you can do whatever it takes to crush the competition.

The next group of managers, headed by Melinda, Bill's boss, also listed being a team player first on its list. When Pat asked Melinda what it meant for her to be a team player, she replied: "It means to share ideas, to listen to each other, particularly when we disagree and have to work together collaboratively."

Bill described a view of the team that requires staying in your position in the hierarchy and playing your position well with no questions asked. Melinda, on the other hand, defined a good team player as someone who concentrates on fostering collaboration and support without concern for her exact place on the team. When Pat asked Bill how Melinda's definition struck him, he offered a surprising answer: "Manipulative." And Melinda's take on Bill's view of teams? "Mindless." That, concludes Pat, explains why a debate will often erupt between men and women about who is and who is not a team player. From Melinda's perspective, process matters more than roles when it comes to determining a team's effectiveness. For Bill, on the other hand, roles define the process by which the group will reach a decision. Whereas Melinda viewed the team through an egalitarian lens, Bill assumed a strictly hierarchical perspective.

Let the Better Man Win

In Bill's mind, belonging to a hierarchy insulates him from viewing a loss as personal failure. In some respects, the team offers men a safe haven. As Margaret Hennig and Anne Jardim suggest: "A team can even be a place to hide, a place to learn about survival—how to stay on, how to be given another chance; 'After all he's too nice a guy to drop', or 'He's not really producing yet but he's learning fast . . . .' Over and above this, there is a drive to win and of necessity win as a team, not as a lone individual independent of everyone else."

Comfortable with competition and protected by the game face, a man can lose without taking it to heart, or at least without revealing his feelings. Sometimes that means celebrating a team win even though you did little more than warm the bench. Other times, it means chalking up a loss to the simple fact that the other guy outplayed you. Then you move on. The ability to move on stems, in part, from the sheer joy a man derives from competing and playing the game. In *Real Boys*, William Pollack describes a boy's view of what he calls mutual challenge: "Sweating, side by side, boys . . . struggle to achieve their personal best. Competition among boys is more about competing *with* another boy than competing *against* him."

It should come as no surprise that at work, too, men derive comfort from mutually familiar sports metaphors. Even men who never participated in organized sports seem to accept their metaphoric power. Comparing work to sports or war (the ultimate form of competition), as many men do, neatly removes emotion from confrontations and differences of opinion. Just as a man can, without regret, handily defeat a friend at tennis or golf, so too can he clash bitterly with him over a business issue without the fear that it will damage their relationship.

When I asked Brian O'Neil, a company vice president, how he deals with a colleague who challenges him, he replied: "I take 'em to the mat." Resolve the problem, get it over with, move on. Even close friends seem to experience little emotion over digging in their heels and taking a firm stand against one another. Barry Walker believes that as long as male colleagues don't let egos get in the way, they can argue vehemently and remain friends. "If you are initially friends or colleagues who have respect for one another, then duking it out is therapeutic," Barry says.

Women often reap different rewards from competition. In *Women at Work*, Sylvia Senter observes: "Girls' games emphasize skills, not rules. . . . They don't develop any sense of an impersonal, working system within which they function. A girl believes that it's not as important to win the game as it is to play 'fairly.'"

Mariah Burton Nelson, a former pro basketball player and author of *Are We Winning Yet?*, characterizes the competitive gender difference as a contrast between a traditionally male militaristic model and an emerging partnership model for women who play sports. The former relies on hierarchy, ranking, control, and aggression to win the game. The latter, Nelson says, reflects the Latin root of the word *competere,* meaning "to seek together." "The partnership model is a compassionate, egalitarian approach to sport in which athletes are motivated by love of themselves, of sports, of each other."

When I interviewed Frank Andryauskas, a former Staples executive now working in a start-up, at his home, he and his wife, Peggy, agreed that girls and boys play competitive sports with different attitudes about what it means to belong to a team. As the mother of two daughters and a son, Peggy observed, with Frank nodding his head in agreement, "Girls just play soccer differently. *No question about it.* They naturally gravitate toward the sharing and collaborative aspects of being on a team."

Brad Miller, an investment partner and forty-five-year-old father of two, coaches both a girls' and a boys' soccer team. As much as he has tried to apply the same approach to both his daughter's and his son's teams, he found that it simply does not work. "Guys are much more like dogs," asserts Brad. "With a dog, you raise your voice and say 'No!' and the dog will look at you and get it." On the playing field, this translates into: "You screwed up! You're not giving 110 percent! Now, get down and give me twenty pushups, moron!" In coaching his daughter's team, he believes: "If I raised my voice to my daughter that way, it would elicit tears and a bad reaction, so I approach her team differently."

Brad's response mirrored the words used by Tony DiCicco, coach of the U.S. women's World Cup soccer champions, whose performance dazzled male and female fans alike. Having coached male teams as well, DiCicco observes: "Men can absorb tough criticism because they really don't believe it anyway. . . . Women believe it and take it to heart. So I tried to coach positive."

The more interviews I conducted, the more I began to detect hints of the real messages buried in sports aphorisms. I heard, for instance, that "Let the better man win" really means: "Even if I lose, I will be the better man tomorrow." Even as men spoke of the sportsmanship involved in losing gracefully, they made it abundantly clear that they will, first and foremost, do whatever it takes to win.

John Snow, a retired company president, age sixty-one, recalled his most effective business strategies, saying: "I try to put my best game forward. I can be Machiavellian. I can manipulate. That's all part of the game." Furthermore, he says: "I'm a chess player. You definitely have to analyze what the competition is up to and make your countermoves." When I asked John how he justifies a Machiavellian approach to business, he responded: "For the good of the project, the company, the other individual, sometimes you have to manipulate. That's what 'manage' means. Manage means the same as maneuver, or manipulate."

And what happens when the other person beats him at the game, winning the account or customer? For John, an analysis of why a competitor won should remove emotion from the situation. It should certainly eliminate any self-blame. "If a better man beats me at something, I don't hold it against him. I say, 'OK, how did he win? What did he do better?'" He went on to express admiration for a worthy adversary: "When I'm outmaneuvered, I'm outmaneuvered. Shame on me!" In other words, learn from your errors and do better the next time. In vivid contrast, women often tell me they focus first on what they did wrong.

A man coaches himself with the game lingo that protects his ego: "I'm number one" in one instance, "I gave it my best shot, but he just outscored me" in another, and "Tomorrow's a new game" in yet another. This sort of coaching can instill bravery, or at least the outward semblance of bravery.

The Brave Front

The game face won't work as an offensive or defensive device unless a man bucks it up with bravery, be it genuine or fabricated. Acts of bravery help a man conceal any fear, vulnerability, or self-doubt he may feel. The modern stoic male traces his roots to the primitive hunter whose survival depended on his ability both to slaughter game and to protect himself, his family, and his territory.

The pressure to suppress fear, even under dire circumstances, both haunts and pressures young men who yearn to project a stereotypical tough-guy image. In *Real Boys,* William Pollack offers an example of what he calls "the sturdy oak" standard: "If somebody slugs you in the face, probably the best thing you could do is just smile and act like it didn't hurt. . . ."

A law partner, Joe Leghorn, talks about the intense pressure men feel to act bravely: "Everyone has a certain level of insecurity, and men are certainly as insecure as women are. Part of the macho image is 'Boys don't cry.' No matter what, we're supposed to put on the brave face." Consider the positive associations that spring to mind when we think of the strong, silent type, who has power emanating from quiet strength. This preference for not expressing emotions may explain why so many of the men I interviewed declared that they least like to work with a woman who cries in the office. If they themselves let tears flow, they would invite ridicule for violating the male code and appearing too weak and girl-like.

On the subject of men shunning any display of emotions, psychologist Bill Winn told me: "More importantly, they've been trained not to know when they're having them, so it's not even so much an issue of deliberately hiding emotion, but one of not even knowing what's really going on." In Bill's experience, men often use components of bravery, such as anger or aggression, to disguise their true feelings. "More discreet reactions of hurt, dismay, disappointment, and confusion may not come through because the person is blustering with anger or annoyance or irritation."

A man also learns to display the brave front for the sake of the team because such a posture can bring him heroic notice, particularly in stressful situations. In the midst of a recent bank merger, the top brass from each bank projected a united front in the form of cheerful backslapping, bear hugs, and wide grins. How else could they act? However, behind this celebratory façade lurked the scary fact that half of these executives would be out of a job within weeks.

Business sometimes requires a certain amount of fake camaraderie for the sake of the team. Rob Parks, a forty-year-old vice president at one of the merging banks, explained it this way: "If I project confidence and group spirit, I have a much better shot at being asked to stay on the team." Given their upbringing, many men step easily into such strained and awkward roles. Putting on the brave front repeats a scene from their boyhood when the coach called them to the bench and put substitutes in their place. In situations like this, showing disappointment means revealing weakness.

When I spoke to Rob, he told me how he rallied his own troops at the bank. Walking into his office the day after the merger announcement, he found worried staff waiting at his door, wondering: Is our group still in business? Will we keep our jobs? When will we know more? Though Rob understood these legitimate concerns, he consciously chose to maintain a brave front, acting as if he were controlling the situation, even though he felt worried himself. The ability to act calm and collected under extreme duress surely made him a more effective team leader. If a person's confidence appears heroic to colleagues, those colleagues will feel comfortable sharing their fears with that person. Naturally, word gets out that Rob is a strong player with a loyal following who deserves a spot on the newly merged team.

As men encounter cultural expectations about maleness, they find that a brave front helps them gain respect in both sports and in the workplace. However, the brave front also blocks emotion and displays of emotion. As Betcher and Pollack suggest, a man's identity relies on a defense against intimacy, requiring him to erect barriers against intrusion of the feminine, relational, and emotional. "Men are constantly trying to plug up the dikes in order not be swamped by the ocean of femininity."

Can a man's brave front fool a woman? Of course. And misreading it might cause her to doubt herself if his feigned bravery causes her to question an opposing position she has taken on an issue or decision. As someone who prefers not to wear a game face into the office, Frank Andryauskas suggests only one viable counterstrategy: "Exude incredible confidence. The manager with extreme masculine traits just smells doubt." Then begins the contest of fear versus confidence. "If they smell doubt, it's a hunt and it's a debate," Frank explains. "It's an intellectual game to demonstrate that they can shoot down, in a matter of moments, what took you a matter of hours, or days, or months."

When I asked Frank why he sees such behavior as a test of courage rather than a legitimate business review, he replied: "Because I have seen some of these managers argue both sides of the point within two hours. To them, it's a game. To the person on the receiving end, it's a devastating criticism of their thoughts and ideas." While a humiliating and public defeat can certainly erode your professional footing, seeing it as a game can help you regain your balance. Frank concludes: "If you realize it *is* only a game, and it doesn't really reflect how they view you, you do develop more courage." But, you may wonder, doesn't this degrade business into a series of manipulations?

The Manipulative Hand

All sports require both skill and strategy, and an excess of one can, to some degree, make up for a lack of the other. Some men I interviewed firmly believe the better man will win and that the man who wins is the better man, whether he has won through skill or gamesmanship. For many, the end justifies the means. One consultant boasted that he often defeats his competitors even before they enter the game. Gathering competitive intelligence so that he knows their product almost as well as his own, he can "slam the competition before they see me coming."

"I set land mines for the competition," he says. For instance, by bad-mouthing another company without actually naming it, he sets the trap. Having learned the features his competitor's system cannot address, he emphasizes them in his own presentation as features absolutely critical to his client's goals. Then the client drops the bomb on the competitor. Part of the thrill of winning, the consultant says, comes from "just knowing that your competition is going to get asked a lot of uncomfortable questions because you've set this little trap that grows into a big issue they have to address—so they *can't win*!"

One senior executive announced: "I find that women can be very catty and sneaky." When I pressed him and others who share this view to describe a manipulative woman they've encountered at work, few could come up with even one example. They just clung to some vague image of an evil, conniving witch that seemed more a product of imagination than of true experience.

In what many women would see as a role reversal, John Lucas, a marketing director and seemingly confident thirty-three-year-old, found himself outmaneuvered by one woman's power play, an experience he'll never forget. The story involves Carol, a woman with what John describes as a "monomaniacal focus" on taking over the best part of *his* job. During a car ride to a client, John decided to confront Carol head-on. She immediately responded, "Yes, you're right. I want to work on that project and I'm pushing every way I can to make it happen." The reality of Carol's assault on his career began to take a toll on John: "I was losing sleep over it and was extremely upset. I can't believe this lady was trying to take half my job! The gall!"

John attributes Carol's behavior, in large part, to her gender and says: "I've never come across a man who has been conniving that way. Now, maybe they are conniving and I just haven't noticed it. Or, you're friendly enough with them to say: 'Oh, I don't mind. I'll acquiesce because I like that person.'" In other words, men may view a competitive maneuver by a woman quite differently than they would the same move by an man.

Ultimately, Carol did take over a piece of John's job. Blaming her behavior on the fact she thought she needed to pull out all the stops to make herself visible, he says: "It became blatantly clear that she was out for career advancement at my expense. She explicitly laid down some ground rules that basically said, 'Don't mess with me.'" In evaluating his own behavior, he comments: "I was working to further the goals of the team. Carol selectively chose projects that would position her to take part of my job." John soon discovered that Carol had also approached his boss and made a pointed suggestion: "Look, if you keep John on both projects, you'll only have John and Dave working for you, but if you give me one project, you'll have three people working for you and can grow the group."

Although John himself has recently been promoted, he still wonders: "What happened? I was just showing up and working real hard. I did a good job and somebody turned the tables on me. What made it worse was Carol's two-facedness, coming in smiling and asking me for a favor one day, and the next setting up a meeting and 'forgetting' to invite me." Either gender can employ a manipulative hand, it turns out, but men expect women to follow a different code.

Regardless of what we would like to believe, most of us work in environments where rewards depend more on individual rather than team performance, a fact that opens the door for behavior like Carol's. We can also speculate that John's vivid recollection of "the conniving woman" plays some role in how he works with other women today. Had their roles been reversed, would Carol have felt the same way about a manipulative John? Were she to speak out, her colleagues might accuse her of whining.

After describing his run-in with Carol, John went on to reiterate why he believes a man would never behave that way: "While men want to crush the competition, they do not want to crush their own teammates." In John's mind, men are more likely to respect another person's territory. "I've seen men sort of create space for people," he explains. Men, he goes on, approach it this way: "We can all have a piece of the pie and make the pie bigger if you want a bigger piece." In contrast, John says: "Women take more of a zero-sum game approach to work: 'I can't get ahead unless someone else gets behind.'" John offered an explanation for the behavior he sometimes sees in women. "When people feel out of control, they get scared. Among men, there is a sense of honor, a code of honor and ethics."

When I asked attorney Barry Walker his opinion about such a male code of honor, he let loose with a series of rapid-fire responses: "Male code of honor! Those are the words of a male chauvinist pig! Good lord!" Quickly amplifying his point, he continued: "I know more duplicitous, lying, bastard men, many more, than I do women like that. Now that's not to say I haven't met some absolute first-class connivers among women. I have. But men will look you right in the eye and lie to you." That, proclaimed Barry, "is why the concept of a male code of honor is horseshit, absolute horseshit. And whoever said that, I want you to put my quote right next to it."

Where does competition end and manipulation begin? It may all depend on the gender lens through which you view a given interaction. Bad-mouth the competition, and you're a hero; bad-mouth me and you're a traitor. For some men, it depends on whom you hurt or what your intention is. John Snow, the retired executive, sees it this way: "I use the chess metaphor. You're constantly trying to get your power pieces in the right place. That's the game. That doesn't mean you're trying to hurt people."

David Knight, a Wall Street trader, will, with what he terms a light touch, bad-mouth his competition. "I make my clients feel guilty for socializing with another broker." Using what he terms his "hard-ass guilt trip" strategy, he says: "I give them a very hard time, telling them: 'Oh, I can't believe you went out with that broker. She's such a numbskull. Why did you do that? What a waste of your time!'" Would a woman get away with saying that? Not unless she doesn't mind people calling her a bitch. Still, David does what he does because he wants to win, winning is everything, and he must do anything to win. It's almost Darwinian: the fittest (the most skillful, the best strategist) shall survive.

To many men, the business world is a tough, competitive, and often heartless, place where survival hinges on doing whatever it takes to get ahead. Among the strategies I heard for getting what you want, "start your own rumor" struck me as the most unusual. One man called upon both his wife and colleagues, at several points in his career, to float informal "leaks" about himself. In one case, he asked his wife to make conversation at a social function with someone who enjoyed a close friendship with his boss. When his wife made a seemingly casual remark about not wanting to relocate again, the man, of course, asked her why she felt worried. She then replied: "Gee, I can't believe Jon's being pursued so aggressively by a rival company. They actually put an offer on the table. Can you believe that?! I hope my husband doesn't take it." Although no such offer existed, a manipulative approach did exactly what Jon planned: "Word got back to the vice president and I got a raise out of it. Dinner and promotion too."

At another company, Jon saw a prime opportunity to enhance his own worth as soon as his boss gave notice. "I went to my boss's boss and started asking questions about whether my compensation plan would change with my boss's departure: 'Are you going to change my bonus plan? Will my responsibilities increase?'" Although Jon opened his discussion under the guise of needing the information before he made an offer on a new house, he really wanted to negotiate a better mid-year bonus. By posing the questions he did, Jon says: "The other guy's thinking, 'Why is Jon asking this? Maybe he's thinking about leaving.'"

Boys learn at an early age that people do not always play fair. Some men who act like straight shooters may, in fact, be hiding a few duplicitous tricks up their sleeve. As Bruce Kohl, a journalist, pointed out: "Yes, women can be catty, but all they can do is talk about it. Men can actually manipulate a situation because they usually have the power to do so."

"I Owe You One"

Manipulation feeds on power and information, which many men eagerly acquire. They feel comfortable with it because the male code begins teaching young boys how to use it in the game. Win or lose, "You give a little, you get a little: You pass the ball to me this time, and next quarter, I'll pass it to you." One senior woman at Fidelity Investments observed: "Men trade favors. They really understand quid pro quo, but it's not anything that's blatant."

At times, the trading of business favors among men seems more carefully engineered. Whenever his boss or his boss's boss visits his site, Sean McNamara, a thirty-one-year-old high-tech manager, maps out a specific game plan for socializing. Sean explains: "He comes out here and gives me his expertise, so I've got to offer up whatever he wants on the personal side."

A female colleague who heard Sean's comment thought for a moment, and then offered an observation of her own: "I don't know why, but Sean's wording just bothers me—sounds like some kind of prostitution or something." When I asked Sean about this, he immediately confessed to a certain amount of showmanship when interacting with colleagues. Following the "work hard and play hard" strategy, Sean comments: "I'm 3,000 miles away from all the people who are decisionmakers and 5,000 away from the CEO in Europe. You've got to find out what they like to do both personally and professionally, mostly professionally. I want the power players to leave here saying: 'Wow, what a trip! We saw this customer and that customer. We had a good time with Sean and got to see Vegas too.'" More than male bonding or pure socializing, Sean sees carefully orchestrated evening entertainment as payback for the presence of his boss.

Many men admitted to some discomfort with the notion of "passing the ball" to a woman at work. When it comes to reciprocity among colleagues, some men raise a red flag for women. Said one man, "It's just easier for me to approach other men than it is to approach women. I'm more comfortable trading information with my friends and the people I socialize with." In addition, with someone whose values you understand, and perhaps even share, a person is less worried about running the risk of looking foolish or being rejected.

Expressing profound resentment toward a senior woman who seemed to miss the expected symmetry of trading favors, John, the marketing director, recalls an incident that infuriates him. "This woman tricked me," he says. "It was a beautiful Sunday afternoon," he states with vivid recollection. "After Joanne called me on my cell phone, I had to leave my wife at a concert in Central Park for an evening meeting with one of her customers—which had nothing to do with my job." Sitting on a plane headed to California, John found himself asking, "How the heck did she get me to do this?"

When I asked John to answer that question, he said: "She's nice and she's a rank up. She looks a rank down and calls people she knows have information she wants, and says: 'Hey, I have a big important client, very important. You're the expert on this. We'd really love to have you in front of the client because you're such an expert.'" As John sees it, Joanne built him up so he would start to believe he was a hero and think, "Oh yeah, I'm here to save the company."

As he ate his airline dinner, John says, it suddenly dawned on him: "Wait a minute. I'm not here to save the company. I'm here to make Joanne look good." What about John? Didn't he get anything out of the trip? When he returned to the office, Joanne made a point of complimenting him in front of his boss and his boss's boss. "She wrote special notes about what a good job I did," recalls John. "Maybe it's my ego talking. But I felt I deserved those compliments anyway and they weren't the equivalent of me getting on an airplane at the last minute for her."

And what does John think Joanne should have done to reciprocate? "It should have been a similar sacrifice and a similar benefit to me. At a certain level of sacrifice, you're asking too much. You should almost have, up front, a contracted agreement on how you're going to pay the person back." In John's mind, Joanne made the mistake of not verbalizing the reciprocity built into the favor.

Would John have responded differently to a man whose request he considered too big of a favor? Perhaps Joanne's gender and the fact that she is not technically on his team have sensitized John to the idea of being used by a woman. For her part, Joanne may, in fact, have simply defined the team differently, focusing on the welfare of their division, even if John did not directly report to her.

Not surprisingly, John admits that trading favors happens more naturally with men: "Between men, there tends to be more of the buddy thing, 'I'm helping my buddy.' Naturally, there's a bit more distance between men and women. Women have to ask for smaller favors—or something. . . ." From the get-go John misconstrued what to Joanne seemed a perfectly reasonable request. She was doomed before she opened her mouth.

Home Games

The game face also allows a man to exert control over his territory in the home. Most men, as Bill Haber explains, arrange the compartments in their life: "At the end of the day, that war is done. You become yourself again and get on with your life. You put on your war face again the next day." Does the fact that a man neatly separates his public and private self make him an impostor in all venues? Not in his mind.

"Our personal lives never, ever have to enter our business life," Bill emphasizes. "In the male mind, you go to work, you fight for whatever it is you want. You try to appear reasonable while creating an environment that's unreasonable so you can get more than the other guy." Bill also describes how creating a distinct workplace persona allows him to compartmentalize two important aspects of his life: "The person I try to be when I'm working is a really giving, really patient person who is fair and ethical about everything." At the end of the day though, Bill goes from Dr. Jekyll to Mr. Hyde: "When the guy I'm buying a car from calls to tell me the car's out of stock and presents a reasonable alternative, I tell him: 'Go to hell. Give me what I want. I'm the customer.'"

A clean break between the public and private self allows men to do what some women can only envy: defeat role conflict and avoid guilt. In the office, the game face helps a man keep it all superficial; in the home, he can relax his guard.

Can men really compartmentalize a bad day in the office, or do they merely tuck their feelings below the surface, safely out of sight of those who might detect their vulnerability? According to Barry Walker, they definitely do the latter. "I store it. But that's a male thing—to hide it." Where does the worry go? "Into the pit of our stomach. That's why we have heart attacks so regularly. We contain it. We don't talk about it with the boys." When men do show emotions, they often express them in a different form. Anger, for instance, can cover a man's hurt pride or defeat on the job. "We vent about things that are not necessarily troubling us. We'll find an excuse to get pissed off about something as a reaction to being wounded, but it won't be the subject that caused the wound."

Barry admires women who practice the healthier strategy of seeking counsel from friends after a miserable day at work. "Men might say to one of their nearest and dearest, 'Boy, Joe Blow really pissed me off today. Let me tell you what he did.' But that type of interaction between men happens twice in a millennium."

Even men who seem fully in control may, in fact, simply restrict where and when they express emotion. Roger Sims, a physician, observes: "I'm not sure men have an easier time letting go, but I am sure they're less expressive of it." When they do vent it, Roger says, emotions erupt in the form of action or escape. "A man might go home and run ten miles, or he might let go by getting drunk, but he is unlikely to go home and talk to his wife, and say 'Oh, this guy didn't do the right thing by me. I'm very upset.'" That would run counter to men's training, from an early age, not to display their feelings openly.

In Ryan Murray's view, learning to let go may be an acquired skill, but it is one worth striving for. "Working is one phase of your life. It's a very rewarding one financially and from a sense of achievement, but there's another whole life out there. So if you take negative aspects of your job home, it impedes your ability to enjoy other aspects." Ryan, whose life outside the office includes training for the Boston Marathon, adds: "That's not to say that when I'm out running, I don't think about 'How can I solve such and such?' or 'How can we come up with a new product?' But that's because I want to think about it, as opposed to it eating at me." When you let frustrations at work eat at you, you invite a destructive force into your life: guilt.

While men do sometimes feel guilt, they express it differently than women do. As a professor, town selectman, husband, and father, Peter Enrich feels the strain of a hectic schedule both at work and at home, and he confesses that he sometimes falls prey to guilt that he has not accomplished enough in either area. Still, Peter refuses to "let guilt wear me down. It can motivate me to a certain extent. It pushes me to do some of the things that need to be done, but it doesn't really eat away at me."

Bob Gault, fifty-five, a senior law partner who struggles to spend quality time with his three children on top of a seventy-plus-hour workweek, admits to the same feelings of fatigue working mothers regularly carry into the office. Guilt, however, does not gnaw at him. Bob explains: "I've got enough fatigue to take care of 50 percent of your survey! Am I tired? Yeah, I'm tired. Am I going to get through it? Yeah, I'll get through it."

Bob refuses to succumb to the temptation to strive for perfection on all fronts. A balanced, and at times downsized, set of personal goals, coupled with the confidence that he does the best he can as both parent and lawyer, allow him to get through the day without shouldering the heavy burden of guilt. "I don't feel guilt because I think I'm doing the best job that I possibly can. I do wish I could do more at both ends, but I can't. I don't look back with any regrets. I will never look back and say, 'Gee, I missed my kids' growing up,' because I'm not. And I'm making a good enough income and doing a good enough job here, under all the circumstances, so I don't have any guilt."

A thirty-four-year-old father of two announced with great pride: "Guilt is not in my vocabulary." He quickly cautioned me: "Please don't tell my wife I said that." I have never, in either of my surveys of women at work, 325 in one sample and 900 in the other, heard a mother proclaim: "Guilt is not in my vocabulary." Hearing that would have shocked me. A few men I interviewed did express regret for not spending more time with their children. Yet even they seemed able to reconcile their role conflict: "This is just the way it is. I'm doing what I need to do to make a living and support my family," versus "I feel terrible as a mother for working so much." None of the men seemed worn down or overwhelmed by a nagging sense of unfulfilled expectations, refusing to carry any more baggage than absolutely necessary.

Rob Parks, the banker, observes: "Of course, women feel guilty. No matter what life choice she makes, some guy is out there criticizing her." If she leaves on time for a day care pick-up, they call her uncommitted. If she works long hours and hires a nanny, they label her a bad mother with poor values. And if she works three days a week, she's not committing herself to a career. No wonder women question their life choices. Rob concurs: "Guys don't face this kind of pressure."

So, should women emulate the male ability to don the game face and compartmentalize competing priorities? Barry Walker thinks so: "A lot of carrying the weight of the world is self-induced. There are some of us who relish that role. We want to be mother/father confessor. We want to be everybody's friend, listen to everyone's sob stories, and involve ourselves in their lives. And when people take advantage of that, we claim to be burdened by it."

For many women, a tendency toward perfectionism, an inclination to take things to heart, and of course the reality of multiple roles conspire against a "Game over, move on" approach to work and life. Many of the men I spoke to asked the rhetorical question: Why carry unnecessary baggage? In *A Little Book of Big Principles*, Wil Brower talks about people who feel the weight of the world on their shoulders, burdening themselves with the assumption that they lack control. Wil's recommendation? "Don't go around picking up rocks and putting them in your wagon—they get heavy real soon."

Code Breakers

Men love sports imagery because they feel so comfortable with it. Like the protective gear they may have worn on the playing field, the male code at work equips men for survival and for winning. The code dictates supreme self-confidence even when knocked down, a knack for deflecting self-blame, and an ability to wipe the slate clean at the end of the day.

A woman competes just as ambitiously as the man in the next office, but she often follows a different set of unspoken rules. By understanding what matters most to the male team, even if she never officially accepts their rules, a woman can begin to exert her own influence, broadening the range of behaviors that build a winning team.

Code Breaker #1

Rely on your understanding of why the men around you act the way they do to reduce frustration and to clarify focus on your own goals.

In the process of conducting the research for this book, I witnessed firsthand how men use competition as a motivating factor, for themselves and for others. When I called an East Coast investment partner, he at first hesitated over my request for an interview. Then he said: "I'll tell you what. If you can persuade Ed, a business partner on the West Coast, to agree to an interview, call me back and my secretary will put you on my calendar." Once both Ed and I had met his challenge, Brad willingly spent two hours chatting with me on the telephone. In this situation, I rejoiced in the competitive spirit that landed me two interviews for the price of one. And I could not help but think: "Isn't competition among men a wonderful thing?"

Code Breaker #2

Since you cannot change a man's love of the game, channel his competitive spirit in the direction you *want to go.*

Steve Grossman, CEO of MassEnvelopePlus, has observed women who use, to their great advantage, the power attached to symbolic elements of the team. "All the style and substance, words and body language that go with 'we're a team' are time-honored techniques to get people on your side." Steve has watched women win over disbelievers simply by stepping forward to acknowledge their interest in joining a team or task force. How do they accomplish this? "On day one, they reach out and say, 'You know, I'm really pleased we've been given this opportunity to work together. I know that teamwork, synergy, and collegiality are the only way we will succeed.'"

A woman's initial reaction to Steve's advice might be: "Hey, wait a minute! Why do I have to celebrate all this 'Yeah, team' guy stuff? Why does the woman always have to make nice and give in? I just want to do my job without buying into all this game stuff." But let's face the reality. Many men thrive on the gamesmanship that often drives work cultures.

Code Breaker #3

Be aware that a man may expect a woman to play by a different set of standards. In many instances he fully expects that she should behave according to standards higher than what he would set for another man.

Competing with a woman represents new territory for many men, who get caught off guard by expectations they do not understand. Even a young man like John Lucas, who attended an Ivy League college where bright and talented women sat next to him every day and who works with many women managers, seems confused by how they play the game. In the case of flying cross-country for Joanne, he may have reacted too sensitively to the idea of being used by a woman. Might he have taken a request from a male superior to visit his client as a compliment rather than an insult?

Among themselves, men build unspoken reciprocity into the trading of favors. The male mind expects reciprocity, especially from a woman to whom he grants a professional favor.

Code Breaker #4

When you approach a man for a professional favor, clarify everyone's expectations. Ask him direct questions: What do you hope to get out of this? Does this seem fair to you? Spell out the terms and conditions just the way you would in any business contract. Eventually, as you get to know male colleagues and as they get to know you, the process should become less contrived.

Consider the positive power of reciprocity. Mary, a human resource manager, put trading favors into practice when Cynthia, a woman she had bailed out of a political struggle, called her to say: "I want to tell you how much I admire the honesty and integrity with which you handled that political situation. I'd love to take you to lunch to thank you." Mary paused for a moment before she responded: "If you're willing, you know what would be even better? Writing a note to my boss would really mean a lot to me." Cynthia agreed, telling Mary: "You know, I'd be honored to write that letter and I think I'll send a copy to the company president as well."

Code Breaker #5

Set your own boundaries on what feels comfortable and right, and what feels phony and manipulative, as you attempt to balance personal integrity with professional clout.

You'll often see a fine line drawn between what the male mind considers effective and what it labels manipulative. A man who acts like a straight shooter may turn out to be a first-class manipulator who uses Machiavellian tactics and behind-the-scenes maneuvering to get what he wants. For both men and women, the "win at any price" mentality has a dark side. Has either gender cornered the market on manipulation? No, neither can claim absolute integrity. You may find it useful, however, to know that many men still harbor the stereotype of the conniving woman in their minds, even those without firsthand experience of the phenomenon.

Code Breaker #6

Choose your battles carefully. But when you encounter an issue that's important to your cause, rally your best resources.

First, ask, "Is this is a battle worth fighting?" Then seek advice from a trusted colleague who will help you define an effective counterstrategy of your own.

Had John really wanted to keep the part of his job that Carol took away from him, he might have approached his boss with a plan rather than a problem. Instead of saying "How could Carol have done this to me?" he might have stated both the facts and the plan: "As you have heard, Carol would like to take over this account. Because I have built a long-standing relationship with the client and can show you the numbers to prove it, why not let Carol take on that other project instead?"

Code Breaker #7

You don't have to play like a man to understand him. But you should feel comfortable borrowing his best tricks.

For a man, separating work territory from home territory allows him to remove his warrior gear at the end of the day. When he takes off the gear, he divests himself of the kinds of stress a woman would more likely drag home. As women lead more teams, on the sports field and in the office, we can take the best lessons that emerge from productive teams, learning that no one wins all the time, that heart sometimes triumphs over brains, that talented teammates can perform individually, yet still learn from one another.

Code Breaker #8

Consider the advantages of the male code. Even when men lose to the competition, they neatly deflect self-blame by analyzing what the other person did right rather than focusing on what they themselves did wrong. This emotional distance fuels a fierce determination to win the next round.

As one man suggests: "Competition does not have to be a masculine theme. Competition is a human theme. Embrace it. Business is competitive." I would revise his statement to say: "A woman likes to win just as much as a man, but she likes to win differently."

Understanding the reasons a man wears a game face removes fear of the unknown. While taking note of what works for men, we can remain true to ourselves and rely on our own game plans.

Code Breaker #9

Once you've learned how a man competes, feel free to compete on your own terms.

Perhaps you will want to assume the outlook Nina DiSesa uses to lead McCann-Erickson, the world's largest ad agency: "Competing in a man's world is what I want to do. I'm very much in touch with my male side. I'm really competitive, and I find confrontation stimulating. But I keep those qualities in check. I use my feminine traits—empathy, collaboration."

Also think about the inspirational vision that led the U.S. women's soccer team to their jubilant 1999 World Cup victory: playing hard but playing fair; "leaving egos and individual jealousy aside"; focusing collaboratively to give their all for the good of the group; exhibiting "sportsmanship, class and determination to win"; competing with "drive, pride, no thoughts of insecurity and a future that may never know glass ceilings."

Cracking the male code gives women the information they need to exert their own imprint on the field of play. Analyzing how a man competes hinges on understanding the delicacy with which human traits rest on a double-edged sword. A complex set of factors, gender being key among them, reinforce the light in which these traits are seen and evaluated.

3

The Double-Edged Sword

Balancing Feminine and Masculine Traits

Even men who run billion-dollar companies confess to some trepidation about learning to work comfortably alongside their female counterparts. When I spoke to Tom Chase, CEO of an international manufacturing company, he readily admitted: "It's harder to work with women. It's sometimes very challenging because the women I work with tend to ask different things of me than the guys do." Tom then quickly points out that the difference he sees does not involve intellect at all. "It's a style thing and it adds complexity to deal with a woman who thinks about things more broadly."

Whenever Tom interacts with a man, he knows exactly what to expect. "It's very clear. I'm looking for an answer. Boom! I've got my answer. 'Good-bye, see you later.'" The interaction tolerates little complexity. With a woman, however, "It is not unusual for a conversation about the same problem or challenge to be more multidimensional. The expectation she has of me is more than 'I just want the answer.' 'I also want to know more about the background, the context.'"

Tom discovered new respect for hearing a different voice when he attempted to steer his organization away from the old command-and-control model toward a new community-based approach to decision-making. In the process, he began to see his work culture differently and started to listen more deliberately to his wife and to the one senior woman on his team. When Tom first raised the subject of how to change the company's "classic jock mentality," three out of the five senior men immediately reacted: "Why are we talking about this stuff?" Even Tom concedes: "It's frustrating for me because, in a way, I don't want to talk about it either."

Changing the work environment led to a profound change in Tom's own attitude because doing so forced him to listen to voices that he had ignored in the past. As Tom's wife suggested to him: "Think about the fact that you're asking your managers to play by rules that aren't the locker-room standards they know. It's hard for them to want to play under the new rules."

Tom readily admits that he cannot rely on male instincts alone, the way he does with most male colleagues, when he tries to grasp a woman's point-of-view. "It takes more effort to have the same conversation," he says. "Sometimes it drives me crazy because I'm in a rush and I feel the pressure of the minute-by-minute stuff. But I have rarely found the extra time to be a bad investment." Gender-based stereotypes, he knows, can easily compromise his objectivity and distort what he sees and hears.

Now that Tom has trained himself to hear the different voice, he can freely admit that, on some days, he gets highly annoyed over the longer time it takes to talk to a woman. "I can't fire off the hip the way I would with my male colleagues," he confesses. "There are times I maneuver a conversation differently with a woman because I know it's not going to be a five-minute conversation. It might be with my male colleague, but I know it's going to be a ten-minute conversation with my female colleague." Although Tom succumbs to occasional impatience over the fact that a woman's mind works differently than his does, he also welcomes her unique perspective at critical decision points. What he once saw as a weakness (longer conversations), now looks like a strength (a more complete picture).

Tipping the Behavioral Scale

The delicacy with which human traits balance on a double-edged sword explains, to some extent, the difficulty of sorting legitimate business concerns from gender biases. Add in the role expectations we bring from our personal lives, and you multiply the problem tenfold.

Strength, and weakness, depend on point of view. For instance, sensitivity can refer to a woman who reads people well and understands nuance, or it can conjure up images of an hysterical woman who acts on raw emotion. A man's just-do-it mentality can mean setting a clear course of action in one situation and trampling over vital details in another. With a minute tipping of the behavioral scale, the same personal quality that brings positive results one day can bring chaos the next.

The way we see ourselves and the way we believe others see us work powerfully together to mold our behavioral expectations. Among the men I interviewed, several revealed that they worry about whether or not their behavior aligns with expectations for "taking it like a man." In particular, they expressed profound discomfort about exhibiting "female" behavior, often viewed as weakness in a man. As one man, a university dean, felt compelled to remind me: "Yes, I'm sensitive, but I'm definitely not a wimp."

Rick Williams, a software developer, questioned his less-than-totally-masculine image, saying: "I feel ashamed for not having more ambition." Discussing the cultural pressure to adhere to the expectations for an aggressive career-driven male, he said: "One of my big fears is how to motivate my daughter. I'm worried that I don't seem ambitious enough for her. I think it's going to be important for her to be strong and confident and ambitious in whatever she does. How do you convey those qualities without being that yourself?" Interestingly, Rick resists pressure to conform to a stereotypic testosterone-driven image himself, and he feels just as strongly that his daughter defy stereotypes that might limit the goals she sets for herself.

To be stereotypically masculine, suggests psychologist Leslie Brody, means to be competitive, decisive, risk-taking, independent, assertive, domineering, ambitious, and at times even aggressive. She explains, "Men who are perceived not to have these characteristics are less popular with their peers, less attractive to the opposite sex, and may be less successful in their chosen careers. Moreover, their own self-esteem may suffer." In contrast, she says, "women are more popular and attractive to others when they express vulnerability, comfort, and concern for others with the quality of interpersonal relationships taking precedence over their individual achievements."

Since men work on a different emotional plane than their female colleagues, they often exhibit a love/hate reaction to traits they deem unique to women. On some days, Ben Adams, head of a customer service division for a large company, expresses deep admiration for the attributes he sees in the female mind at work. On others, he grows frustrated over how these same qualities, in a different context, turn negative.

Ben himself often faces the dilemma of doing it fast versus doing it right. As a result of overseeing six direct reports who are women, Ben has come to see the value of paying more attention to process: "My first instinct is to look at the facts and make a quick decision. I've learned that it's best to run it by the women in my group to get a more thoughtful take on the situation." Ben believes that, if he were supervising only men, he would less likely recognize the value of paying attention to the subtle issues that he sometimes misses. "It makes the process a little slower," Ben concedes, "but rather than having to back out of a decision I've already made, I get it right the first time."

Because of his experience working with women, Ben believes he has evolved into a more effective manager. He now balances a macho bulldozing get-it-done approach with what he considers a more feminine one that helps him pause to consider the many ramifications of a decision. On the other side of the equation, Ben still believes that too much process and too much attention to detail can become both cumbersome and unproductive. As an example, Ben says that women sometimes get off track by paying attention to irrelevant details and involving themselves in issues that he considers none of their business.

A woman's awareness of nuance in other people's behavior, Ben believes, can too finely tune a woman's antennae for her own good. "Although women tend to be more forthright about saying what's on their minds," he says, "they're also, at times, more judgmental about whether the people around them are pulling their weight." While women may openly react with a sense of righteous indignation toward people who do not pull their weight, men hold their tongues, Ben believes, because "they usually don't notice them in the first place."

For men, caring less can signal more control. David Kohl, a Dallas insurance executive, observes: "Men are often reluctant to get close to people—not on a buddy-buddy level, but in terms of being genuinely interested in what's going on in people's lives." A tenuous balance persists between caring too much and caring too little.

Jim Barnes, a senior executive in investments, and a former marine working in the most macho of work settings, took me by surprise when he said: "Men have to let the feminine side out. If you try to box it in, it's too linear. It's too narrow. There's more stuff out there." In Jim's case, his wife detected something in him that he himself had failed to see. "I had to learn to find my feminine side to learn to really listen and to be up front with my business partner when something bothers me. Now I understand what my wife has been trying to tell me all these years!"

Learning to talk to his wife enhanced his long-term business partnership with Burt, a trusted colleague and friend, Jim says: "When we started our copartnership ten years ago, everybody in the firm said that it wouldn't work, one too many egos involved. But our wives said it would, and we believed them."

Discarding Marine Corps assumptions about hierarchy, the two arranged a fifty-fifty split in work duties, largely because Jim transferred to his professional life communication skills he had honed in his personal life. "Men look at the world differently than women. What Burt and I do that most men don't is to actually talk about things. If we have a difference of opinion, we'll argue our side, and then we'll shut up and listen to the other guy—which most guys don't do because their ego gets in the way." Jim concludes: "That's why relationships break down."

While Jim clearly sees the benefits of looking at the world through another person's eyes, not every man has experienced a revelation like Jim's. And neither Jim nor Burt has abandoned his own unique strengths. As Jim explains: "Although we communicate differently with our wives than we do with each other, I think a lot of the lessons we've learned from each other have actually helped strengthen our marriages, and vice versa."

A man may find himself simultaneously drawn to and threatened by a particular quality he sees in a woman. The very quality he admires becomes threatening, particularly if he does not see it in himself. When, for instance, a man relies on a woman as a caretaker of details, he resents her friendly reminders as much as he admires her tenacity. Cast in a role that connotes power, a woman poses yet a different kind of threat, perhaps mirroring too closely how a man sees himself.

Each role a woman displays elicits a different set of responses from a man, ranging from comfort to threat, or a confusing combination of two colliding emotions. He may expect the sensitive woman to balance his action-oriented gruffness by adding the people side to the equation. Yet if, in a man's eyes, the woman becomes *too* nurturing, he may find her behavior stifling and intrusive.

Each of us carries some measure of so-called masculine and feminine traits. For both women and men, our most compelling traits balance precariously on a double-edged sword. The edge on which they rest depends on who exhibits the behavior, who observes the behavior, and the reaction it elicits.

Can either side strike a balance between both the complementary and contradictory nature of the masculine and feminine sides we each carry? Can we tip the scales in a different direction when the need arises?

Acknowledging Old Stereotypes

Not only do men perceive a woman differently, they may evaluate negatively behavior they'd rate as a plus in a man. Mark Kramer, a professor, admits to such a double standard when he says, "If a woman is strong and directional, the guys say 'Oh, what a bitch.' For a man with the same style, we would say 'Hey, he's just getting the job done.' Men, whether they admit it or not, are guilty of this perception. And that's something men struggle with."

Emotional displays also do not sit well with men, although coldness and aloofness don't work either. "There's a certain type of career woman who can come across as unapproachable and men don't like her," observes Mark. According to Mark, a woman can find herself in a "damned if I do, damned if I don't" predicament as she attempts to find a style comfortable both for her and the men around her. However, the double standard described by Mark, and shared by many men, gets more complicated and contradictory the more you look at it.

Certain stereotypes have stalked businesswomen from generation to generation, and these characterizations often contain stark contradictions. *The Woman Executive,* written in 1958 by Margaret Cussler, put it this way: "Women executives are pictured often as cold and chic statues, ruthless and calculating in their business technique, yet apt to explode in a fiery tantrum or retire in a feminine pout. They are called too aggressive and too yielding, too feminine and too masculine, too emotional and too icy, too rigid and too indecisive, too personal and too impersonal. It makes little difference that these stereotypes contradict each other; to the person who fears the executive woman the contradiction seems logical."

When I read this quote to women today, they shake their heads as they hear words that ring true for their own work experience. Perhaps fear of the unknown, of the consequences of a woman's decisions at work, conjures up these contradictions. To complicate it all, a man may expect certain behaviors from a woman trailblazing the path in any profession. Several CEOs I interviewed suggested that men do, in fact, hold strong expectations for women pioneers.

Are these expectations valid? What are the implications for women who try to measure up to the unrealistic expectations conjured up in the male mind?

Paul Meyers, who heads a $50 million company, describes Jane, the first woman he invited to make a presentation to his board: "She is hard-core, smart, tough as nails, absolutely tough as nails." He added: "I like her and I have a lot of respect for her." Laughingly, Paul recalls the first time Jane called his home and spoke to his wife, who after hearing Jane's trademark abruptness, handed him the phone with a sarcastic, "Boy, was *she* ever pleasant!" Paul has learned to accept Jane's brusqueness, concluding, "It's just her personality. Once I got to know her, I thought she was terrific."

Paul admits that for anyone on a fast career track, toughness almost always factors into the success equation. "No matter what, you're going to have to be tough—not nasty—but you're going to have to be able to take a certain amount of crap and be willing to be self-reflective and say 'Boy, I really screwed that up' and think about the reasons why you screwed something up. And most people, men and women, have trouble doing that." In the case of corporate boards, where women compose only 11 percent of the members, Jane's hard-as-nails style may partly explain why she has succeeded in almost exclusively male territory.

Tom Chase, another CEO, describes the first woman to join his board of directors in masculine terms: "She is, by head and shoulders, the most aggressive, hardest-hitter on our board. The guys wanted the smartest person we could find. They are intimidated by her, but not by her gender." Outlining her strengths, Tom says: "She is a strategist, a real hard-edged operational person." Interestingly enough, Tom paints a very different picture of the second woman appointed to the board. "She is a heavy hitter, but more of a humanity person with an interest in our community work. I would characterize her as having humility as well."

Both Paul and Tom imply that pioneering women may need to demonstrate to their male peers the hard bottom-line business skills deliberately displayed by executive men. Of course, a masculine style requires no translation for men. Eric Stephens, an executive vice president for a biotech firm, admires women who seem to revel in a distinctly masculine style. Describing one woman's forceful presence as the head of business research, he observes: "She adopted what I would call the male persona as a manager. She adopted it so well that she out-cursed most of the guys. She sort of out-toughed the guys, and that went over great. She was charming, but tough at the same time." Recognizing that she may not have felt perfectly comfortable with her persona, Eric comments, "Having said all that, it was also clear that she was putting on a bit of an act, but people didn't really care. It qualified her to be part of the crowd."

The effectiveness of a woman's style in male-dominated offices depends very much on the context in which she displays it. In certain situations, a style comfortable for her will threaten her male colleagues while an "act" will garner their acceptance. A 1996 Catalyst study of 461 women at the level of vice president or above in *Fortune* 1000 companies confirmed this: "It is noteworthy that, besides superior performance, the only strategy regarded as critical to advancement by a majority of women executives was developing a style with which male managers are comfortable."

In some settings, out-toughing the men might backfire, proving too threatening and a direct affront to the male code. As enthusiastically as Eric expresses admiration for his rough-talking female colleague, he also promptly points out that her style would backfire in a different setting. To illustrate his point, Eric cites the example of a woman at the firm who used an understated, low-key approach to gain respect from what he calls a very tweedy group.

Exploring why this woman's style works so well with a predominantly male group of physicians, Eric says: "She's very data-driven and results-oriented, and an excellent tactical marketer. But she's willing to sit down and take the time to connect with these guys to gain their trust, and she doesn't use anything of a sexual nature. She's the furthest away you could imagine from that type of relationship builder. But neither is she one of the guys." In other words, she acts like a woman, but avoids the sort of chumminess men might misconstrue.

Men admire the stereotypical invincible woman for two reasons. One, they admire qualities they like in other men, such as being tough and straight-shooting. And two, they welcome qualities they often do not see in their male colleagues. Among the executives he counsels, psychologist Bill Winn detects a common theme: "Men particularly enjoy working with women who are results-oriented and can pitch in and drive whatever the bottom line is for a business—who can make a good, logical, coherent case for a company's direction." What the executives imply to him, but do not voice directly, is their appreciation for the very presence of women. As Bill explains: "Men will use the presence of a woman as an excuse to talk about whether or not people are working well together, issues that men are more likely to avoid." A man, whether he admits it or not, on some levels values female colleagues who compensate for weaknesses in his own set of skills.

The woman men would most like to work with walks on water. She is forthright, but not too pushy. She is strong, yet feminine. She is sensitive in managing people, yet tough in making decisions. She can take a firm stand on issues, yet remain unthreatening to the men seated around the conference table. How can a woman meet such lofty expectations? And, more importantly, what can she do to change assumptions about her roles that contain inherent contradictions?

The Beholder's Eye

Conflicting stereotypes can create a field of landmines for women at work. Men who accept such stereotypes do not see women clearly, and they probably will never do so unless they develop a clear understanding of their own behavior.

No two women think and act alike. Neither do any two men. Obviously, stereotypes assume they do, and such assumptions about gender can do a lot of damage. In the face of wildly inaccurate, disparaging, and even demeaning stereotypes, people might long to disassociate themselves from the group to which they belong. Images of the nagging woman or the heartless man cause us to wince at unflattering traits too readily attached to a particular group.

When gender-based stereotypes cast us in a positive light, we tend to embrace them. For instance, we may identify, at least in our fantasies, with the exaggerated portrait of a Superwoman painted by someone who admires us. But when a man complains about an hysterical woman, we recoil at words that negatively pigeonhole women.

Certain stereotypes limit a man's view of a woman at work, and thus limit her status in the organization. For example, a lone woman may turn into a token woman, without anyone explicitly using that label. In *Men and Women of the Corporation*, Rosabeth Moss Kanter explains why token status harms women: "The token does not have to work hard to have her presence noticed, but she does have to work hard to have her achievements noticed." Based on his own experience, David Kohl, insurance executive, agrees, saying, "I think there's a general misconception in business that whenever a woman comes into a position, the reason she's there in some measure has to do with the fact that she's a woman. Generally that dissipates as people get to know the person, but typically men jump to that first conclusion."

One misconception often fuels another. In David's case, he goes on to say that many men assume that women promoted as tokens will give preferential treatment to women who follow them. "Some women don't realize that they can't show a particular preference toward women, any more than they do men, because that undermines their credibility. I've seen situations where women are more favorably biased toward other women, which is a stupid thing to do. They let it be known that they are on a mission to promote women and that's their agenda." This, David believes, opens women to unfavorable stereotyping: "You can't trust a woman because she will always favor her own sex."

Women who enter predominantly male territory must not only struggle to prove themselves on the job, but they also must demonstrate that they do not embody the negative stereotypes many men carry in their minds. Philosophically, a man may champion qualified women, yet he may still fail to recognize the subtle labeling that hinders an objective view of women at work. This built-in tendency poses a real hurdle for most women. How can I break down a stereotype without contributing to another?

Analyzing successful executive women, the authors of *Breaking the Glass Ceiling* answer that question this way: "It was essential that they contradict the stereotypes that their male executives and coworkers had about women—they had to be seen as different, 'better than women' as a group. But they couldn't go too far, to forfeit all traces of femininity, because that would make them too alien to their superiors and colleagues. In essence, their mission was to do what *wasn't* expected of them, while doing enough of what *was* expected of them as women to gain acceptance. The capacity to combine the two consistently, to stay within a narrow band of acceptable behavior, is the real key to success."

The alarmingly narrow band that circumscribes a woman's "acceptable" behavior easily tips a man's view of her behavior toward the negative side of the double-edged sword. For David Kohl, it took first-hand experience working for a woman, an event not of his own choosing, to ease some deep-seated fears. David confesses to a complete reversal in his opinion: "I was surprised when I first worked for a woman. I expected all these things to be different, but they weren't. She was terrific! She treated people fairly and I didn't even think about whether my boss was a man or a woman." Men, he openly admits, often let unfounded stereotypes color their initial business relationships with women. "For example, men have the perception that women are moody. I went in with that assumption. And I never found it to be true."

How a man evaluates a woman hinges, to some extent, on how he views himself. Literary agent Mike Snell suggests that a man's ability to work well with women reflects his own level of professional confidence. When he sees a man treat a woman colleague poorly, he wonders, "Is this guy treating women the way he does because he's a chauvinist or is he a chauvinist because he's insecure?"

When the Boss Is a Woman

Insecure men may feel particularly threatened by women who hold positions of authority. Mark Kramer, college professor, says that , like many men, he has a hard time accepting direction from a woman. "I've almost always worked under a woman. And when I finally started working under a guy, I felt myself saying 'Wow, what a relief!' It felt so much more relaxed. I felt less was at stake." When I asked him to explain the difference, he responded: "I felt more judged by women. I felt they were working out issues with power whereas the guys felt more comfortable with it."

As Mark saw it, his female bosses had set out to prove something. "To me, this looks like a weakness," asserts Mark. "When you're proving you should be there, instead of just being there, it makes me wonder." Mark chuckles as he refers to what he terms one woman's need to over-control: "She would constantly send out memos and at one point sent out a notice—without a hint of irony—that said 'Recently people have been sending out too many office-wide memos. This needs to stop.'" Women, of course, can make as many mistakes compensating for their insecurities as men make.

A large part of a man's alienation from his female boss may stem from the much higher level of comfort he feels with a male boss. "I feel less challenged, on the personal front, by a man," explains Bill Haber, sales director. "Whenever I've reported to a woman, I've had to spend a lot more time explaining what I'm doing." Bill expresses particular frustration about working for Anne, who he says put him on the defensive by misinterpreting the reasons behind a slip in his performance.

Unaccustomed to working closely with a woman, Bill began to envision a wall between Anne and himself that he had no idea how to dismantle. During the time he reported to Anne, Bill enjoyed an excellent track record, with one exception. For two months in a row, his sales dipped well below quota.

As Anne addressed Bill's performance, she attempted to uncover the underlying causes. "Bill, what's going on with you?" she queried. "You're out there. You're in front of the right people. You're saying the right things. You look the part and it's not happening." When Anne used words that in his mind seemed to question his stability as a person, Bill took offense: "There was nothing going on with *me* that was causing problems so I would talk about the business factors that I felt were responsible. But what Anne really wanted to know was: 'What's going on with *you*, Bill? Let me get inside *you*.'"

Men come to work armed with ready responses to codified behavior. Caught off base by what he saw as Anne's violation of his code—the male code—Bill reacted to Anne's probing as a personal attack. "It pissed me off. I felt like she was saying that who I am was causing this failure." How would a male boss have handled the same situation? In Bill's view, the whole interaction would have consumed all of ten seconds. A man would have said: "Anything else going on in your life, Bill? Anything weird with you that could be causing this?" Bill would have responded: "Nope. Next topic?" When I asked Bill how Anne resolved her concern about him, he replied, laughing: "She never did. She kept thinking: 'Something must be going on with him. He's just not telling me.'"

For women, highly personal gentle questioning serves as a form of support. For men, it can turn into sheer torture. In their book *We Have to Talk*, Samuel Shem and Janet Surrey, who are husband and wife, describe scenarios most likely to create an impasse in male/female communication. For a man, it's getting too personal. "When she asks me what I'm feeling, it's like a five-hundred-pound gorilla has just walked into the room," admitted one of the subjects of Shem and Surrey's research. The result? "Things go dead, each participant retreats into his or her self . . . . Women's yearning leads to men's dread."

What was really going on between Anne and Bill? Each may have felt caught off guard for different reasons. Given Bill's stellar work history, Anne probably assumed that his setback must stem from something other than a business factor. What Anne saw as seeking a possible explanation for Bill's performance, Bill took as an unwanted intrusion. Perhaps Anne could have ended the standoff with Bill by addressing their communication problem, saying, "You seem to be uncomfortable with my questions, Bill. Let's drop this subject. Why don't we have lunch next week so we can talk about your new customer prospects?"

Other factors besides gender may have been operating between Bill and Anne. In situations where two intelligent people see two distinct realities, they might bear in mind that gender does not account for every workplace miscommunication. Sometimes styles or personalities simply clash. Other times, when gender does factor into the equation, a complete void in trust can completely ruin a business relationship.

Bill also felt very uncomfortable when he worked for Joan, whose boss happened to be a close buddy of his. In this case, Bill believes: "Joan was threatened by my relationship with her boss. Every time she saw us getting along, she felt that because we were guys, we were bonding and I was jockeying for position to screw her out of her job." Emphatically, Bill explains: "This couldn't be farther from the truth. It was her own paranoia. She was harder on me because of it."

As he told more of his story, Bill seemed to perform an about-face, revealing a legitimate justification for Joan's concerns. "Maybe when guys feel closer to each other and feel like they have more in common, the guy *is* more likely to get a promotion before a woman." By first calling his boss paranoid and then acknowledging good reasons for her suspicions, Bill reveals yet another of those deadly contradictions. It's like the old story of the paranoid who discovers that someone really is following her. A personal alliance can, as Bill suggests, lead to a man's promoting a male friend over an equally or more highly qualified woman.

Not every man sees red flags rising when he reports to a woman or when he thinks about promoting her. Ryan Murray, a community bank vice president, knows that his own experience differs from that of most men: "For the first fifteen years of my career, I worked for a company where the president was a female. I didn't think of her as anything but the president of the company. I grew up in an unusual environment where maybe 10 percent of the workforce is male." Today, Ryan moves easily among both male and female colleagues, with a high degree of comfort. The reason? "Having worked for a woman, I just learned to respect people differently."

"I've been fortunate in the environments I've worked," Ryan concludes. "There were always women who were either contemporaries or senior to me. From the time I was straight out of school, I was never in that loop of people who perceive an aggressive woman as a bitch in the workplace. That just isn't anything that would ever dawn on me." Ryan adds: "I mean, what choice do I have? You know! I have a feisty sister and a strong mother, and a strong-willed niece. But it all boils down to respect. And that's an individual thing."

Men do interact with women other than those at work, and those interactions may go a long way toward explaining why they think and act the way they do.

He Already Has a Mother

A man's past relationships with women, especially his mother, strongly influence how he deals with women in the present. His view of his mother as nurturer, his sister as supporter (or antagonist), his wife as caretaker of the details can cause him to ascribe inaccurate motives to women with whom he works. Although I did not explicitly question men about their mothers, many volunteered information on the subject.

Mark Kramer, professor and arts director at a community theater, expresses extreme irritation as he describes Ellen, the board president: "We're sitting here worrying about whether we have the funds to open the next show and she gets up, in the middle of all this, to pass around the coffee and the cookies! And I wanted to scream out: 'Don't be my mother! One is enough!'" Clearly, he resented Ellen's behavior.

When I relayed this scenario to a woman, she analyzed the meeting's dynamics differently. "Did Mark ever consider the possibility that the board president was, perhaps, simply trying to diffuse the tense atmosphere in the room by distracting people with food and coffee?" In Mark's mind, tension should naturally attend the budgetary process. From Ellen's perspective, that tension stalls clear thinking and good decision-making. Whatever the case, a man can ascribe emotionally charged meaning to a woman's behavior, especially if it reminds him of his mother.

When comparing Ellen's style with that of her male predecessor, Mark observes: "The male president brought in a written agenda. The female agenda is for everyone to take a minute to 'check in with themselves,' to see how everybody *feels* before we start the meeting." Mark says that he recoils when people reveal highly personal information such as "My dog just died" or "I love my new job." He thinks, "*Who cares*? I couldn't care less! And I think that in a volunteer organization, people's real personalities come out, but I resent this when I'm putting aside time to get something done for the organization."

From Mark's standpoint, the female president's style hinders group performance: "She is very good at tapping into feelings, but hardly ever sees the overall picture." How does Mark think she should behave? "I want leadership," he emphasizes. "I want someone to say: 'You do this. You do that.' And if someone needs to be criticized, just say it; don't soft-pedal it."

Why does Mark find a man's power displays less irritating than a woman's display of interest in personal connections? Quite simply, because he's a man.

Leslie Brody is not at all surprised by Mark's opinions. As she explains: "A man needs to de-identify with women to establish his own identity. In order to develop an identity, he must become 'not female.' The pressure on men to de-identify and also to put women down means that what they reject may be women's strengths."

The men I talked to expressed the greatest discomfort with any woman at work who conjures up strong, and often negative, images of women from their personal lives. Woman as nag tops the list.

John Lucas, a marketing director, acknowledges his tendency to overlook the nitty-gritty aspects of a project. He also talks about the negative images that race through his brain as soon as a female colleague begins to remind him about details he has forgotten: "Nag, nag, nag, nag. I don't feel comfortable organizing other people. I think it's almost condescending, sort of stepping on toes and patronizing." Then he adds: "But my mother has no problem doing that!"

One male manager immediately requested anonymity after sharing his technique for tuning out annoying people. "Perhaps it was the way I was raised, but my mother always used to talk and talk and talk and you had to learn to tune her out if you wanted any peace of mind." About applying this technique in the company where he works today, he says: "You've got to filter out the grief you get from a difficult boss. You have to learn to tune out the name-calling and insults that are extraneous to the job." Even when the toughest boss has castigated him harshly, he says, "I just key in on the problem and ignore everything else."

While some men harbor stereotypically negative images of women's roles, others seem to welcome a "mother" in the office. Peter Drake, co-founder of a healthcare investment banking firm, believes that a soothing office presence diffuses the intensity of his firm's highly charged environment. "One of my female partners does an outstanding job of putting men at ease because she is very approachable. She's very honest, but she is very non-threatening. I actually call her 'The Jewish Grandmother' because she puts people at ease." Hmm. Sometimes, it turns out, a mother can come in handy around the office.

On the other side of the psychological coin, a woman who does not measure up to standards a man associates with a woman's roles can also disappoint him. Jim Pratt, who works in finance, felt deeply disappointed when a colleague failed to live up to the positive image he had instinctively attached to her because of her gender. "I trusted Kate the way I trust my sisters," he said. "I was duped by her because I never saw her as a threat, the way I view my brother, and other men who always want to beat me at the game." In Jim's eyes, a comforter should not turn into a competitor.

Peers at the firm, Jim and Kate took on the task of developing a strategy that would launch a new service. The project appeared to be going smoothly until Jim discovered that Kate was making decisions without consulting him and then forwarding them to their boss. He felt betrayed that a woman, of all people, would stab him in the back. "I did not expect pride and politics to enter into the equation as much as they did. I generally tend to identify with women as a sort of familial presence as opposed to a competitor, or someone I need to guard against." With a male partner, Jim would have taken a different tack. In working with men he finds: "The rules are a little bit clearer, with more defined constraints to the relationship." With a man, Jim says, "I would not have let my defenses down."

Analyzing what got him into a messy partnership with Kate, he says: "In most interactions, there's something about the person that reminds you of someone in your family, and that's a powerful association. Thinking back to my own family, my relationship with my brother has been mostly competitive. My relationship with my two sisters has mostly been cooperative, collegial, pleasant, and unguarded." With his sisters, Jim says, he never engaged in the power struggles that, to this day, plague his relationship with his brother.

That, Jim thinks, may explain why he would instinctively view a man differently from the way he saw Kate: "I would not make the same error with a man because if I were to associate him with anybody, it would be my brother who I competed with for toys, for money, and in many dimensions. So I would be looking at: What's this person's agenda? How can I best meet my agenda given what *they* want?" Man-to-man combat he understood, man-to-woman combat he did not.

Joe Leghorn, an attorney, believes that many men resist accepting women as colleagues because on some levels, they fear them. "I think there are still a large number of men who are threatened by women. It goes back to the grade-school mentality: 'I'm not going to be beaten by a girl.'" In Joe's eyes, "The men who are the least supportive of women carry a certain discomfort with not knowing how to deal with women as equals." Joe suggests that men may also feel threatened by women because of their past experience in social settings: "There's another phenomenon from the male side which most males will never admit. At some time in their life, often in a dating situation, they have been intimidated by women—not that it was real, but it was perceived." Such threats can cause a man to build walls around his ego and to pull up the emotional drawbridge.

A Man's Office Is His Castle

In their effort to separate the personal from the professional, some men erect sturdy mental and physical boundaries. Mark Kramer, for instance, has purposefully excluded from his workspace any vestiges of his life outside the office. Thus, whenever he walks into a woman's office that looks like a second home or a cozy family den, "It sends signals to me that perhaps she would really prefer to be at home." As Mark explains, "I think women need more reminders of home—knick-knacks, pictures, plants. The first thing you notice is 'Wow, you look like you don't want to be here.' For women, it's important to have a comfortable work space that reminds them of plants and growth, warmth, kids staring at you." As far as he's concerned, Mark says: "If a workspace is really, really homey, I don't feel comfortable in it."

Hearing this reaction, Leslie Brody comments: "I wonder what Mark's scared of." A woman creates a comfortable environment at work, and a man reads hidden motives into it. Perhaps he reacts so strongly because the woman has violated the male code of maintaining distance between home life and work life.

Similar reactions apply to roles as well as decorations. At work, men often avoid the same roles they try to avoid outside the office. Psychologist Bill Winn points out that many men, as they concentrate on building a career, rely on their wives (many of whom also work) to manage family dynamics and personal relationships. He says the tunnel vision that protects a man at home makes him more vulnerable at work.

Women, Bill believes, often understand vulnerability much better than men. In Bill's view: "The myth of being in charge and having things go your way gets exploded earlier for women than it does for men. For some men, work provides a refuge from the difficulties of raising a family and dealing with relationships. But it also provides them with the false sense that the good life will go on." If a woman assumes the primary role managing a family, where she cannot control such issues as sick children or elderly parents in need of help, she has certainly experienced life's limitations up close and personal.

The castle-building that allows a man to feel in control of so many aspects of life can render him unexpectedly vulnerable, Bill suggests. The self-styled invincible man suddenly finds himself defenseless when faced with unforeseen setbacks, such as job loss, because he, unlike his female counterparts, has not maintained strong networks outside his work life. As Bill sees it, men let two factors conspire against them: "First, they've relied on their partners or spouses to keep social relationships going and don't have a support system for themselves. Second, men often have a harder time confronting frailties or limitations because acknowledging loss is unmanly."

Bill cites the extreme example of a stoic male, trained to suppress feelings, who nearly did himself in. "An executive came to my office for help in maintaining sobriety over the holiday season. He said he had been in a dark well for the past two weeks because he'd decided he couldn't call me and should tough it out." Recognizing a person in serious trouble, Bill asked him: "What made you think you couldn't call?" His client replied: "Well, I had a plan I was supposed to stick to, so I thought I couldn't call."

Well-schooled in what William Pollack terms "the boy code" in his book *Real Boys*, boys grow up with a "gender straitjacket that prohibits boys from expressing feelings or urges seen (mistakenly) as 'feminine'—dependence, warmth, empathy." With their ability to maintain a cool emotional distance and stick to the facts, men can seem almost invulnerable to emotions. Or do they just put up a good front, as Mike Snell, a fifty-three-year-old literary agent, says: "We wear more masks than women do. Just because a man doesn't share his feelings doesn't mean he doesn't possess them."

According to Barry Walker, an attorney, "Men take things absolutely as personally as women. There are as many thin-skinned men as there are thin-skinned women. However, the male psyche will do everything in its power to prevent a man from admitting that he has been wounded." When I asked Barry what he takes personally in a business setting, he replied, "Everything."

A man likes to appear invincible and not subject to emotional upsets. Beginning with the "big boys don't cry" message men constantly hear from an early age, men grow up to believe a real man does not allow himself to appear vulnerable through a display of emotion. Psychologist Bill Winn summarized this important part of the male psyche: "If I'm too emotional, I'm unmanned." Many young boys have been taught, particularly on the playing field, to equate emotion with lack of control. As Sylvia Senter explains in *Women at Work*: "Men, consequently, view emotionality as an inability to control oneself, an inability to behave rationally." This, in turn, explains why a man labels a woman out of control at the mere hint of an emotional reaction in a work setting.

A man's self-insulation in the office works against him when he applies business strategies to situations outside the office. Talking about that sort of transfer, Sean McNamara, a technical manager, says: "Men are not as sensitive as women. I do better in my professional relationships because they are defined by certain criteria–action items, contracts. Issues are very clear." While Sean succeeds in the black-and-white sphere of business, he finds himself challenged in the gray area of personal relationships: "I get in personal situations where I try to treat a relationship more like a business transaction. And it doesn't go over very well."

John Snow, retired company president, points to the tension that exists for people who manufacture quite different and at times conflicting public and private roles: "If you relate to women in a certain way, hopefully a healthy way, you can't relate to them one way in the workplace where you're spending eighty hours a week and another way where you're spending your discretionary and recreational time."

As a senior executive, Paul Meyers describes his professional style as "very blunt and very direct—and one that works phenomenally well." While expressing admiration for women who share many of his business traits, Paul also confesses: "A man may want a woman on a partner track to be very strong and very tough, but that's not the kind of person he wants to go home and have dinner with." In other words, some men expect women to behave one way at work and a different way at home. As Margaret Hennig and Anne Jardim conclude in *The Managerial Woman*: "A proposition developed from such a point of view would state that a successful woman cannot be a successful executive and a successful woman executive cannot be a successful woman." This potential dichotomy adds yet one more layer to the already complex puzzle of why some men may never feel fully comfortable working with women.

Joe Leghorn sees a distinct correlation between how a man behaves at work and how he leads his life after-hours. About men who resist accepting women as peers, he says: "They go home and expect a hot meal on the table. Their attitude is 'That's what women are for.'" When I asked Joe how his own attitude differs, he commented: "I come from a family of professional women. My grandmother owned her own pharmacy back in the 1920s so I've always dealt with women as professionals." Once again, a man's history of relationships with women helps explain his approach to working with women.

Details, Details, Details

Of course, we all carry aspects of our roles at home into the office. If a woman has fulfilled the traditional function as the caretaker of the details at home, she may naturally do the same, to some extent, in the office. If so, she may find herself in the same Catch-22 there that she faces at home: If she fails to remind the man to attend to details, they may fall by the wayside; and if she does remind him, he may see her as a stereotypic and unwelcome nag. It's a classic point of marital contention: dispute over details. Who should assume responsibility for them? Do they need to be done at all?

Leslie Brody observes that positions of power enable people to delegate details. If a woman feels uncomfortable with power, she will find it harder to say "You do this for me," rather than "I'll just do it myself."

John Lucas, who works in a *Fortune* 500 company, described how easily a strength in this regard defaults into a weakness, or at least a perceived weakness. In one breath, he defines the value that female coworkers bring to his team: "The women I work with lay out their customer proposals in such a compelling way, with seventeen different scenarios for implementation, that you'd be a moron to disagree with them. They hedge their risks by being more methodical, making sure they've dotted all the i's and crossed all the t's." Men, he believes, gravitate toward the opposite approach: "'Here's the vision.' And they give you one choice and you get excited about it and move forward, oftentimes to a fault." For John, mixed-gender teams offer a clear benefit: "They equal one another out so the job gets done right."

Like many of his peers, John will more likely assign coordination and logistical roles or process to women. "I don't know if they enjoy it, but they're good at putting together the plans and making sure everybody is doing things, sort of cracking the whip." For his part, John dislikes performing that role. "I can't be bothered with all the details. Oh man! You've got to nag people about them. Why should I have to remind someone? He should just do it. I don't want to be a house mother."

Reflecting on his experience as a member of an arts board, Mark Kramer believes: "The women are more detail-oriented, but not end-result oriented. The female members of the board always get lost in the details." Mark cites a recent discussion about a public event: "Before we've even gotten to how we're going to pay for it, or how it will be organized, the women are talking about how they can furnish the lobby and what kind of material they can put on the wall." When I asked him how he reacted to this line of discussion, Mark replied: "I just sat there in disbelief."

To insure that people pay attention to the right details, Mark recommends leading the discussion toward the organization's mission statement. This tactic, he says, forces focus on the important and away from the mundane. "Everything we do should be focused toward whatever that mission statement is. Then we can ask questions like 'If we do this, won't it go against who we are as an organization?' versus getting lost in the details or worrying about stepping on someone's toes."

In the male mind, getting it done, at times, matters more than getting it done right.

Ben Adams, who manages a primarily female staff, sees those irritating details as a crucial part of doing the job right. "Women," he contends, "tend to be a lot more steady in following through in their work. They take a project right straight through from beginning to end, with progress reports along the way, rather than being the rogue male and just diving into something, without thinking, and not doing it right." Not every man forgets about details entirely, but for many, too much attention to details gets in the way of action. And action occupies center stage in the male code.

Law professor Peter Enrich attributes a woman's detail orientation to the best of intentions: "I don't think of it as details versus the big picture, but as a willingness to get involved. All the women I work with convey the sense 'I'm part of my institution. I should throw myself into it.'" In other words, what some might label as unnecessary focus on the small things, others might see as total immersion in their work.

Dan Harris, who buys and sells businesses, ranging from $20 million to $300 million, factors gender into his hiring decisions, believing that a focus on details represents an advantage for certain jobs, a disadvantage for others. As an example of the latter, he cites his companies in advertising and the motion picture industry "where pennies aren't important at all—you're always dealing in big numbers." His service businesses exemplify the former.

Describing a woman who runs a $25 million service business, Dan refers to her as "a very, very tough manager, " but he sees significant differences between how she functions as a manager and how a man would. "She's in a business that requires enormous amounts of time worrying about very small amounts and very small percentages, like a 1 percent difference in a deal is very important," explains Dan. "I find men don't do that as well as women."

As Dan admires a quality he sees in more women than men, might it also work against his openness to hire a woman into a big-picture job? When Dan acquired his service business, he specifically searched for a woman. Even if not deliberately, might he have excluded a woman from being considered to run one of his $300 million companies? Would he worry about her ability to manage the big numbers and the big concepts? Might he also, on the basis of role stereotyping, exclude a man from a detail role in his business?

Big Boys Don't Cry

Sex-role stereotyping constrains a man's behavior just as much as it does a woman's. From the time little boys can talk, they often boast about their ability to take a hit without leaving the game. As their coaches insisted from grade school on: "You've got to play hurt sometimes." Consider how insulted a man feels when someone tells him: "You're acting like a woman," or "You sound like my mother!" Phrases like this may echo insults endured at an early age: "You're throwing like a girl" or "You're acting like a sissy."

Bill Winn told me: "If men acknowledge their emotions, they worry about behaving like a woman, which is a negative epithet. Words used to describe women are somehow second class, so men will avoid behavior that is 'womanlike.'" While men readily accept a man who blows up or storms out of a meeting with an outburst of anger and aggression, they disdain other emotional displays in the workplace.

In answer to the question, "What's the worst thing you've seen a woman do at work?" a majority of the men I interviewed answered: "When a woman cried." Tears spark less compassion than discomfort or even anger. They certainly have no place in the male code. If big boys don't cry, then the invincible woman shouldn't either.

For Mark Kramer, encountering a woman's emotions at work undermines clarity and control. From his experience: "Even the president of my arts organization has on occasion gotten really choked up and started crying." In his view, people can release their emotions, but only in private. "As much as I feel for anybody, I don't want their altered emotional states in my workplace. If you do that, even once, you set up this atmosphere where you're among the walking wounded." Mark especially resents the emotional impact on his own behavior: "Now I'm going to be walking on eggshells in terms of telling it like it is or rushing to get something through."

Worrying too much about people's feelings, some men told me, slows them down. Describing how women can ruin the tone of meetings with their emotions, Mark declares: "We don't have time to baby-sit everybody. When we have to overrule someone, we don't have time to stop and worry 'Oh no, someone's feelings are going to be hurt.'" Women, he believes, enlist optimism as a defense against hurt feelings and personal offense. He sees a man's more cynical view as more honest: "Opinions tend to be more realistic when they recognize the negative. Nothing is worse in an organization than a cheerleader saying 'Well, it will all work out'—but it always won't."

CEO Steve Grossman concedes that he has yet to master this one area as a manager. "As someone constantly on the go, who rarely comes up for air, I probably don't demonstrate sufficient sensitivity to the emotional fragility of employees. Women, in general, have a better instinct for knowing that somebody's in trouble and needs somebody just to sit and say, 'What's wrong? Let's take a walk. Let's go for a cup of coffee.'" In Steve's view, men often remain blind to issues that a woman sees instinctively. "By being less sensitive and less willing to drop everything when a colleague is in trouble, men don't nurture relationships as successfully as most women." And that can undermine effective management of human beings.

Leslie Brody says that "people in positions of power can afford not to be as aware of what inferiors are feeling." She points to recent research suggesting that even when superiors fully comprehend their subordinate's feelings, their position allows them to choose whether or not they will pay attention to them. In this case, the man holds the power to select the role.

Code Breakers

When a woman walks into the office each morning and walks into the home each night, she often encounters a different set of expectations than a man does, expectations that are reinforced or challenged by both men and women.

The roles we play often shape our behavior, and that behavior in turn shapes our culture. Can a woman select the roles she wishes to play, on her own terms rather than someone else's? What can a woman do to reinforce her own business instincts if she finds them challenged by stereotypes and misconceptions swirling around her?

The comfort with which a woman fulfills her various roles in life and at work usually depends, to some extent, on the support of the men around her. And the roles men play often distort their views of women.

Men often describe women at work in contradictory terms. As a participant in the Women and Public Discourse series at the Radcliffe Public Policy Institute suggested: "Women are defined as nurturing, maternal and kind, or they're described as hard, frigid and cold." Men at work, another participant observed, wield power more comfortably than women: "The very image of authority in our culture is associated with men . . . . When a man exercises authority, he's also enhancing his masculinity. Any sort of power a woman wields may well enhance her image of authority, but it also undercuts her femininity."

Acknowledging how so many human traits rest on a double-edged sword can help both sexes broaden our range of effective behavior in the workplace.

Code Breaker #1

Recognize that we often learn our best, albeit most frustrating, lessons from the most tense interactions between men and women.

In the case of Bill Haber and his boss, Anne, each perhaps reacted too emotionally because each unknowingly pushed the other's hot buttons. The more Bill resisted (and misinterpreted) Anne's questions, the harder she pushed. Both let a rigid pride in their own way of thinking mute the voice of the other person.

When a man conjures up stereotypically negative images—woman as domineering mother, woman as nag, woman as emotional wreck—he may overreact and launch into his own exaggerated behavior.

What's a woman to do? Should she start taking it like a man? Absolutely not, says Mike Snell, literary agent. As he sees it, the worst mistake a woman can make is to proclaim: "OK. Now that I'm in business, I've got to act like a man." In Mike's experience, this strategy often creates more problems than it solves, magnifying the challenges a woman faces as she enters male territory. A woman can, instead, use her knowledge of dangerous images a man may attach to her, based on gender alone, to inform her business strategies.

Code Breaker #2

Avoid letting a man's stereotypes tempt you to adopt a persona untrue to yourself. Your successes and confidence come from the comfort you feel in your own skin.

While gender differences can represent healthy and productive tension between the sexes, they can also pose a threat to men. A woman often walks a tightrope between a style that feels right for her on one side and a style that does not alienate or threaten men on the other. A trailblazer into male territory carries the extra burden of close scrutiny by her male peers, who may expect her to overachieve.

Code Breaker #3

Be aware that the same message coming from a woman often ignites a markedly different reaction when coming from a man.

As one executive I interviewed admitted: "What men in business can get away with in terms of an 'I'm the boss' attitude and 'I'm in control' approach, women have to find other ways of accomplishing. All too often, a double standard applies to women, particularly in leadership positions." For instance, "Aggressive behavior by male managers is frequently ignored, whereas the same behavior by a woman often draws critical comments."

While some men caution a woman against coming on too strong, others advise her not to be too soft. In a hospital setting, Roger Sims, a physician, has observed a reluctance among women to give direct orders, leading to trouble in keeping the sometimes rebellious troops in line. Instead of saying "I want you to do X, Y, and Z," women speak "in a more indistinct language so it's hard to understand exactly what's being said to you." Roger recalls one supervisor, in particular, who totally lost control of her group: "The rounds would go on and on with no particular focus. I desperately wanted more direction and more control to make the rounds shorter, more to the point, more concise."

While Roger may not have responded to indirect orders and indirect power, a woman probably would have. In her book *You Just Don't*

Understand, Deborah Tannen explains the source of this tension. "Often, the labeling of 'women's language' as 'powerless language' reflects the view of women's behavior through the lens of men's." A woman will often make requests with indirect language that to her exhibits politeness but to a man looks like a weakness, a lack of clout.

We cannot, in every situation, talk to a man the same way we would to a woman. We may need to think about a more deliberate approach, recognizing that a communication wall can only exacerbate a situation already mired in gender role confusion. When you find yourself at odds with a male associate, stick to your business goals.

A man who expects competition from another man may not gracefully handle a showdown with a woman. When a man casts a female colleague in roles familiar to him, such as mother or sister, doing so often distorts how he treats that woman.

Code Breaker #4

Remember that roles from the home can carry unintended and potentially explosive messages into the office.

A man may easily cast a woman in a role familiar to him, but that makes it very hard for her to be herself. Easy for him to expect her to worry about the details, hard for her to defy that expectation.

Many women, early in their careers, find that skillfully managing details brings recognition from bosses and colleagues. Yet, as their careers progress, this strength betrays them if they can't let go and delegate responsibilities. Susan Galler, president of a consulting company, cautions against getting buried in the details. "Don't forget that the work will always get done, but you'll never catch up, ever. Catching up is not the goal. Seeing the big picture is the goal."

Don't ignore the details, but don't get lost in them either. Details become particularly treacherous when they cast a woman in the role of supporter, rather than leader.

Code Breaker #5

Beware of gender landmines that explode for no other reason than the fact that you are a woman. Refuse to allow negative stereotypes to default into self-fulfilling prophecies.

A woman wielding power, delegating tasks, and rewarding or penalizing performance can invite gender-based stereotypes. In *The Managerial Woman*, Margaret Hennig and Anne Jardim pose an important question: "Finding a style that will work effectively, that doesn't come across as too 'masculine' (hard, tough, aggressive, unfeminine) or too feminine (not tough enough, overemotional, not enough of an initiator) is Catch–1001 for women in male work groups. How do you set standards for the quality of relationships you expect subordinates to meet if you are uncertain about the style you should yourself adopt?"

One woman, who refuses to allow confusing and contradictory expectations to mold her behavior, has arrived at this conclusion: "I'm probably never going to act in a way that men find totally acceptable so my best option is to find a style that works for *me*."

Regardless of the specific steps you take to implement your knowledge of conventional stereotypes, the knowledge alone will give you a certain degree of comfort, perhaps even control and power, in situations where men may be acting out the male mind without realizing it. Here, a little knowledge is not a dangerous thing, but a powerful thing.

4

Excess Baggage

Maneuvering Adversity and Adversaries

A little over a year ago, Brian O'Neil, a thirty-six-year-old father of four, found himself fighting for a job he didn't even want. When his annual performance review at a high-tech firm offered a scathing critique of his work, he came out swinging. "The first thing that came to mind was survival. I said 'OK, I'm in trouble.' I've got four kids and a big mortgage. I can become depressed. I can put my tail between my legs and sulk home, and then tell my wife 'I think I'm going to be out of a job soon.'"

When you come under attack, suggests Brian, "You can curl up in a ball and do nothing or you can get up and start swinging."

Although Brian loved the content of his work at the company, his long-standing philosophical disagreements with his boss came to a head. Once his boss began to hurl pointed personal insults his way, Brian admits, "My first reaction was to strangle the guy." Instead, Brian chose not to react immediately, telling himself, "Let's take a step back." Once he decided that he needed to regain some semblance of control over his job security, something clicked in Brian's mind. Here's how his thought process unfolded: "First, let's understand what the game is. If I go in there and start defending myself, I'm just going to get into a verbal fight—especially since my boss is known for managing by negative reinforcement." Seeking a better alternative, Brian reverted to his tried-and-true mode of operation: "I'm going to win. Guys are going to win. We're put on this earth to conquer."

With a clear focus on the goal most important to him, keeping his paycheck until he could find another job, Brian walked into his boss's office the day after his review and said, "I don't agree with much of what you put on paper. We can sit here and discuss every little detail, but the result won't be conclusive. What we need is some kind of decision right now." Using these words, Brian hoped to play on his boss's insecurity instead of his own.

Brian threw down the gauntlet. "As they were threatening my security, I threatened theirs because I knew the company wasn't prepared to lose another technical manager at that point in time." To test that assumption, Brian said, "Let's decide whether we're going to work on this in a positive direction or if it's not going to work and we should call it a day right now." As I listened to Brian's story, I began to see that his "start swinging" approach meant taking charge of what appeared to be a situation fully out of his control.

As a next step, Brian launched into what he terms "the sneaky part," during which he used words that said one thing, but meant another. Ending his meeting with a smile and a handshake, Brian told his boss: "Great. You want to work with me. We can be friends, right? Beautiful." In conveying a peace-making message that really meant war, Brian set up the appearance of loyalty to the team. In reality, he kept two thoughts in mind, "I need to buy myself more time so I can figure out what the heck to do next. And, inside I have a lot of emotions telling me 'I want to beat the living snot out of my boss.'"

When it comes to this sort of conflict resolution, Brian believes a woman would have handled it differently. In his eyes: "Women are more likely to let conflict get under their skin. From a woman's point of view, it becomes a lot more introspective. 'What have I done wrong. What could I do better? How do I save the situation?' All these things have nothing to do with the chess game."

For Brian, formulating his work strategy as a chess game helped him to suppress some potentially destructive emotions and to see more clearly all the options available. "I continue to play the game because I know what my hidden agenda is. I don't have a lot of emotion in this game. I can look at my possibilities and see what moves are available to me. This gives me the advantage, as long as they don't have a hidden agenda I haven't figured out." Brian's resolute refusal to fold under intense pressure got him exactly what he wanted. His boss gradually "got off his case and started on the next guy." Brian began to receive positive feedback from his boss just about the time he landed a promotion at a rival company. Dealing with his condescending boss, Brian suppressed his emotions and shifted the power to resolve the conflict from his boss to himself.

How we react when adversity strikes our work life provides a true test of our mettle. When asked about his definition of success, Sumner Redstone, the chairman and CEO of the media conglomerate Viacom, a billionaire many times over, told a reporter: "Success isn't what you do when you're on top of the world. It's what you do when you're down on your luck." Marty Bennett, still, at twenty-nine, in the early stages of his career, makes a similar observation: "I've learned more from making mistakes than from being successful. Everybody can't be successful all the time."

Another man I interviewed, Ryan Murray, now a vice president at another bank, squarely faced the closing of a large community bank where he was employed by choosing his own course of action, rather than letting others do it for him. As the number-two person at the bank, Ryan's first response was to "hold it together" for his own benefit as well as for that of his loyal staff. As Ryan reflects on his six months of unemployment, with sporadic consulting jobs to pay the bills, he says that, yes, he was worried about finding another job in an industry that was downsizing across the state, but no, he never took losing his job as a sign that he was somehow incompetent, or worse still, a bad person.

As he launched his own job search, Ryan reached out to his staff, many of whom had worked with him for more than a decade. Before the bank closed its doors, Ryan told his people: "Hey, this company is going out of business. Now is the time you need to start managing your life." Then he gave his group the support to do just that, helping himself as he helped others. Taking his advice to "move to Plan B" proved easier said than done, so Ryan arranged for psychologists and career counselors to meet with individual employees as well as their family members.

Concurrent with his own job search, Ryan wrote a handbook for his former staff on how to find a new job. As Ryan recalls this difficult time, he says: "There were some, both men and women, who just sat there thinking, 'Life sucks. It's over. What am I ever going to do?'"

For his part, Ryan examined the problem from two different angles. "One says my life is over, the other says life goes on."

Like many men, Ryan views the world through a prism that propelled him into a take-charge, never-say-die mode, rallying a competitive, and in Ryan's case, a team-building spirit. Like Brian, he followed the mantra: I will do everything in my power not to lose; even if I lose my job, I'll keep my pride intact; and when someone or something threatens me, I will do everything in my power to regain control. Ryan attributes his own rational and methodical perspective to an attitude that says "OK, this is a little blip in my career plan. It's not the end of the world. I still have a pulse." Hello, Plan B.

In his book *Real Boys*, William Pollack suggests that organized sports teach many boys to minimize the agony of defeat. "Sports take boys who thought they would always have to cover up their feelings of loss and vulnerability and show these boys that losing, and the pain that goes with it, are part of life, that one can be honest about one's disappointments, and that all one can do is just get up again, head back into the field, and continue to do one's best."

When confronting the nasty aspects of work, a man's goal remains the same: to remain confidently in control, or at least to create that impression for others to see. Many men I talked to described their absolute determination *not* to fold under the pressure of workplace challenges we would all rather not face: difficult situations, troublesome people, mistakes, criticism, any type of adversity. The true measure of a man's power, men told me, is whether he maintains control even in the most dire circumstances.

We have all been in situations where resolution seems hopelessly beyond our control. We think we must stick with a difficult boss until we find another job. We must hang onto that miserable client to meet our sales goal. In situations like these, men protect themselves in several ways as they channel their emotions into regaining control.

The Discipline of Restraint

Like most human traits, a competitive spirit encompasses a spectrum of behaviors, from positive steps to insure survival to negative and unprovoked aggression. When a man assumes a fighting stance, his mind concentrates on action rather than emotions. In other words, testosterone takes over.

Andy Friedlich, a health care consultant, believes that women face a supreme disadvantage when confronted by a very aggressive male. "There are times when I've seen women get bowled over because of an aggressive man who does not look at women as equals and is used to steamrollering over them." When faced with a person like this, he suggests: "You have to be able to disarm them. That's when a woman has to learn how to stand up for herself. A woman cannot afford to bow to intimidation." Why not? Because, "Once somebody has walked over you, you lose credibility."

As an example of someone who manages conflict gently but powerfully, Andy describes Eileen, a female medical director at a Boston hospital whose responsibilities include contract negotiations with an all-male group. According to Andy, most of the men enter the negotiations with a hard-charging, guns-blazing style that conveys, "Here's what I want, and I won't settle for less." Eileen, however, takes them by surprise when she does not fire back with an ultimatum of her own.

When Eileen needs to "dig her heels in", Andy says, she deliberately rebuffs the approach many men take: "No! You're not right! You guys don't know what the blazes you're talking about!" Instead, Eileen counters aggression with a clear, yet firm statement: "Yes, I understand your position; however, this situation is not analogous to the other case because the cost structure is different in the following areas."

Describing one particular negotiation, Andy says Eileen appeared "more relaxed, more willing to blow in the breeze while these guys vented and blew off their steam. Initially this caused her to appear as the weaker party," but the final results ruled in her favor. "The perception that she was in a weaker position made the men drop their guard. That's when Eileen would step forward with her facts. And because of the way they were presented, these guys would have no recourse but to agree." As Andy saw it, Eileen engineered the situation by arming herself with detailed facts, in contrast to the men who had entered the negotiations armed with aggressiveness.

Whether or not our jobs require formal negotiation, we all, at some point, need to bargain for advantage during conflict. When Ryan

Murray was promoted to chief operating officer of his bank, he encountered ten members of senior management who rarely communicated or cooperated with one another. "There were all these little kingdoms," recalls Ryan. To make matters worse, several of the people who now reported to him had been his bosses earlier in his career. Ryan decided to confront the infighting head-on. "The only way I saw to change the situation was to force them to work together. As juvenile as this may sound, I wrote a strategic plan that required four or five people to work together as a team. I looked at all the personalities and purposely put people together who hated one another."

On day one, Ryan says, "I had people screaming at me. 'There's *no* way I'm going to work with that person!' But I made it clear that their options were somewhat limited. They could either work it out or go find a new job." By forcing people to choose between the frying pan and the fire, Ryan was pursuing one clear objective: get results or get out. "If they won't work together on a simple strategic planning project, well, hell, they ain't gonna work together the rest of the year!" Over a ninety-day period, Ryan says: "I had people who absolutely detested one another going out to dinner as a group. I was forcing each one of them to develop a different level of respect and understanding for the other person's abilities." With no blood spilled on the bank floor, Ryan says, "It worked." By confronting, without hesitation, a sticky issue that lent itself to no easy resolution, Ryan transformed the contentious group into a functioning team.

When I asked Roger Sims, a physician, if he faces dissension in his current job, he instantly replied: "Oh, of course. All the time." Only recently has he begun to experiment with a positive rather than a negative response to contentious people. While Roger has tended to respond to conflict with a sarcastic retort, he now makes a deliberate effort to unravel the source of the dispute rather than to engage in it, putting out the flames rather than fanning them.

Like Eileen, Roger refrains from jumping into the fray, buying himself time to analyze and strengthen his own position. "Sometimes you'll find out another piece of the puzzle as to why someone reacted the way they did. You can even approach the person after the meeting and ask directly: 'Why did you react like that? What was going on? Did I miss something?'" In some cases, Roger finds resolution in a frank airing of differences. In others, he gains control of a volatile situation via a more circuitous route.

In Roger's experience, letting an adversary initially save face works to your advantage in the long-term. When confronted by one staff member "who challenged me on a hundred different fronts as I tried to conduct staff meetings," Roger restrained himself from lashing back with words that might have publicly humiliated the troublemaker. Instead, he allowed the insubordinate employee to save face publicly, believing that doing otherwise would cause others to jump into the fray, escalating the tension still more and relinquishing control to this highly difficult person. When he let his adversary save face, however, he increased his authority as a boss to resolve the conflict, which he did during a private follow-up meeting.

Whenever Roger cannot exercise direct control in response to a situation where the potential for political problems looms large, he follows a different strategy. Still, he resists his first inclination to respond emotionally. Admittedly, Roger learned the discipline of restraint the hard way. In his younger days, he gave into his first impulse and went to battle on issues he could not possibly win. The result? He lost big. "You take a public stand that you have to back down from, in public. Or, you're just ignored as a loose cannon, which sets a bad precedent for the future."

As Roger explains: "You need to figure out what your power base is and who's behind you. If you're really going to go to battle on an issue, you need to know who your allies are and how much power you have." Only after you have lined up your constituents, Roger emphasizes, do you go to war.

Ryan Murray summed up the strategy that seems to work for many men: "It's the ability to remain open-minded and to be able to respond as opposed to react." Ryan sees the difference in approach as not just an issue of semantics but of choosing a rational plan founded on action rather than emotion. Bottom line? "There is always a Plan B out there."

Bonding with an Adversary

Sometimes Plan B's feel counterintuitive. For example, if you cannot defeat an adversary, why not bond with him?

When Paul Meyers, CEO of a $50 million wholesale company, faced a volatile customer and a big mistake all rolled into one huge problem, he invoked a "kill 'em with kindness and understanding" policy. With an eye on the more critical issue, long-term success, not the crisis of the moment, Paul made carefully orchestrated moves aimed at regaining the trust of this important customer.

The problem began with a production delay at one of his Mexican factories. When Paul contacted his customer in New York to relay the bad news, the customer "went ballistic": "I'd rather burn this whole division down than do business with you! I have other options you know!" Rather than taking the reaction personally, Paul adopted a different view: "I knew there was a lot of theater in what he was saying." In reality, the two had agreed to such a tight delivery date that "I knew he was screwed if I didn't come through. In reality, I had him over a barrel." Nevertheless, Paul scripted a humble approach to the customer, telling him: "I know you have other choices and I know we screwed up, but we will do whatever it takes to regain your confidence."

This seemingly generous spirit actually represents a survival tactic. In tight spots like this, Paul says, he tries "to play to something that hopefully will be a strength for the business, which is the ability to be humble." As soon as you get overly aggressive, he emphasizes, "you get kicked and you're out of the game."

Brad Miller, a forty-five-year-old investor, meets the challenge of difficult people by doing something they would never, in their wildest dreams, expect: He makes nice. "I love dealing with difficult people," Brad explains. "They cannot handle niceness. When someone is nice to them, it just totally discombobulates them." As an example, Brad describes with some humor a group of people he works with whom he fondly calls "the shouters."

Brad disarms the shouters with charm, bringing them on board by "agreeing with them even when I don't agree with them." As he begins business negotiations with these testy folks, Brad immediately concedes one point. "You know, you're right. Why don't you take that point so that we can move on?" At that moment, the shouter may feel like "My god, it was easy to win that concession. Maybe I can let my guard down." This, says Brad, offers him a golden opportunity: "That's when I jump in for, I won't say the kill, but I can jump in and really influence the situation."

Marty Bennett, a sales rep who sells to physicians, uses humor for two seemingly contradictory purposes: first, to bond with even the most adversarial customer, and second, to keep a safe emotional distance from people who push his patience to the wall. In referring to one particularly volatile customer, Marty says: "On some days I walk in and he's just a real ass. And on other days, he's in a great mood." On the bad days, Marty takes a step back, (in this case, he means that quite literally) and "lets the guy vent and get off his chest whatever is bothering him." On these days Marty decides to cut his losses and not even mention his products. "I know the next time might just be a better opportunity," he says.

On the days when he finds his customer in a better mood, Marty uses humor to set a different tone and even to acknowledge their previous not-so-pleasant interactions. Joking to the physician, he says: "Maybe we should put a little red light/green light outside of your building so if it's red, I won't come in. If it's green, I'll make sure to run in." And on this day, his customer laughs "because *he* knows he's very moody."

After a bad day in the office, Marty mostly avoids excessive self-examination. Rather than assuming that he has somehow offended an irritable customer or done something wrong, Marty first considers every other viable explanation. As he constructs emotional distance between himself and an erratic personality type, Marty thinks about this basic analogy: "I walk into any situation and it's like the weather. You have to be prepared for good days and bad days and you may never know what to expect." That sounds sensible, but what if you stroll into a hurricane?

A Jerk Is Just a Jerk

Sometimes, not even generosity of spirit will win people over. Many men told me they will much more likely label someone a dope or a jerk rather than spend more than a split second analyzing that person's psyche. When sales director Bill Haber encounters a supremely difficult person, he just cuts his losses. What can I do to spend less time with him? Do I really need to do business with him at all? How can I replace him? Even when the challenger happens to be a really big customer, Bill does not believe in suffering the company of a fool any longer than absolutely necessary. "If some guy is an idiot, I am a lot more effective in the long run by saying 'I don't think I'm getting anywhere with him. So next.'" In other words, remove the jerk from your life, and get on with it.

For Ryan Murray, reacting to a difficult colleague makes less sense than simply not letting the adversary get under his skin. Be the big person, he suggests: "You have to kind of bite your pride. Although you think the person's a jerk, you have to be able to say to yourself 'The only way we'll be able to work together is to have some level of respect.'" As a manager of a large staff, Ryan makes every attempt to treat a difficult person the way he treats everyone else. He does this for two reasons. First, he says, "I take a deep breath and try to approach whatever the topic is in a way that will foster communication with the other party, as opposed to build barriers." Second, Ryan says, "I try to treat the difficult person the same way I treat the easy people. Because the thing a difficult person wants is to be treated differently."

When a man cannot either eliminate or manage a jerk, he sometimes opts for head-on confrontation. Richard Shell, a negotiation expert and professor at the Wharton School of Business, suggests that confronting a difficult, bullying, or competitive person head-on sometimes offers the best strategy. "Show them that, in your own way, you can be just as bullying and as assertive as they are. And chances are, they will escalate a bit, but then the competitive bully, having seen that you can match them on that front, will move to a second bargaining style that will be something other than bullying."

As an observer of hundreds of negotiations, Richard has seen a fighting-fire-with-fire approach succeed for both women and men who must deal with a bully. First, Richard advises, skillful negotiators "quickly show that you've got the stuff to stand up to them and that you won't proceed until they change their tenor." Seven out of ten times, Richard suggests, this will do the trick. But, he admits: "Three out of ten, the bully is completely irrational and there is nothing you can do about it. Find someone else to deal with, change jobs, go home and weep, or do whatever you need to do to handle a very tough situation."

How do these negotiation strategies apply to real-life, everyday business situations that at first blush seem out of our control? How do we work with a client who lies to us or a colleague who stabs us in the back?

Dean Mechlowitz, who works in telecom, has faced more than his share of dishonest customers. Once he discovers their deceit, Dean wastes not a single moment agonizing over that person's motives or intentions, rejecting any inclination to send a message that would never register with an unprincipled person anyway. Instead of saying, "How dare you! How could you do this to me after I've been so fair to you?", Dean focuses on finding resolution in his company's best interests.

"How can I put myself back in the driver's seat?" Dean asks himself. He uses words such as: "My understanding from our conversation on x date was that you had given me the verbal go-ahead. I'm very disappointed in the way you have proceeded. We acted on the information you gave us in good faith. Here's what needs to happen to get back on track." Redirecting the process in a direction where Dean regains control over the outcome matters much more to Dean than making accusations.

As a literary agent, Mike Snell deals with a lot of high-strung, difficult people and just factors their behavior out of the equation, reminding himself, "That's just the way he is. Don't worry about it. Go back to work. Don't waste time trying to 'fix' a jerk." But Mike says that dishonest or unethical people prompt a different response. "My reputation is so bound up with my clients' reputations that I can't afford to let someone get away with lying or cheating. I fire them immediately."

When it comes to issues of trust and betrayal in business, Mike protects himself by trusting his gut feelings. When one business associate let him down, every instinct told Mike to sever the relationship and never look back. "When this person betrayed me, he talked me into overlooking it and promised it would never happen again." But it did. With hindsight, Mike says: "Damn it, why didn't I listen to that inner voice the first time?" When faced with an untrustworthy client today, Mike nips the problem in the bud. "Whenever I have seen unethical or improper behavior on the part of a potential client and overlooked it, I've paid for it. If this is what I'm seeing in the good times, in the honeymoon phase of our relationship, imagine what it's going to be like later." Having learned that unethical clients can create a negative ripple in business, Mike firmly recommends: "Better to cut the relationship short early on than to let it fester and get worse.

It's the old saying: 'If you screw me once, it's your fault. If you screw me twice, it's my fault.'"

A Mistake Is Just a Mistake

Just as a jerk is sometimes just a jerk, a mistake is sometimes just a mistake. While not endorsing careless mistakes, law partner Bob Gault makes this observation: "Even the very best lawyers make mistakes, so all you can do is your best. And realize that 99 percent of the mistakes will never have any major consequences at all."

We all, of course, make mistakes, but does a woman tend to take it harder than a man? I asked each man I interviewed "How do you react when you've make a mistake?" Nearly every one responded with the same answer: "I just say 'I made a mistake.' And I fix it." When men make mistakes, they may scold themselves by saying "I did a stupid thing," but they don't think, "I must be a stupid person." Brad Miller, who works in the high-stakes field of investments, advises his staff: "Treat the problem like a cancer. Respond quickly and immediately. Like cancer, if you let it grow, it will eventually eat you up." And, he emphasizes, "Don't make the same mistake twice, but don't carry baggage either. Just get it over with."

Ben Adams, a thirty-four-year-old customer service manager, was one of only a few men who confessed to letting mistakes gnaw at him. "I will rarely show it outright. I get upset, but rarely, if ever, discuss the problem with anyone else." Where does Ben find forgiveness for his errors? "It just goes away eventually. It's really something I just deal with myself." Despite this emotional inner turmoil, Ben does not let fear of making a mistake paralyze him with inaction.

On this subject, Bill Haber asserts, "One of the most powerful business skills you can have is to free yourself of the fear of making mistakes. Making mistakes is the only way we learn." While men seem to focus more on resolving the problem rather than berating themselves over it, they also caution against trying to cover up errors. When you make a mistake, admit it right off the bat. I heard this advice from nearly every man I interviewed. John Snow, retired company president, put it this way: "If you try to hide a mistake and you wait until the boss notices and nails you, then you're in for some rough sledding." The wiser person says: "I've done something stupid. Now here's how I'm planning to fix it."

Greg Block, a director at an international commission, also believes in acknowledging mistakes quickly and honestly. It's not always easy, he says, because "Corporate cultures seldom provide a supportive environment for self-criticism." On the other hand, Greg cautions, acknowledging mistakes does not get you off the hook if you make too many of them. "If I were committing a lot of them, I would be much more discreet about which ones I owned up to!"

As someone who has supervised many women, Ryan Murray, the bank vice president, observes: "When I tell a woman she's made a mistake, she either feels hurt or it wears in her subconscious longer than it does for guys. But a lot of the reaction depends on the person's level of security or insecurity." As Bruce Kohl, journalist, points out, a majority position can strengthen feelings of security. "Men," he says, "don't have to be as circumspect about how they do things because of the power and support they have in most workplaces. Women may develop a fear of making *any* mistake because the consequences, quite frankly, may be more dire for them."

Barry Walker suggests that men may say one thing about mistakes yet think something quite different. For himself, a blunder sparks this thought first: "How could a smart person have done such a stupid thing?" His second thought grows more introspective: "You beat yourself up over it. You give yourself hell for making the mistake." But to the outside world Barry tosses off a flip remark, such as "Well, that's why they put erasers on pencils." As Barry admits: "You don't really mean it. It's a blow to your ego to make a mistake."

When I raised the subject of mistakes with Peter Drake, co-founder of a health care investment firm, his answer took less time than my question. "I deal with it completely honestly. I try to analyze what I did wrong and I try to communicate it. Then I completely let it go." In other words: I control the mistake; the mistake doesn't control me.

Risky Business

A man looks at risk the same way he looks at mistakes. Either is preferable to inaction. Yet, if the price of inaction versus making a mistake seems unacceptably high, then the price of inaction versus taking a risk seems exponentially higher. As Mike Snell sees it: "Making a mistake might cause you to say 'I won't make that mistake again.' But avoiding risk in the future can cause you to make the biggest mistake of all. Making no decision is worse than making a bad one." Men feel as comfortable taking risks as they do making mistakes because both represent action.

Roger McPeek, now retired at age forty after selling his successful start-up, voices this opinion about taking risks: "If you're not making mistakes, you're not trying hard enough." Entrepreneurs roll the dice every day. Mike Snell, who specializes in books for entrepreneurs and small-business owners, observes gender differences in the magnitude of risk an entrepreneur will take. "A man will, without batting an eye, go to the bank and borrow $200,000 whether he needs it or not. A woman will lie awake night after night for three weeks worrying about borrowing $1,000 when she really needs $100,000." In analyzing the results for these entrepreneurs, Mike observes: "More men failed because they over-risked and more women failed because they under-risked. The women are too cautious and worry about every penny." The men go out on a limb even when reason should tell them to do otherwise.

On the subject of female entrepreneurs, Mike suggests: "I think it gets back to the fact that most women harbor some maternal instincts. They're very concerned about the health and psychological welfare of themselves and their families. I think a woman extends into a business some of those feelings." In Mike's view, a woman sometimes cares too much for her own good. A man, he believes, will more likely say: "So your business blew up. Do another one. Job didn't work out? Get another one." This puts you in more control than believing "My whole life is going down the drain."

"When it comes to making a really big mistake in business, a man will not feel as destroyed by it," says Mike. Dan Harris, who has served as CEO of two $300 million enterprises, agrees and describes his approach to the risk/reward equation: "I've always believed that people don't succeed unless they've been right on the edge, hanging on with one fingernail. And if you haven't had that experience, you can't be a very good entrepreneur." To illustrate this point, Dan describes a terrible decision he made early in his career when he rejected a business proposal from a *Fortune* 500 company that he soon learned would have made him a millionaire many times over.

When I asked him how he recovered from such a costly decision, Dan replied: "Well, you just forget it. It was just a bad decision. If you want to play the game, you better damn well realize that you're going to have failures." He adds: "Of course, you can't afford too many of those." Given the level of detail with which Dan told this story, it became clear that he hadn't actually forgotten this mistake, but he didn't let it break him either. Instead, it spurred him on to make millions in television and other media ventures.

Glenn Sears, a vice president at a well-known Silicon Valley firm, works in an arena where risk figures prominently, but mistakes could spell the end of a career. From his perspective, you minimize risk on two fronts: with a contingency plan to fall back on, and with clear accountability for each step of the process. As he points out, the small stuff can sometimes kill you. "A lot of times if something isn't going right on the smaller scale, it's just the tip of a bigger problem. Being sensitive to those small signs and following up on them minimizes the risk that something severe will go wrong."

Barry Walker points to a fundamental reason why men may feel more comfortable with pushing the envelope and going out on a limb. "They have less to lose than women. They're already there. They've been there a long time." And if a man stumbles in a risky venture, he can often turn to a buddy nearby who will help him get back on his feet.

Barry believes that at least part of the difference between how women and men approach risk and the possibility of failure comes from the built-in lens through which we view our potential: "For men, it's in the nature of the hunter. If you're going to get your prey, you have to go out and take a chance. If the prey turns and bites you? Lick your wounds, then get back in the hunt."

Damage Control

A healthy ego allows a person to use mistakes as an enhancing tool rather than a diminishing event. The type of respect accorded to a man who admits his error may originate in the experiences of young boys on the athletic field. "Yes, I should have passed the ball" wins much more respect than whining about how the other team played unfairly. Coming clean about a dropped ball or a missed shot clears the air and tightens the bond with teammates.

"Never make excuses when you screw up with a customer," advises Dean Mechlowitz. "That only makes matters worse. Just say, 'Yes, I was wrong, but here's what I'm going to do to fix it. And be assured, this will never happen again.'" Most customers, he believes, will forgive one mistake, assuming it's not monumental. But from then on, they expect no more errors.

Concerning damage control after a setback, Bill Haber suggests: "Don't be too preoccupied with looking powerful or not admitting fault. The best approach is humility. Men respect humility in other men." The question arises: Do men also respect similar humility in women, particularly if they hold female colleagues to a higher set of standards?

Owning up to a mistake not only reflects honesty, it can help insure survival. Step forward before an adversary does, Bill says. "Beat your competition at admitting when you screw up, because there's internal competition no matter where you are. This way, no one can argue with you."

Although Bill cautions against over-apologizing, calling it a sign of weakness, he also contends that accepting responsibility for a mistake can become a badge of honor. Bill put this delicate principle into practice when his CEO made a special trip to a branch office to review the loss of an important deal. The CEO basically said, "This company doesn't lose deals. What's going on here?" One director answered: "Hey, we were competitive in the technical process. It wasn't our fault." Another manager offered: "We communicated every step of the way. It wasn't our fault."

By the time the CEO got to Bill, they were sitting alone in the conference room. "So why did we lose the deal?" asked the CEO. Bill thought for a minute before he answered: "Well, there are a lot of reasons I could give you, but in the end I think I could have been closer to the customer and I could have done a few things differently. I know we don't like to lose deals, and I take responsibility for not doing some things that could have saved it." The CEO took Bill by surprise when he said: "Thank you." Bill, of course, asked: "For what?" The CEO said: "Thank you for being the first person, when I've traveled halfway across the world to come here, to take some responsibility and be accountable. Don't misunderstand me. I don't want to lose deals. I don't want to come here and hear 'I'm sorry' every time, but if you realize what you did wrong, we know you're not going to repeat it in the future."

For Bill, admitting a mistake scored points with the top gun. The right packaging of his words, no emotions, short and sweet, exquisite timing, after the CEO had already heard excuses from others, worked in Bill's favor. "In the end, even though what we were talking about was a failure, it was a win for me," Bill says. "I built a better relationship with the CEO and won his respect." Bill's ego clearly did not overrule his better judgment.

The Teflon Ego

Just as readily as Bill Haber accepted the blame for a team loss, other men feign incredulity: "Who me? I had nothing to do with this." They assume you can avoid the consequences of a mistake by denying that you have even made one. When I asked law professor Peter Enrich how he deals with mistakes, he smiled and said: "My wife would tell you I never admit that I made one." He concedes there's some truth to her opinion. "I am very reluctant to admit that I made a mistake," he says. "I'm much more inclined to say 'It was a reasonable strategy, but it didn't work out.' I'm probably very bad about taking responsibility for blowing something." Peter says that he rationalizes the error by analyzing the situation rather than criticizing himself or someone else. "I've never been as interested in apportioning the blame as in figuring out how to fix it." And, he adds, "I'm certainly not inclined to apportion the blame to me!"

If you deny that you have made a mistake, then it stands to reason that something or someone else did it: the team, the weather, just a bad day. Ray Ingalls, a business manager in high tech, observes that as a gay man, he often finds himself thinking about issues differently from the other men in the office. Like many of his female colleagues, Ray says he tends to personalize mistakes and feel the weight of the world on his shoulders. Most men, he believes, find it easier to displace blame. "Maybe it's a coping mechanism that men use so that they can move on and continue, without obstruction, towards whatever their next goal is." If the dog ate your homework, then you can move on to the next assignment.

While some men seem willing to accept a mistake that they themselves made, they don't so easily accept someone else's criticism. Why shoot yourself when you can shoot the messenger? Nobody really enjoys criticism, but the way we process it determines its effect on how we perceive ourselves as well as how others perceive us.

Men carve out emotional distance from criticism by making it not about them, but about the other guy. In his role as town selectman, where criticism sets the tone for many meetings, Peter Enrich adopts this approach: "If I'm on my game, the way I react when I'm functioning best is to be diagnostic. Where are they coming from? Why are they experiencing me like this? Their evaluation doesn't sound like me. So what's happening with *them*?"

In particularly volatile sessions, Peter uses the classic technique of diffusing criticism by listening carefully and then summarizing his critic's comments. However, Peter cautions that the tactic can appear Machiavellian. "I feel sort of condescended to when I feel somebody is doing that to me, but I find that when it doesn't look too blatant, it works very well."

In his own experience, John Snow, now retired, responded to criticism from a boss or board member in one of two ways. In one instance he might say: "Yeah, you're right. You got me. What can I tell you? Hopefully, I learned a lesson from it." But when he thought his boss was wrong, "I'd fight him tooth and nail, and say 'No, I don't think you're right. I am certain I am right. You're overlooking this important point.'" In the latter case, John took care to deliver his message in a way that did not come off as too defensive or combative: "I'm pretty rational, too, so I didn't get emotional. But I wasn't afraid to put a logical rebuttal on the table." In other words, you can't dent a man's ego if he's coated it with Teflon.

When a man delivers a negative message to another man, does he sometimes increase the firepower in order to pierce the Teflon? Ray Ingalls thinks so, especially when the man is delivering a poor performance review. "Many of the male bosses I've worked for have been punitive in performance evaluations as opposed to constructively critical." As to the motives behind this behavior, Ray suggests: "Maybe they believe that a way to motivate good work is by sort of punishing you." This approach may reflect the mentality of "you have to pay a price for a loss" and "just play through the pain" that some coaches drive home on the athletic field.

By denying they have done anything worthy of criticism, men go one step further and deny that criticism angers or upsets them. As Ben Adams, the head of a customer service group, sees it: "The majority of men are probably defensive at some level. They don't really believe that they've done anything wrong. They say 'Yes, OK, I'm listening' but they're not really paying attention to what you're saying. They're thinking how wrong *you* are."

While men might deny criticism, Ryan Murray, the bank vice president, believes that women get too emotionally invested on either end of criticism. "When a female disciplines a subordinate, there tends to be a tone of 'I don't want to hurt your feelings. I'm sorry about this.'" When a man delivers a negative message about performance, Ryan says: "He is more apt to say 'These are the issues and this is what we need to do about it.'" As for this difference in approach, Ryan comments: "I think it comes down to the maternal instinct that women have."

Mark Kramer, the college professor, has noticed a distinct difference in the ways women and men on his community arts board react to criticism. "I tend to get a bigger reaction from women who tend to look crushed and retreat. I feel like I have to soft-pedal the criticism just to keep them in the game." In telling a woman what she did wrong, Mark will wrap words of support around his critical message, saying something like: "Well, I understand why you want to do this, but—" or, "I acknowledge your position and your reasoning, but—"

When speaking to a man, Mark does not hesitate to use direct statements: "I think you're wrong." In considering how gender influences his response, Mark observes: "For women, I feel like I have to acknowledge their participation first, more so than with a guy." With men, he believes, "I know they will be more outcome-oriented and not take criticism personally."

Insults among men occur naturally, both during games as boys and during bonding as adults. For many men, experience with "playful criticism" explains why insults and critical messages do not necessarily cause emotional injury. The worst insult one boy can hurl at another boy? "You're playing like a girl." That, suggests Pat

Heim, management consultant, doesn't hurt much, either. "Boys grow up getting constant criticism and have learned to compartmentalize it. Because women haven't learned to compartmentalize it, we see this criticism as being about my whole being, my very core, everything I am, rather than 'My boss just doesn't like this part of the report.'"

Men also grow up mocking themselves as part of the game, often calling upon self-deprecating humor, or even insults, to rescue themselves from a miserable situation. This is a tactic that serves the purpose of throwing the first punch, in this case at themselves. "Be your biggest critic—at least publicly. And you don't even have to mean it," suggested Bill Haber with a laugh.

Deep down, most people, regardless of gender, would prefer not to hear criticism. When he actually deserves criticism, Barry Walker reacts one way. When he doesn't think it warranted, he reacts quite differently. "I get pissed. But I very rarely show that I am bothered by the critique. I think it's human nature, not gender, to be offended when you're criticized, particularly when you perceive the criticism to be unfair." At the same time, Barry wants colleagues to approach him honestly when he has done something stupid: "I don't want to be surrounded by people who kiss my ass."

The wisdom of experience has taught Barry to welcome criticism before he rejects it. He cites as an example a judge who, many years ago, called him into his chambers after a trial in which Barry admits: "I was a hotshot and I just lambasted some poor police officer. I was unmerciful to this guy." The judge gave Barry some advice: "I want you to listen to me. You get a hell of a lot more with honey than you do with vinegar. Remember that. Good day." Barry took the judge's critique to heart and learned to calibrate his style more carefully. He now reflects: "My reaction to criticism, even though I'm offended by it, probably deep down even by fair criticism, is absolutely one of gratitude."

When a man sees a critique as valid, he may dissect it to see what he can learn, but he rarely takes it personally. By adopting a perspective that protects him from feeling overwhelmed when things do not go as planned, men like Barry Walker remind themselves on a regular basis: "I'm not perfect, but neither is the next guy."

Just Say No

Men use a variety of strategies to define boundaries between themselves and the unpleasant and sometimes unforgiving aspects of their jobs. "Here's what I do. Here are my boundaries. Cross them at your peril." Discussing his male colleagues who rely on this approach, Peter Enrich, law professor, observes: "I don't think there's a single woman [I know] who has said or done anything remotely like this." Another man made the point that at both work and at home, his wife finds it exceedingly difficult to say no. In his view, for his wife, saying no brings so much guilt that she finds it easier just to give in and agree reluctantly.

For some men, Peter says, refusing to do something can also represent fear of the unknown. "No" can mean "I'm not going to go near that stuff. It's not what I know how to do. It's not what I like to do. Let me stay where I feel comfortable."

According to Peter, women, less comfortable with their place in the organization, think they can't say no to requests at work because they'll be letting down the institution. Men, he believes, more readily assume an identity that separates who they are from how much they do for the organization, defining the roles they will play rather than allowing the institution to do it for them. Peter sees male colleagues as more willing to declare: "This is who I am and don't expect me to be anything different because that's not me."

Management consultant Pat Heim observes that men feel quite comfortable verbalizing a direct "No." Women, she contends, prefer to embed their response in several apologetic sentences, saying something like: "I'm in the middle of a huge project right now. If I don't get this done, I'm dead meat. I could help you after the fifteenth, but I can't help you now." In Pat's view, a woman's discomfort with wielding direct power can make it harder to say no. Add to this a desire to appear helpful and caring, and a direct no, suggests Pat, may feel like too high a price for a woman to pay.

Gender differences in how we say no often raise the odds for mixed signals. The effectiveness of our message depends not only on our delivery but on how the recipient views and processes our words. In her book, *You Just Don't Understand,* Deborah Tannen describes the reality behind the myth of the over-apologetic woman, suggesting that women may appear to apologize when they tell someone no. "There are several dynamics that make women appear to apologize too much. For one thing, women may be more likely to apologize because they do not instinctively balk at risking a one-down position. This is not to say that they relish it, just that it is less likely to set off automatic alarms in their heads." And men often interpret a woman's words inaccurately, Tannen says. "Women frequently say 'I'm sorry' to express sympathy and concern, not apology."

For Marty Bennett, who works for a pharmaceutical company, saying no without apology is a sign of strength. When faced with a high-pressure customer, Marty handles the situation from the standpoint of time management. "I want to make sure that I retain the respect of the customer. I set limits by letting them know that my time is as valuable as their time." To weigh the true urgency of a request, Marty first factors in the customers' relative importance and where they fit into the scheme of other priorities. He feels no qualms about a response that says, "I can't do it today." Period. No apologies, no explanations. Marty adds: "Even if the person is a good customer, you may have other fish to fry so you need to balance out everyone's needs. It's not going to kill them if they have to wait a day or two." To put himself firmly in control of customer expectations, Marty says: "I prove to them I'm the best person to buy from. I always under-promise and over-deliver." Like many men, Marty follows a code that puts himself rather than someone else in the decision-making role.

As a man who practices a collaborative style, Frank Andryauskas, now a partner in a start-up and a former Staples executive, has learned how to maintain his own powerful position as an outsider in competitively charged organizations. Essentially, he has learned to say no to people who prefer that he transform himself into someone other than who he really is. As Frank explains: "A simple understanding of basic personality grids and of where you stand on the grid helps you understand that a difficult interaction is not a condemnation of you, but a natural exchange that's taking place between personality types." With this outlook, Frank says, he suffers no lingering self-doubt, wondering whether he should tailor himself to fit the culture.

With even the most challenging bosses, Frank has learned "to stand a little more courageously in the heat of the moment." Adopting an intellectual perspective about what he can and cannot control allows Frank to draw his own line in the sand on what he will, and will not, agree to do for the sake of the bottom line. Believing strongly in a principle-based philosophy about work, Frank comments: "Would you rather manage your own destiny, or be trapped in a destiny that's being dictated to you by someone else? And to the extent that you have the luxury of that choice, it is better to stand strong and take the risk, in the worst possible case, of dictating your own departure rather than continuing to live with humiliation."

Once again, the powerful guise of comfort, confidence, and control underpins the male code. Ryan Murray offers this insight: "There are few things in life that are the end of the world. And even fewer things in business."

Code Breakers

Investor Peter Drake describes his style as "direct, factual, and never mean spirited." When he finds himself on the receiving end of criticism, Peter's thick skin allows him to deflect a fairly high degree of insult. "Being called stupid is nothing in this business. Being called a toad is nothing too. Being told to 'F— off and die' is a little harder to accept." When confronted by a client who spouted these brutally cruel words, Peter simply replied: "I'll have to call you back." His real message? "I'm sorry I have to work with you, so I need to assess whether I can dump you as my client." Five minutes after the initial exchange, Peter redialed the client's number, telling him: "You know, we've known each other for a long time and you are entitled to your opinion. But when you are abusive and you haven't done enough business with us, the only thing I can say is, 'I don't ever want to talk to you again. That's it. The relationship is over. You're not a big enough client to treat me that way.'"

While most of us may never enjoy the luxury of delivering a response like Peter's, we can certainly take steps to bolster our negotiating position as we work our way through the trials and tribulations that attend every work environment.

What gave Brian O'Neil the courage to stand tall, and, in fact, end up in a much stronger position after his devastating performance review, was a belief in himself. Never losing sight of his technical strengths, he employed them on two fronts: first, to redeem himself professionally and prepare to leave the company on his own terms, and second, to use his prized skills as a software engineer as a point of leverage to buy time and regroup.

Code Breaker #1

Recognize that the best defense is often a strong offense.

Wisely letting an adversary save face can yield huge dividends over the long term. In some cases, the adversary finds someone else to taunt. In others, he or she becomes an ally. And sometimes the time you have bought yourself with your generosity of spirit immediately elevates your own position.

Men often use heavily scripted and carefully crafted responses to maneuver around political landmines, volatile people, and untenable situations. Negotiate from a position of strength by not backing yourself into a corner when someone confronts you.

Reacting instantly and emotionally to a problem situation or person can pour kerosene on the flame. Instead, hold back a bit, fully assess the situation, buy time to do some fact-finding, then readdress the situation more confidently. In one situation, you may decide to let someone else win the battle so that you can win the war. Once Brian O'Neil determined that his relationship with his boss had deteriorated beyond repair, he temporarily retreated as he initiated an active job search.

Under a different set of circumstances, such as a heated disagreement about business strategy, Brian might have returned to an unresolved conversation armed with new data to support his position: "You know, after running these numbers a second time, I see a stronger case for going forward with this plan. Here are the facts that support it. Take a look, and why don't we set up a time to meet tomorrow?"

Code Breaker #2

Choose your battles carefully. Before men go to war they retreat to line up their soldiers, analyze the battlefield, and confirm their power base.

Sometimes it makes more sense to walk away from the challenge than to stay and take the heat. When confrontation occurs, buy yourself some time to fashion a considered response. When a difficult person confronts you, transform your position into one of control by telling yourself: "I am not going to let myself react. I refuse to let this person unnerve me. If I do lose it, it just makes me feel terrible. The adversary could care less about how I feel. I bet that person won't be tossing and turning at night, replaying the scene over and over."

An emotionally distant stance often enables men to take power out of the hands of the difficult person on the other side of the table. At the other extreme, men also assert their power by responding with intense aggression, aimed to intimidate. How can a woman best respond to an aggressive male? Consider the options.

Code Breaker #3

Do not expect a highly aggressive person, regardless of gender, to accept a different view of the world. You can either find a way to ignore the person, you can work around him, or you can strike back. But whatever you do, don't expect the person to change.

As Professor Richard Shell explains in *Bargaining for Advantage*: "Competitive people are hard to 'convert' to cooperation because they almost always see their counterparts as competitive. They adhere to 'rules of the game' that reinforce this belief." Even if such an approach runs contrary to your natural inclination, remember that meeting aggression with aggression often works.

Code Breaker #4

When faced with extreme personalities, temporarily adjust your style to speak in a language and style they will hear and understand.

Try what has worked for Frank Andryauskas, whose own collaborative style got no results in meetings conducted by highly aggressive people. Position yourself and your words with a tone that says: "You really need to hear me out on this issue. I am absolutely certain that my approach will benefit the bottom line."

Richard Shell offers an explanation for why Frank's approach often succeeds: "When two competitive people negotiate, they clash, bargain hard, and take risks. But, surprisingly, they can often get the job done because they understand one another." In other words, a woman may sometimes need to speak in a language that the man on the other side of the table will understand. This simple communication tool need not change your underlying game plan.

Code Breaker #5

Don't let a difficult person or a difficult situation steal your thunder or your self-assurance. Remind yourself that sometimes a jerk is just a jerk.

In teaching seminars on how to deal with difficult people, Naomi Deutscher, a consultant, recommends a two-pronged approach. First, "Stop wishing the difficult person would change. Remember that punishment, retaliation, and manipulation will not change anything." Second, defend yourself by taking control in a way that allows you to formulate a new game plan. "Protect yourself. Don't act in the heat of the moment." If all else fails, Naomi suggests: "Cut your losses. Distance yourself mentally or physically from malicious, hateful, or extremely manipulative people."

Not only do men cut their losses with others, they also, in effect, cut their losses with themselves. Men seem to spend less time on self-criticism than many women do. When a man stumbles, his first inclination is to blame a poor strategy rather than to blame himself. This depersonalizes and deflects any negative impact on himself.

Code Breaker #6

Never hide a mistake. It will only come back to haunt you. If you make a mistake, be the first to admit it, fix it, learn from it, and move on.

Freeing yourself from the fear of failing opens up new opportunities. Being the first to admit you've made a mistake should be coupled with the politically wise strategy of presenting your admission as a plan rather than a problem. Women, in particular, get singled out for over-apologizing. Choose your words carefully when you need to own up to a problem. For instance, telling your boss "You won't believe what happened. I never anticipated these results and I'm really upset about them" will only make the error look bigger than it is. Saying, "Here's what went wrong and here's how I'm going to fix it" positions you as a realistic problem-solver.

In many situations, short and sweet fares better than long and drawn-out. One day, I heard an interviewer ask Oprah Winfrey how she has learned to set limits on herself and on others. "I had to learn that 'No' is a complete sentence," she said. Less can sometimes mean more.

Code Breaker #7

Remember that perspective brings control. Changing our perspective means changing the level of control we feel, even in highly volatile settings.

What you do is not who you are. As strongly as many men channel their egos into their work, they employ that same ego to fortify themselves against blaming themselves for people and situations they cannot control. Never relinquish confidence in your abilities. Even under the worst set of circumstances, you may have more control than you think. There's always a Plan B out there.

As we learn to interpret how the male gender lens perceives workplace interactions, we can respond in a way that clarifies our own gender-based responses and encourages productive alliances where gender is not an issue.

5

Insult and Inquiry

Mixed Signals and the Great Gender Divide

Sometimes dismantling the barriers between men and women at work takes little more than the ability to distinguish an elk from a deer. Diana Foster, a consultant at an international firm, laughs heartily as she tells her animal tale. As so often happens, Diana and a male colleague visited a prospective client as a team to allow the client to choose the lead consultant. While waiting in a conference room, Diana says that she tried hard not to stare at what looked like a deer's head mounted on the wall. Before the two consultants even began their pitch for the engagement, Diana's colleague, who had correctly identified the dead animal as an elk, began discussing bow hunting with the client. As luck would have it, her colleague had come across an article on hunting elk while on a weekend canoeing trip with the guys.

"And, he got the job," concludes Diana. Now, while other factors may have been at work as the client made his decision, connecting on a personal level definitely helped close the deal.

While Diana disdains any interest in anything remotely related to hunting, she understands the power of human connection. She may not know one mounted head from another, but, still, she says: "I can bring some things to the party that most guys can't. People will talk about their personal life with me, while they don't seem to open up with men until they have known them for a long time. So I can take advantage of that."

What can women do to "bond" with their male customers or colleagues? What, in a man's mind, prevents him from feeling as comfortable working with talented women as he does with talented men?

Surprisingly, the younger men I interviewed expressed the greatest annoyance about having to work alongside women. David Knight, a thirty-two-year-old vice president at a well-known Wall Street firm, explains his view: "There is a constant overhang, or concern, that if I say something wrong, I'm going to get sued, or it's going to get back to one of my bosses if I joke around too much, a constant fear that I can say or do something that will get me in trouble around here. I hate that. I'd rather there were not women working here." In vivid contrast, a small number of men in my sample grew up in cultures where women represent both bosses and colleagues and where working with them has become second nature.

Bill Haber, a thirty-one-year-old sales manager, discussing the common gripes men share about female colleagues, offered this comment: "Men fear that women will abuse the new-found power our society has given them."

That response answers every other question about the complex factors that can work against productive alliances between women and men at work. Among the men who admitted to profound discomfort in working with women, three themes emerged as the source of their apprehension: behavioral cues that provoke conflicting interpretations of the same event; controversy about affinity on the basis of gender; and backlash from what men see as political correctness pushed too far.

As men described some of the challenges that emerge when they conduct business with women, they addressed a wide range of issues: differences in how men and women communicate, business socializing, the old-boys network, and lines that cannot be crossed. As men increasingly encounter the female mind at work, each of these factors can potentially set off yet another gender landmine.

The potential for explosion lies in the fear of the unknown. In the judgment of some men, a new sharing of power with women in business represents a *shifting* of power as women demonstrate new models for how to conduct business. When outsiders become more powerful, the insiders hunker down.

Bruce Kohl, a thirty-two-year-old journalist, believes that heightened awareness of gender issues in every aspect of life has created a backlash among men, particularly in the workplace. "The bar has been raised. People are bombarded with more messages about gender, but ironically, I'm not sure it's helping." Observing other men at work, Bruce says: "There's a perception that says 'I don't want to be consumed with how I'm relating to the women in my office because I have to think about it in my home. My wife's watching Oprah and we're talking about this stuff, and it's making me crazy.'" Bruce concludes: "We're talking a lot more about this stuff, but no one is really listening and trying to understand one another."

What can a woman do to forge solid, productive relationships with the men in the office? Bill Haber advises women: "Don't be dangerous. Do feel comfortable joking around with men and having a good time with them. Don't ever let a man get abusive. Do give men the benefit of the doubt."

Like Bill, many men seemed eager to transfer the burden of gender-based conflict to a woman's shoulders. While overzealous political correctness can be annoying, it can easily default into yet one more excuse for not accepting women as full and equal peers. Men seem to struggle most over business transacted outside the office: over a drink, at a conference hotel, on the golf course. John Lucas, a thirty-three-year-old who works in a *Fortune* 500 company, comments: "I would never go out for a drink after work with Carol because that could be perceived as inappropriate. So then I think I shouldn't go out for a drink with Bob because it looks like I'm excluding Carol. I resent that."

Some men pay lip service to their company's egalitarian policies, yet practice something quite different. Even before a woman steps into the office, men may prejudge her as a troublemaker. When I began my interview with Gary Pierce, a fifty-three-year-old management consultant for a well-known international firm, he opened our conversation by telling me: "Talented women in this business have no problem getting ahead." Ninety minutes later, as I put on my coat, Gary dropped this bomb: "You know, whenever I see a resume from a woman that says she belonged to one of those feminist groups in college, I automatically put it in the trash."

When I asked Ryan Murray, the forty-two-year-old banker, "Is there anything that drives you crazy about working with women?" he laughed out loud, and immediately asked me: "Do I have to limit my response to only one thing?" Ryan had opened our interview by expressing pride in the unusually high number of executive women in his profession. Having worked with and for women throughout his career, Ryan clearly felt comfortable enough to joke with me and secure enough to feel certain that I would not misinterpret his humor. Humor itself emerged as an alliance-building theme among nearly all the men I interviewed.

Some men expressed resentment over having to learn a new set of rules when it comes to working with women. The same men who remarked that they enjoyed flirting with women at work also revealed frustration about what they see as the unnecessary intrusion of regulated behavior in the workplace. While many acknowledge that sexual harassment does occur in many work settings, they also discussed the negative impact of confusion and fear about harassment on interactions between men and women. This fear, particularly of getting sued, some suggest, forces them to bond more tightly, and exclusively, with other men at work.

Many men interviewed confessed that a heavy layer of political correctness has only served to push the old-boys network further underground, barely moderating its effect on either men or women. David Kohl, a Dallas insurance executive, suggests that an old-boys club persists largely because men tend to play with men and women tend to socialize with women. Each naturally gravitates toward people most like themselves. "When you talk about doing business," he observes, "the phrase most often used is 'You must build relationships.' How do you do that? When you deal with the dynamics of the old-boys network, men go out together, play golf, have drinks after work, go to lunch, go hunting. I'm guilty of that one. There is no sexual tension in that environment." David adds: "You don't find women nearly as comfortable in those environments. They're left to figure out on their own: 'How do I build a relationship with these men? And how do I do it in such a way that I'm not putting myself in an uncomfortable position?'"

To answer those questions, women can follow one of the classic Dale Carnegie tenets: "Remember that the other man may be totally wrong. But he doesn't think so. Don't condemn him. Any fool can do that. Try to understand him. Only wise, tolerant, exceptional men [and women] try do that."

Walking on Eggshells

For some men, behind the bravado sits a reserve of yet more bravado. And behind that bravado lurks backlash against the very presence of women.

David Knight asserts: "I won't hire a woman assistant. I'm allowed to hire someone for like eighty to a hundred grand a year to be a junior sales person and assistant to me. And I refuse to hire a woman. During the day, this is such a fast-paced operation, and I have so much to do with twenty accounts in two states, there's no way she would last. I would just beat the crap out of her with 'Do this. Do that.' The girl would be in tears within months. There are very few women cut out for this job."

A male assistant, David believes, will not dare cry or complain because "he knows he'll be called a sissy." Working with women, he says, would prevent him from being himself, a price he says he cannot afford to pay: "It's a woman's prerogative to be sensitive, which is such bullshit. Who has time for that bullshit? I have three people on hold for me and we're yelling back and forth on the trading floor, and if she forgets who's on the line, I'm going to yell at her."

If some men see women as intruders into an exclusive male bastion, others perceive women as mere tokens. The latter perception, thinks David Kohl, insurance executive, may explain how carefully women's behavior comes under scrutiny, particularly when they first comes on board: "Who gets into their inner circle? Who do they go to lunch with? Who do they share confidences with? Who seems to know information from them before others?" David adds that men also scrutinize women's hiring preferences: "Now most women will typically bring in other women, but at the same time they're bringing in people they know, they are working to exclude men from that loop, or at least that's the perception other men have."

Political correctness also seems to have spawned a lot of paranoia among the men I interviewed.

John Lucas, a marketing director, believes quite firmly that the political correctness conundrum has forced men to avoid too much public socializing with other men. For this, he blames women: "Concern about backlash hinders communication, when the person I'm talking to just happens to be male. We both recognize that when there's a bunch of women around, we shouldn't be talking like close friends. *That* would be inappropriate, to strike up a friendship and help each other out at the office." So, John steps gingerly around the issue, thinking to himself, "I could have so much more fun with the guys if I didn't have to worry about women watching us."

Paul Meyers, thirty-two, observes: "There is always this thing about walking on eggshells between men and women in the organization with the threat that is always there, that you're going to get sued for sexual harassment." His friends, he says, laugh at him when he offers this observation. "They tell me that I am such a straight arrow that I have nothing to worry about, but I do think there is always sexual tension when men and women work together in an organization." In his own company, Paul pays close attention to boundaries that employees can and cannot cross: "If you have an organization that is very young like ours, and you have a lot of young, sensual people who are primping themselves, the sexual tension gets heightened." As CEO, Paul tries to set a balanced tone that conveys respect: People should engage in a little fun and appropriate humor while at work, but no one should be made to feel uncomfortable or fearful about their surroundings.

Mark Kramer, a professor, also believes that political correctness, gone too far, has created some backlash: "I carefully avoid sexual language in my classes. I think guys feel hamstrung. And I don't think you need to be a pig to feel uncomfortable. But I think there's a resentment that goes along with the PC atmosphere right now that I think women are getting the brunt of it, whether they know it or not." Unfortunately, he believes: "A lot of times, men want to avoid women in the workplace in terms of hiring or whatever, not so much because it's an all-boys club, but it's almost as if there's a sexual-harassment spy there."

When a man first meets a female colleague, Mark says, he may think: "Here's a person who's going to get me into trouble." Mark admits that his male colleagues regularly trade stories about their "vague fear" of working alongside women. Word spreads quickly as men inform one another: "Did you hear about this woman who got a guy fired because he said something she didn't like?" These perceptions, he says, influence the realties of the hiring process even when untrue: "Would a guy rather hire a man where there's no chance of being sued? Or hire a woman where there is a chance of that happening?" In Mark's view, some of the laws originally designed to protect women's rights have hurt them as much as they have helped.

When he works in his arts organization, Mark anguishes less about what he can and cannot say than he does at the university. In the latter setting, he believes, he will more likely encounter that "career-woman type who can come across a bit cold." In an academic setting, he says, "A lot of men feel: 'I'm going to make a mistake if I let my guard down,' especially with very educated women because I think they are much more hip to the nuances of language. There's more room to transgress with them." Mark also teaches a theater class. He discusses with some humor a dilemma he attributes to political correctness: "I teach an acting class that deals with human emotions and most scenes are governed by power and sex, but I have to eliminate half the topics, half of life. I can't afford to take that risk."

Carrying fear of political correctness to an extreme can certainly provide yet another excuse for men to avoid working too closely and too collaboratively with women. In Bill Haber's eyes, a man has no choice but to adopt an attitude of presumed guilt on the issue of sexual harassment. "If you have a discussion or even a debate about sexual harassment, I think every man feels like they have to start by admitting some fault. The last thing we want to do is to cause problems in working with women, yet we respect the process a lot less when we feel we have to enter into any kind of discussion at a disadvantage." The result? "I feel like I have to start from a negative position with women."

Bill believes quite strongly that misunderstanding about what constitutes sexual harassment, on the part of both women and men, exacerbates tension between the two. Bill recalls a woman with whom he worked in a highly competitive sales environment: "She was looking for stuff to use to get ahead. I certainly didn't have any feelings of being attracted to her and actually never even thought about it. But I once put my hand on her shoulder, kind of a tap the way I would with any person, man or woman. She freaked out and said: 'I'm going to report you if that happens again.'" As a result, Bill says: "I remember being totally uncomfortable with her the entire time I worked with her." Bill also advised the other men in the office: "Hey, be careful with her. She's dangerous." While admitting that his interpretation of this experience caused him to move more cautiously when getting to know female colleagues, Bill concludes: "I'm sure they didn't have that in mind when they thought about legislation for sexual harassment."

Talking the Talk

Not only do men act differently around women, they also speak differently to women, adding yet another mountain range to the great gender divide. Tom Chase, the thirty-nine-year-old CEO, describes how he interacts with a male colleague with whom he will more likely enjoy a long work history than he will with a woman: "We bash each other right in the head when we disagree, saying, 'You idiot. This is ridiculous!' We yell at each other and it's over with." In contrast, Tom takes a step back before he confronts a woman: "I just know that I have to be thoughtful with a woman and can't fire off the hip the way I can with a male colleague."

Sean McNamara, a thirty-one-year-old technical manager, does not think twice about his telephone demeanor when he calls a male colleague. According to Sean, the conversation usually proceeds along the lines of: "Hey, how's it going? I need a quote on XYZ. Can you send it to me? Thanks man. I appreciate it. Bye." With a woman, Sean believes, the same request requires a different tack: "No way could I be this direct. In my experience, it takes a little more time, a little more sensitivity." When he speaks to a woman, Sean will often include words like: "Is this OK? Can you prioritize this? Where does this fit with your other priorities? Yes, this is really important. I'd appreciate it if you could do this by tomorrow."

Women speak their own language, too, of course. While a man will make a bluntly direct request to a man, a woman will often package her message to either gender with words that soften its impact. In *You Just Don't Understand*, Deborah Tannen explains it this way: "Because their imaginations are not captured by ritualized combat, women are inclined to misinterpret and be puzzled by the adversativeness of many men's ways of speaking and miss the *ritual* nature of friendly aggression."

Not taking the time to measure his words sometimes lands a man in hot water. While Sean thrives on a blunt, no-nonsense style, this approach backfired with an assistant who reported him to his boss. What Sean viewed as a strictly business style, his assistant interpreted as demanding and rude. Confessing to perhaps excessive directness when he first started working with her, Sean recalls: "I was like boom, boom, boom. I need this. Can you do that? Thanks. Good bye." Although Sean says this style succeeds with men who work in support roles, he believes: "Women have to be dealt with using a much higher degree of sensitivity." In speaking to women on his staff today, Sean will likely begin a conversation with: "Hi, how are you doing? Thanks for taking care of that for me last week. You really did a great job. Can you take care of something else for me?" Evaluating his behavior, Sean admits: "I'm basically polite because my Mom raised me right, but when it's business and you need to get things done, I guess I was a little too demanding."

Receiving bad news in performance reviews, men told me, really separates the genders. As a customer service manager, Ben Adams observes: "Men seem to withhold their feelings and don't really express that they're angry or upset about what I'm saying. Whereas the women I've counseled, even on the smallest things, tend to get a bit more emotional, sometimes even to the point of crying." Ben observes: "The majority of men are probably defensive. They don't really believe they've done anything wrong, or they just say 'Yes, OK, I'm listening.' But in the background, they're really not paying attention to what you're saying. They're thinking about how wrong you are." Of one thing, he feels certain: "Men rarely express their true feelings."

As a manager of both men and women, does Ben vary his approach along gender lines? "I normally find myself backing down a little with the women. When we're in a confrontation situation and I'm explaining how their performance affects their job, women tend to get more emotional. When that happens, I take a softer approach to get my point across." Among men, Ben suggests that the rules allow a fight-fire-with-fire approach. "I find it easier to speak with a man in a conflict situation like that because there's kind of an aggression on both sides."

As he navigates gender differences in communication, Ben keeps his eye on the goal of making the points he needs to get across as a boss. "The end result comes out the same," concludes Ben. "I just achieve it a different way." Ben recognizes the clear pros and cons embedded in the differences: "It just might take a little longer with a woman than it does with a man. Because the man is typically fed up, he just wants to get out of there. They don't believe you. But the women want to know, 'What can I do to fix the problem?'"

In the perfect world, how would Ben prefer his staff behave? "Ideally, I would like both the man and the woman to accept the criticism and come back with their version of what they see as solutions. Then the two of us would communicate to come to an agreement on how to move forward with the issue, rather than letting emotions get in the way, on the man's side getting angry and on the woman's side getting hurt."

A difference in interpretation can also exacerbate tension between men and women as colleagues. For men, conflict and confrontation may precede connection and affiliation. Deborah Tannen suggests that mutual struggle among men represents a form of bonding. "To most women, conflict is a threat to connection, to be avoided at all costs. . . . But to many men, conflict is the necessary means by which status is negotiated, so it is to be accepted and may even be sought, embraced, and enjoyed." Yet conflict with women may greatly upset a man who resists being told what to do by a woman.

Occasionally, Bill Haber gets into an argument with a female colleague when he tries to justify his behavior: "I'm not yelling! What are you talking about? That's not yelling. I was just talking." In the majority of situations like this, Bill simply moves on to the next subject with no resolution in his mind or the woman's. As to lasting repercussions, Bill says: "I usually just bury it. It's a challenge for men, but that's how we're told to react. And my concern, and I've debated this with my instructor, my mother, and a lot of women in my life, is that this causes a pattern that, long term, makes men ignore women."

Bill's comments bring to mind the stereotypic image of a man in front of the television, watching a football game, totally oblivious to his wife's telling him the garage is on fire. Extreme patterns of behavior like this become particularly dangerous when they are reinforced in both the office and the home, perpetuating and reaffirming the great gender divide.

When I asked Bill, "If you thought your female colleague would listen to you, what would you say to her?", he thought for a moment. Then he replied: "I'd say men do go through a range of emotions in the workplace that are natural for them, that are different from women's. These emotions are not an attack and are not terrible." Bill's advice to women? "When a man's expressing himself, give him room to explore a range of emotions without interpreting it as anything having to do with you and without taking it personally." Remember the game face and the mask of invulnerability?

In Bill's opinion, women attribute too much substance to a man's emotional response. "When we raise our voice for emphasis or mimic someone to communicate effectively what was happening, we're not trying to belittle people or portray a negative perception of women." He adds emphatically: "We don't think that much! We're just talking! Don't freak out about it. It's just the way we communicate." From Bill's perspective, the smart woman does not react at all. In other words, he seemingly would prefer that the women in the office let boys be boys.

In some cases, it may not be quite so simple. The way a woman speaks, the way she tells a joke, and even the way she dresses enter into the complex equation governing how men perceive her.

Walking the Walk

Although I never asked the men I interviewed to share their thoughts about a woman's appearance, they frequently brought the subject up when answering such questions as: "What can women do to enhance their business success?", "Is there anything you'd like to say to women, but have only thought about?", "What advice would you pass on to your daughters?"

While human nature may cause anyone to admire a good-looking person of the opposite sex, most women I know seek recognition for the brains rather than the beauty they bring to the office. That creates a quandary when not only men but the media pay too much attention to what female executives wear. When a *Business Week* cover story proclaimed Abby Cohen "the prophet of Wall Street," it cited "the demure business suits and sensible shoes she wears." Announcing

Carly Fiorina's appointment as Hewlett-Packard's CEO, many articles included descriptions of her "elegant designer suits."

"Don't be afraid to use what you've got," Bill Haber advises his female colleagues. When I asked him to elaborate, he explained: "Some women who are good looking don't want this to enter into their success level. Why not? As men, we don't understand that. If people think you're pretty and want to do business with you because of that, great. That doesn't have to affect how you operate morally."

Bill, like several of the younger men I interviewed, believes that appearance deserves a place in a woman's arsenal. In his mind, it boils down to using any advantage to beat the competition. "It's a battle out there," Bill says. "Don't be afraid to use what can be a powerful asset." However, Bill quickly cautions against crossing sexual lines to gain a competitive edge: "I'm not talking about turning on the charm. I just meant that women can use their attractiveness, or femininity, or their differences from men to complement business, to make closing the deal more interesting without compromising who they want to be."

On the subject of women's using their sexuality to advantage, I asked Bill a hypothetical question, "What happens if I'm a peer of this beautiful, young blonde woman and I'm not nearly as attractive physically? Does that put me at a business disadvantage?" Bill's response? "Well, I don't have sexy legs that guys are going to be staring at, so I never even think about my appearance being an issue. What do I say to you? You've got to do business like the rest of us!"

One forty-four-year-old executive casually dropped the word "hot" into his description of a senior financial analyst. As men talked about a woman's physical attributes, I often found their examples offensive. Why can't a woman just do her work the way a man does? A man's typical reaction to the dilemma: "She can in some ways, she can't in others. Live with it."

Most women I know react defensively to advice telling them to "use what they've got," thinking "I want to win a promotion with my brains, not the fit of my suit." Deborah Tannen designates appearance as a marker unique to women, and she offers a perspective on why the way a woman dresses grabs so much attention, even in the workplace. By a marker, Tannen explained at a women's leadership forum, "I mean the idea that women can't be neutral, that whatever we do attracts notice and misinterpretation." A man can appear more neutral in most workplaces, in terms of his demeanor and his physical appearance. "On the other hand," suggests Tannen, "as soon as a woman comes in, you notice her appearance, and start forming an impression about the kind of person you think she is based on her choices."

So what about the men who genuinely respect women as colleagues and friends? With admitted awkwardness, some men told me they censor what they consider normally innocent interactions with a female coworker. Is it OK to compliment a woman's outfit? Will she think I'm coming on to her? Marty Bennett, who works for a pharmaceutical company, has noticed that women seem particularly uncomfortable when a man compliments their appearance. In Marty's view, they wrongly construe his remark as an insult or affront. "Sometimes a person will say to me 'Oh, that's a great tie' or 'that's a nice shirt.' And I don't think of it as 'Oh, wow, this person really likes me.' It's sort of like they are comfortable enough to make a positive comment to you and that's all it is. I've seen some women get uncomfortable because they read more into what is just a nice gesture." A man's advice about a compliment like Marty's? "Accept it or shrug it off."

"Did You Hear the One About . . . ?"

This brings us to something men admire a lot, a healthy sense of humor. Mark Kramer, the thirty-three-year-old college professor, comments: "I think humor is a good equalizer. If you want to get closer to men, humor can help. Being humorless just allows for more distance. But I also understand that a woman may feel the need to compensate for their gender, thinking 'I'll appear more serious if I don't joke around.'"

Like so many behaviors in the workplace, however, humor's sword boasts two edges. Depending upon who exposes the humor to whom, humor can in one instance remove barriers, and in another, affirm them. In her book, *They Used to Call Me Snow White . . . but I Drifted*, Regina Barreca explains how humor can both form bonds and draw dividing lines: "If your group's joking tends to focus on the foibles of another group's style or structure, you're using humor to cement the bond between you and your colleagues by contrasting your 'right' way of doing things against your opponents' 'wrong' way."

More than one man I interviewed offered the suggestion that "women need to lighten up a bit" in the office. Literary agent Mike Snell observes: "I can't remember the last time a woman told me a joke, except for my wife, Pat. Men tell each other jokes all the time, at the golf course, over lunch. I don't know why women don't tell jokes much, though I think it's natural to take yourself and life more seriously when you're not at the top of the mountain." In Mike's view, humor comes more easily to those who feel comfortably in control.

Regina Barreca sees another reason why women may feel uneasy about some forms of humor. "The idea of humor-as-disguised-hostility is one of the reasons women have for so long been told they themselves can't laugh at a good joke: we've been hearing the underlying hostility of those jokes and have often been unable or unwilling to overcome our distress. It's difficult to hear the 'funny part' when what you're really hearing is an attack." If you don't laugh at the "funny part," men may think you're a humorless dragon lady. Yet, if you do, you're seen as applauding the joke's attack.

Barry Walker, a sixty-two-year-old attorney, talks about the dragon lady stereotype: "These guys have got to understand that if you've been kicked in the butt time after time, and if you really are trying to achieve something you believe a man can achieve without being challenged by others, you will be deadly serious about your job. And because you're so deadly serious, you will find very little in it that's humorous." In his own experience, women, as a group, receive a bad rap: "I have met women in the workplace who are absolute hoots. Because they've reached a certain level of self-confidence, they can let their hair down and be natural. I also know guys in the workplace who never smile, who never laugh. They are so impressed with their own self-importance that it's beneath them to have fun."

Bruce Kohl believes that most work cultures require women to be more circumspect than men about what they say and how they act. "For men, it's easy to say, 'Yeah, women can be humorless' because men come from a position of power. They can be jolly and have a great time because they can be looser about what they can get away with." Power authorizes you to use humor to your advantage, permitting you to poke fun at yourself and at others. Bruce adds: "Women are not going to be funny when men treat them poorly."

Depending upon your status in the hierarchy, humor can either connect you to others or isolate you from them. Locker-room humor, for instance, automatically excludes most women. In some situations, men use humor as a display of power. As Susan Stewart suggests in a *Parenting* article entitled "Laughing Matters": "The superiority theory maintains that when we laugh, we set ourselves above what we're laughing at and feel good about ourselves." In this case, humor works with people who share the same values, a similar view of the world, and comfortable positions in the hierarchy.

Unlike male counterparts, women more likely experience the negative effects of using humor, because, as so many men freely admitted, women at work are often held to a higher standard than their male colleagues. Women may, in fact, take their jobs more seriously, knowing their behavior is scrutinized under a microscope. According to psychologist Leslie Brody: "Men can afford to be humorous because no one is going to judge them for using bad humor. A woman who exhibits humor might not be taken as seriously." The heart of the issue, explains Leslie, resonates with power and status. "Humor is the privilege of a higher status, and women are treading in territory that has traditionally not been theirs."

Another psychologist, Bill Winn, points out that bonding-by-humor often becomes exclusionary. "In the old-boys network, men are able to crack jokes that women are outside of, or the butt of, so humor becomes a disadvantage for women." All humor depends on subjective funny bones, often relying on a private code for full appreciation and participation. As Susan Stewart's article on humor suggests: "If you laughed at my little joke, you recognized and connected with my humor, which gives me a kind of social status and encourages me to tell more jokes, which I'll do as long as you keep laughing." Regina Barreca makes a similar point in her book: "Humor can help to confirm the rules and the boundaries of your in-group through its 'tacit delineation of mutually accepted norms of behavior.' Humor can and does reinforce the rules of the group."

Management consultant Pat Heim observes that men also use humor as a means of welcoming new members into their group, in much the way women use personal conversations. She describes an example where six male engineers thought they were welcoming their new female supervisor with their unique brand of humor. As

Pat explains: "They were really glad to have her on their team. Every morning, as a way of showing that they accepted her, they moved her desk to a new spot." After about a week of overlooking this prank, the woman went to her own boss, and asked, "Why is the group harassing me?" After learning that the joke reflected warm acceptance, she understood the men's message. In Pat's view, it's not that women don't enjoy a good joke, they just enjoy their own brand of humor. "The bonding that women can do verbally—'I'm glad you're here' or 'Nice to be working with you'—the men do through humorous action."

Humor, in just the right doses, can be turned into a plus. When asked about the subject of humor, Marty Bennett responds: "Oh, humor is *so* big. If you can show a sense of humor with your customer, it's really going to help soften the relationship in terms of making it much more comfortable between the two of you." Marty likens his initial meeting with a customer to a job interview. Humor, he believes, goes a long way to putting a person at ease as you seek common ground: "You have to be smart about humor. You just can't start making jokes about nothing, but if you pull out topics you both can relate to, it makes the communication process much easier." Marty also believes that bringing a little fun into the business process helps him stand out from other vendors. "Customers remember someone with a great sense of humor."

Marty points out that you need not become a stand-up comedian to bring a little levity into the office. He describes one female coworker who successfully deployed humor when interacting with people who had let deadlines slip. Using a light touch rather than threats to make her point, "She would leave voice-mail messages that would say 'If you don't call me back, I'm going to sing on the phone the next time I call. You definitely do not want to hear that!'"

Brad Miller, an investor, recommends humor when times get tough. "In any relationship, personal or professional, there are ups and downs, cycles of good times and bad times, and you have to find things to laugh at." At work, that sometimes means laughing at himself, particularly in the heat of tense business negotiations. "I think I have a knack for that," says Brad. "It's important, at the right time, to make a self-deprecating remark. Sometimes, that just blows people away, that you just dumped on yourself. And by doing that, you just gave yourself the upper hand." The element of surprise in a humorous defense, explains Brad, can keep people talking when they really want to yell at you. "When people laugh, they've let their guard down, and you can talk to them reasonably, at least for a little while. Then you can maybe start to sway them to your way of thinking."

Matthew Arnold, a management consultant, also employs humor as a barrier breaker. "I'm not talking about starting every presentation with a joke," he insists. "But I know that it helps my work if people have a good feeling about me initially before they hear anything of substance from me. As a consultant, people don't know you and there's a lot of insecurity about changes we might recommend. They may not be up front with you if you don't put them at ease."

Greg Block, an attorney for NAFTA, views humor as a healthy escape valve from the Dilbertesque absurdity that crops up in all organizations. "It's a great attribute in the workplace because so much of your workplace life is just as absurd as Dilbert portrays it. Without humor to force us to take a step back, it can be pretty depressing."

Humor's greatest strength lies in its ability to provide a fresh perspective. Laughing privately about a miserable boss or finding some humor in the faux pas you made in front of a client can help relieve stress. Executive coach Bill Winn advises: "Humor is a critical talent for both men and women. It can let you step aside from whatever trauma or drama or dilemma you are in and see it from another angle. If you are able to laugh at yourself and not take yourself so seriously, it gives you more flexibility to see the really important issues."

Humor, when used wisely, can produce tremendous influence. It can diffuse high drama in crucial negotiations. Self-deprecating humor, when deployed in moderation, can convey that a person feels comfortable in his or her own skin, allowing others to feel confident in that person as well. People who believe in themselves can take a swing at themselves with a style that allows them to appear more powerful in the eyes of their audience. Which brings us to an entirely different kind of swing.

To Golf or Not to Golf

A funny thing happened on the way to the eighth green: four men developed a lasting bond. Can a woman join the fun? Among the forums where men can appear both powerful and connected is the golf course. To golf or not to golf, that is a question many women ponder as they consider how to build effective business alliances with men. I use golf symbolically, to stand for all those games men play, from duck hunting to squash.

As an avid golfer, Barry Walker, the attorney, comments: "If a woman shows an interest in golf and wants to play, I will instantly invite her to play." When I asked Barry if he invites women because he's enlightened, he replied with a laugh: "No. I'm a male chauvinist pig just like everybody else. It has nothing to do with enlightenment. The practicality is that a lot of women, just like a lot of the men I know, have power and influence. And they're fun to be with. Now what better combination could there possibly be?" Barry also has a ready answer to women who worry that if they can't play well, they can't golf with the men. "That's BS," he emphasizes. "They don't have to be good. Any reasonable male golfer doesn't care whether they're good or bad as long as they're fast, as long as they don't embarrass them by holding up the entire golf course, if they know when to put the ball in their pocket when they've taken a few extra shots on a hole."

When I asked Barry about transacting business on the golf course, he described the benefit as more about laying a foundation for business, rather than sealing the actual deal. "It's a bonding thing. It's a place where people can develop confidence in each other, to see whether they're compatible, whether they think alike." Barry sees part of the magic of golf as an opportunity to evaluate a person's character. "If you play with somebody who moves the ball with their foot or finds a ball in the woods when you know it's impossible for them to find a ball, you learn about their honor. You learn an awful lot about people on the golf course."

When Jim Barnes asserts that "business is a contact sport," he means that almost literally. Jim, a fifty-year-old in the business of managing other people's money, talks about the clout behind the swing of a golf club in a business that lives or dies on client referrals. "The only way you get referrals is for them to get to know you as a person, to respect you as a professional, but also to like you and trust you," he says. "My business partner spends every Wednesday golfing. He takes clients and referral sources out so it's a huge part of the business. Ironically, in all the years he's been golfing, I don't think he ever golfed with a woman." Describing the socializing that occurs in all-male forums, Jim says: "It's like the grown-up graduate locker room. You get to do the stuff you did in high school on the football team and in the college locker room, ridiculous things, but you get that type of bonding on the golf course. My sense is that if you threw a female into the equation, they'd behave a little bit better." Then again, might not the men resent a woman's presence if it forced them to tone down their behavior?

I asked Jim how he would advise a young female protégé who came to him and said, "I want to build the kind of relationships that will bring in big business." He replied: "Well, this may appear sexist, but I think there's a huge market for women to approach other women because more than half the money we invest is controlled by women. She can prospect and develop relationships with women professionals who can give them referrals and also have money themselves. My guess is that this would probably not be on the golf course, but in face-to-face meetings in the office, in restaurants, in their homes."

The New Old Boys

Not every man wants to play golf. Not every man wants to join the old-boy network. One man who works in a Big Five accounting firm admits: "I know nothing about sports and could care less." He adds: "I think that has slowed my career a bit. I play golf so badly that the men have stopped asking me."

Professor Peter Enrich recalls his job in state government. "On my first day on the job, I walked in the office of a senior official. He and his aide were throwing a football around." Shaking his head now, Peter instantly grasped the symbolic importance of that passing of the ball. "It was really kind of weird. I can throw a football, but it's fairly evident that that's not what I spend my time doing. That established a little bit of distance between us."

Interpreting cues like this, suggests Peter, is critical to picking up on the subtext beneath a man's words. Peter himself often finds it easier to build relationships with women. "I find men sort of distant, and I have less of a sense of where I stand in dealing with them." As the chair of his town's board of selectmen, Peter has seen the old-boys network function in all its power and its subtlety. Peter observes: "There's sort of an old-boy group in town politics where joking around, and teasing, and sort of not quite saying what they're really thinking is part of the style." A go-along, get-along bonding, with a potent dose of machismo thrown in, writes the subtext for how contemporary old boys communicate.

As an outsider to this mentality, Peter describes the unwritten character of this exclusive club: "There's a real locker-room sort of one-upmanship. I think I miss that half the time. It does mean that to the extent that you don't project yourself that way, you're not going to be part of the gang. You're not trusted, you're not included in quite the same way. You're treated as somebody who they work with, but who they never build a close relationship with."

When I asked Barry Walker to talk about myths associated with the old-boys network, he quickly answered: "It's not a myth." He then explained: "Gender-based networks exist, and those networks, I hate to say it, have a base in men's clubs, in country clubs, in church groups, wherever men of the same interest and economic status seem to associate." And, he added, "Men take care of each other." When I asked him to say more about the impact of these associations on business, Barry remarked: "If there's a deal and one member of the old-boys network knows about it, he will first tell somebody else in the network about its availability. He will refer a case to a lawyer in the network or offer him a business opportunity. It really helps us." Barry believes a new "old-girls network" obeys the same rule: "Take care of your own first." In Barry's view, "As more and more women achieve higher levels in their professions, they become power brokers and therefore create their own network."

When I asked John Lucas, a marketing director, "What are the myths and realities about the old-boys network?", he burst out laughing as he answered, "Women decimated it." After joking about women's intrusion into male territory, John, like every other man I interviewed, confessed that the old boys network still thrives, albeit in a less blatant edition. Mark Kramer, a professor, expressed the sentiment I heard from many: "The old-boys network is definitely a reality. It's not a myth at all."

Political correctness may have done little more than drive the old-boys network underground. John, who works in a *Fortune* 500 company, comments: "Women have created a fear that has helped, through adversity, to create an innovative new network of men that's less explicit than an old-boy network." According to John, men now worry more about people saying, "Oh, he got that job because he's buddies with the guy." For that reason, he says, men network less publicly with other men for fear of backlash. Still, they do network.

As someone who works in a female-dominated department, John observes: "Ironically, I think a greater presence of women in the workplace may, in fact, be creating an old-boy network that is more gender-centric. In marketing, as an example, where men are maybe 40 percent of the workforce in my department, there's a feeling 'We're in the minority here, so we stick together.' There's a little bit of bonding and you single out a few friends that tend to be of your gender simply because you know you're outnumbered by the women."

Bill Haber believes that the basic propensity to bond with, and help, people you like is what sustains the old-boys network. "Maybe when guys feel closer to each other, and feel like they have more in common, the guy is more likely to get a promotion before a woman. Is that favoritism? I don't know. Is it wrong? I don't know. I don't think so."

The subject of people promoting those who are most like them gets sticky. If the boss has bonded more easily with one of two people of equal ability, whom will he choose? Matthew Arnold, the management consultant, takes offense at a senior officer in his company who typifies the worst stereotypes about an old-boys network. "He's sexist and to the extent that he's a key interviewer, his out-of-date views are going to affect people's careers. He refers to some women candidates as 'dollies,' not to their face, but to the men at lunch later on. We all kind of turn red." Yet they dare not challenge him because he also holds power over their careers.

In answer to the question "How real is the old-boys network?", Greg Block, thirty-nine, instantly responded: "Oh, I think it's *very* real. Deep inroads have been made, but it's still a strong barrier to women." As someone who considers himself conversant with the new old boys, though not an official member of the club, Greg explains how he navigates this slippery slope. "I grew up in a setting that would make most men in power comfortable talking to me—

sports and suburbia. When I see an old boy, I know there are issues we can relate to without having to worry about searching out common ground so we can develop the personal relationship that all business is ultimately based on."

As to the future of the old-boys network, Greg believes it remains resilient: "There are still a lot of them out there. A lot of them have done their best to conceal and adorn their old rhetoric. But it's the exact same attitude and behavior. It just looks a little different. It's going to take a long time to really even out the playing field." And Greg adds: "It's not just women who are excluded. Non-athletic, poetry lovers have a hard time becoming old boys too."

What do the new old boys say about women on the job? According to Greg, "They take a less-than-flattering view of women's capabilities. They hold the fundamental belief that there is some biological determination that makes women so emotional, so unstable in many ways, that women cannot make important decisions about our country's business or our country's political issues. An aggressive female attorney is 'too strident' or 'bitchy.' The same male attorney is "tough."

Several men described their own frustration watching other men get promoted on the basis of shared allegiance to college or professional sports. Marty Bennett, twenty-nine, described a previous job where men with less impressive sales records won promotions before he did. "These guys were all talking about football teams. I saw a lot of the college alma mater stuff tied into promotions." Marty decided not to compete on these terms: "My way of getting away from it was to find a better job elsewhere. I look at it from the standpoint that if they don't feel I'm a value to the company, I'm on my way to be valued somewhere else and get more respect."

Did women decimate the old-boys club? "I don't think so," answers Brian O'Neil, a vice president in a start-up, disagreeing with John. "They're just another player. They throw another variable into it." Women, Brian concedes, can never fully participate in this network: "It's harder for women. Always has been. It's always going to be harder for a woman to chum up without sexual innuendo. How can a woman go into a bar and drink as much as a guy, or more, and still be respected? For a woman to get into the old-boys network is tough. But if you have something they want, and you're willing to play the game, you're in." The dilemma is: who determines the rules and the playing field?

The Grown-Up Locker Room

Marty Bennett, a sales representative, concedes that since men generally outnumber women at after-hours business forums, those venues often represent precarious territory for his female colleagues. "The guys seem to kid around a little bit more after work when they leave a meeting to have a beer together. The women are a bit more guarded. It's more difficult for them to joke about work."

Marty confesses that many men exercise extreme caution when socializing with women professionally: "It's difficult for men, especially after the whole microscope on the sexual harassment thing." Like many of the men I interviewed, Marty says that men expect women to tell them when they cross inappropriate lines. The smart woman, suggests Marty, takes a direct approach. "If something upsets her and conversation goes in a direction she doesn't like, it's pretty easy for her to steer the conversation in another direction just by saying 'This is making me uncomfortable.' And then she should just join back into the conversation." In other words, Marty believes that a woman should expect respect, but not make too big a deal out of inappropriate comments. It's a delicate balancing act, indeed.

The after-hours smoky bar, the golf course, the tennis court have traditionally offered informal settings where men can conduct business and solidify personal bonds. Certain locations seem destined to magnify gender differences rather than to bridge them. In describing his best tips for client entertainment, a Wall Street trader, David Knight, talked about getting tickets to major sports events like the World Series, Super Bowl, or the U.S. Open. He has also taken clients on hot-air balloon rides. More recently, David says: "I took twenty clients to an Italian dinner restaurant at a gun club. Everybody loves the food and the great service and we go down and shoot little rifles in the basement. I'm taking ten clients on a hunting trip next month."

When asked if he deals with his women clients any differently than male clients, David answered, "Oh yeah!" In making the distinction, David says: "It's pretty basic. I don't curse as much. I am not as crude and lewd. I don't tell them any of my favorite disgusting dirty jokes. I don't harass them. I'm a lot more sensitive."

So what's a woman to do? Clearly, she wants access to the informal channels of communication important to any career, but she does not want to become one of the guys. In some fields, client entertainment to build trust and personal connection is a job requirement.

As Bill Haber sees it, schmoozing works to anyone's business advantage: "When you're having a good time and a couple of drinks go down everybody's throat and everybody is talking freely, you get information that you might not otherwise. That's an advantage to women as well as men. If they have some moral hang-ups that prevent them from getting that kind of information, it puts them in second place." Bill also admits that some men feel embarrassed when women observe what transpires during after-hours schmooze time.

Some men, he points out, define as fun activities that strike most women as distasteful. Several men described standards of behavior that deteriorate during after-hours socializing among men. One said: "Sometimes we'll go to crazy bars, strip clubs. That, believe it or not, is where I do business. It's something a lot of clients like to do." When I asked Bill what he would say to a woman not comfortable socializing with these men, he replied: "Then don't go. It's not a deal-breaker."

According to Bill, men welcome women some of the time in some places, and it's up to women to figure out which activities to join and which to avoid.

Dangerous Liaisons

Mark Kramer, a university professor, thinks a fundamental sexual tension underlies interactions between men and women at work. "Whenever men and women first meet, I think there is always an evaluation on a sexual level. Whether or not you would ever act on it is not really the issue." Quickly adding that he truly believes women and men can be good friends on the job, and nothing more, Mark says: "There's still a kind of sizing up that goes on as soon as you meet someone of the opposite sex."

John Lucas, marketing director, advises women: "Be proud that you're a woman. Show up and exude some sensuality. That's fine. If it confuses some of the men, more power to you because while they're confused, you're impressing people." Describing the ideal woman at work, John, thirty-three, remarks: "Men are comfortable with women who they see as women. They're pretty, they're nice, and it's OK to joke with them and say 'I think you're cute.' And they're not going to sue me. Men like to have a bit of flirtation in their life." He adds: "They're probably married and so they're not flirting any more. So it's nice to go into the office and be able to flirt a little bit. And if a woman can allow flirtations, yet be competent at work as well, then I think men would feel more comfortable." Talking about two women colleagues with whom he can relax, John says: "They're a lot of fun. They're women you'd like to go out drinking in a bar with. They're very genuine. And they're not trying to act like one of the boys. So men have no problem establishing the same rapport with them as they have with any man."

Can rapport turn into something else? When men and women begin bonding, they may find themselves skating close to danger. David Kohl, an insurance vice president, says: "I genuinely think that it's men who get the wrong ideas more often than women." David believes that men should directly and honestly confront their reservations about working closely with women, particularly after hours and on the road. David decided to address his own discomfort head-on when work required him to spend an unusual amount of time with a female colleague: "We were basically running the office. We traveled together. We ate lunch together. We spent time together socially."

To alleviate any awkwardness in their business relationship, the two talked about their ground rules up front. Discussing how they accomplished this, David explains that they started from a premise of total honesty: "We talked about the importance of loyalty in relationships. And I told her that my marriage was strong because of that loyalty. As a general way of operating, I told her I would be most comfortable with our business relationship if she got to know my wife a little bit. So my wife would understand that her agenda had nothing to do with me personally, but everything with trying to get a job done."

As a result, says David, the two colleagues cleared the air, allowing them to focus on their work rather than potential awkwardness in their working closely together: "It's not an easy thing to do, but it cuts to the essence of dealing with someone of the opposite sex. When you're out late hours or staying in the same hotel, it's just not an issue." What made it possible for the two to work so well together? David concludes: "We both have integrity. We're both honest. We don't want anything more out of this relationship than purely business. We got our spouses involved so they wouldn't put any unwarranted pressure on it."

David said he maintains a clear, straightforward approach with himself and others when it comes to working with women. His confidence stems in large part from having witnessed the bad behavior of too many other men. "I honestly see real gender differences between what men expect from working with a woman and what the woman will expect. More often than not, if you pair a man and a woman and put them on a project together, the woman is not interested in the man for anything other than trying to get the job done. They genuinely believe that the man, if he's nice to them, is just trying to do the same thing. But in reality, that may not be the case."

David offers what he considers well-intended words of caution: "Men do different things when they drink and women need to be aware of that and not put themselves in risky situations." In his view, a woman should feel no qualms about avoiding situations where male colleagues may sink to a much lower standard of behavior than they follow in the office. To maintain a decent professional relationship with people like this, David advises: "You might go out to dinner with a group of them, but then excuse yourself when they go for a final round of cocktails at some place that stays open half the night." In his experience: "Some women will feel pressure, feeling that they might be excluded or miss something. Well, they weren't. Actually, the reverse is true. If they stay out for the late drinking, it only serves to diminish how they are perceived by others." This illustrates another of the alarming double standards that still exist in male-dominated environments. The man who overindulges gains respect, the woman who overindulges loses it.

Uncrossable Lines

Many men described the lines that, according to the male mind, should not be crossed in business socializing between the sexes. Their basic message: I want to work with a woman who is feminine but not a floozy, who will have a beer, but is not a lush, who will flirt with me, yet is not sleazy. As they heard their own words, many also admitted that men rarely hold other men to such contradictory standards for behavior.

Brian O'Neil rationalizes the double standard this way: "A guy has a lot more freedom. I can flirt with you a lot easier than you can flirt with me. I can come on to you and say 'I didn't mean it. What are you, nuts?' The onus is always on you to make sure that line is real clear." Why must the woman set the ground rules? Brian comments: "If a woman starts coming on to me, I can point my finger at her a lot easier, even if she just puts a hand on a shoulder. It is much more significant for a woman to do that than for a guy, much more significant. A guy can just say 'I'm faithful to my wife, but I like to fool around a little bit.'"

A lot of the tension hinges on confusion among both women and men about the gray areas of sexual harassment. True sexual harassment should never occur. Period. Just don't cross that line. But the line can blur for either party. When does that pat on the shoulder or highly personal compliment go from innocent banter to real harassment?

The marital and professional status of the parties involved greatly complicates the issue of socializing among work colleagues. One forty-four-year old senior executive offered several examples of where he drew the line differently on inappropriate behavior.

One case involved an officer and shareholder in the firm. As he explains: "This married colleague was sleeping with his secretary. I went to him and said 'It has come to my attention that this is going on.' He denied it. I said to him 'I have e-mail records, OK?' The guy turned absolutely white." At this point, the executive laid down the law: "Listen, I'm not making a judgment about your marriage. I know you are unhappily married. But you are an officer of the firm and you're married. End the affair." The officer later called to say he had halted the affair, but it turned out he had lied. His boss immediately fired him.

But the same senior executive acted differently in a similar situation in which neither party was married and the affair, in his view, wasn't affecting work performance.

"As far as I'm concerned, they're consenting adults. The guy works six days a week, five nights a week. We don't have an official policy on this so I have no right to tell him what or what not to do." Absent official company policy, you can only make judgment calls based on your personal values, he insists. Still, every situation can get sticky.

He cited a third example involving another married officer: "Everybody who works for him thinks he's having an affair with his assistant. Is she attractive? Hell, yes! Anyway, in his review, we went to him and said: 'We're not going to ask you whether you are having an affair, but in our business, perception and reality are pretty close. There is a perception right now that is impairing your ability to manage your group. Know it. Deal with it.'" In this case, the "perception of impropriety" *is* impropriety.

In each case, impact on the business defined the executive's course of action. While he did not condone an unmarried man's dating a subordinate, that relationship did not appear to affect their work, so he took no action. In contrast, he viewed the other situations as negatively affecting both department morale and the firm's image. This prompted him to draw an uncrossable line.

Even when single employees get involved, the tangled web of dating a coworker can lead to problems and dilemmas you would never expect. Sean McNamara, thirty-one, strongly cautions against dating a coworker. While attending a training session, Sean met a woman from another department whom he wanted to date. Concerned about whether dating her would create a problem, he went to the vice president of his division and asked him: "I've met a person at work I'd like to date. Do you have a problem with that? Is there company policy or anything I need to know before I go down this road and date Lauren?" The vice president answered: "No, Sean. As long as you get your job done, it won't hurt your career here. More power to you."

As it happened, Lauren's boss was Sean's peer, a woman who, in his view, considered Sean a rival: "This woman was a tough cookie. She was pretty ruthless, more ruthless than most men I know. When she found out I was dating one of her people, she immediately thought I was doing this so I could get information about her potential customers." After this, Sean says, Lauren's boss made her life so miserable that she decided to look for another job while serving as a juror on an eight-week trial. As Sean explains: "On the days court is not in session, you're supposed to go back to work. Lauren didn't. She used the time to look for another job. Somebody found out about it and they fired her."

Two weeks later, the company vice president called Sean into his office and announced: "Sean, we have reason to believe that you were aware of Lauren taking the days off that she did. You're a manager and she was not. You are held to a higher standard and you should have come to me and told me this was going on. We would like to ask for your resignation."

Sean now cautions others: "Never date a coworker. It's just not worth the risk of throwing a good job away. Had I not dated Lauren, I would probably still have been chugging along at that company. Lauren's boss left soon after we did and I hear life is grand over there." Much as this experience devastated him at the time, it gave Sean a new perspective about his career: "I thought because my numbers were so good, nothing like this would ever happen. It did. I realized that I'm expendable."

Like Sean, Marty Bennett agrees that managing personal attractions can cause a lot of awkwardness for both men and women. As an example, he says: "I've had customers who are gay men sometimes hit on me, not knowing that I'm straight. I just take it as a compliment and move on." How does Marty manage what could be an awkward and uncomfortable situation for both parties? "I'm secure enough with myself that it doesn't shake my foundation. I use it to my benefit and just talk about work and how busy we are. And that's it. Depending on the situation, I might say 'It might be fun for a bunch of us to go out or maybe my boss could join us.'" Bringing another colleague into the picture, Marty says, generally diffuses the situation without embarrassing the other person. Marty would advise women facing a similar situation: "Don't let it upset you, but at the same time, be strong if they try to get you to do things you don't want to. Be polite about it and say 'No thanks. I'm busy. That's really nice of you, but no thanks.'"

Code Breakers

Every day, we process the unspoken cues and signals that people subconsciously send to one another in the workplace, in meetings, in hallways, in elevators, in the parking lot. Men and women may walk away from the same interaction with profoundly different impressions of what took place as we interpret those cues through our own gender lens.

Women may need to take the first steps in dismantling some of the walls men have put up in response to political correctness, while putting into place respectful and comfortable standards for workplace behavior. Just as earlier generations of women forged courageous paths into the professions, this generation has a new agenda before it, much influenced by entrenched business traditions they may want to change.

Affinity on the basis of gender has become a defense against political correctness for men and a landmine for women. While a woman may be accused of favoring her own gender merely because she is seen socializing with a group of other women, no criticism would be leveled at a man meeting with his male friends.

Knowing that political correctness can default into an easy excuse not to value their presence, women may need to play the role of change agents as we set the stage for open communication and productive alliances among women and men.

Recognizing men's concern, and at times resentment, about what may appear to them to be the foundation for an old-girls network, some executive women carefully avoid what may appear to be an exclusion of men. Thinking about potential political ramifications, one female CEO has been careful to avoid what looks like isolation from men. In her observation: "I have noticed a number of women entering powerful positions who are very bright and they've formed this kind of club. They meet in this little clique, often in the company cafeteria, and discuss how stupid men are. Men sense that and it's uncomfortable."

Code Breaker #1

Mitigate the effects of the double standard by building networks that include both men and women.

As the only woman at the level of company vice president, Jenna Burke considered carefully how she would connect with her male peers. As she watched her male peers bond in the elevator and in the parking lot, Jenna decided that she did not want to simply break into their conversations. Instead, she forged a deliberate plan to build alliances on their shared professional territory. Clipping journal articles to share with her colleagues, inviting them as her guests to professional seminars, and sharing relevant e-mails launched Jenna's master plan. As the men began to respond in kind, they began to treat her with the level of trust and comfort so readily accorded one another.

Code Breaker #2

Recognize that, as unfair as it may seem, women must be the standard bearers when it comes to defining the boundaries for social interactions between men and women at work.

The behavior of a woman may be interpreted differently from that of a man doing exactly the same thing. Nowhere is this more apparent than in forums for after-hours socializing. For instance, a man who drinks too much might be dismissed as just playing too hard. A woman in the same situation, unfortunately, is likely to incite gossip about being a lush. Do whatever you can to avoid situations where your integrity and your job may be jeopardized.

With profound anguish, one Wall Street woman told her cautionary story: "I can't tell you how much I regret my first decision to become 'one of the boys.' It seemed fine at first, and they seemed to like my drinking and swearing right along with them, but after a while they began to think less of me. And now I can't get out of being labeled as someone they consider kind of a floozy."

While men might feel pressure in adhering to what they view as confusing standards for behavior in the office, many attest to an even more complicated story in what happens after work. Many men do not want the burden of deciding where to draw the line in after-hours interactions. In this case, the burden rests on the woman to figure out the definitive lines that should not be crossed. Women and men can alleviate any real, or perceived, pressure of working closely together by first acknowledging it and then agreeing on clear ground rules.

This is particularly important when they spend long hours together or regularly travel to the same location.

Without company policy, there are no easy answers when it comes to dating coworkers, except in the area of bosses dating subordinates. Given the potential volatility created by office romance, caution, discretion and common sense override emotion. Sexual harassment law defines the boundaries that should never be crossed.

Code Breaker #3

Consider the reality that as we take responsibility for business standards, we also hold the power to change them.

Understanding why golf endures as a powerful business tradition is useful even to women who never play the game. This insight can serve as a catalyst for generating new occasions for the forging of alliances.

If you enjoy golf, put your golf bag in your trunk and call a client. If not, find something else. Nancy Mills, a Boston banker, decided she had attended one too many hockey games. Since her lending division depends so heavily on personal referrals, Nancy began to offer her clients a different option with an early dinner and theater tickets. As some of the men followed her lead, they told her, "Thanks for the idea. My wife now wants to go with me for the evening schmoozing." Some women are finding that as more men race to the school pick-up or the soccer game, they appreciate making a personal connection over a business lunch at noon rather than a beer at six.

Code Breaker #4

Don't forget that humor can be a powerful weapon against misunderstanding, misinterpretation, and mistrust.

As one of the most senior women in a well-known Silicon Valley firm, Connie Moore has learned to find some humor in the inroads she has made in a heavily male culture. Connie just laughs when a male colleague informs her that the fact she refers to "shooting a round of golf" explains why she has never been asked to play golf with the guys. With this same man, however, Connie schedules business breakfasts on a regular basis.

Code Breaker #5

Generate new venues where business alliances flourish, and look for those venues right on company ground.

Do we want business networks that will be separate, and perhaps not even equal? Absolutely not. Where and how does a woman forge common ground with men at work?

In describing the first woman to enter his company ranks as senior vice president, Tom Chase attributes her acceptance to one critical and deliberate strategy. Joan first recognized her status as an outsider, and then she broke it down. From day one, she concentrated on forging alliances at every opportunity. During her first month on the job, for instance, she spent nearly every lunchtime in one-on-one meetings with members of her staff and with key players across the company.

As he acknowledged the heavy "maleness" that permeates his work culture, Tom followed the tone Joan had set for integrating herself into a macho culture. In the past, he admits, "we would bring a woman on board by saying 'Here's your office. Good luck.'" When Joan arrived, he used very different words: "Let me show you this business in context. I'm going to take you to Europe, as well as the U.S., to introduce you to all of our general managers and to our best customers." Then, Tom says, "we got on a jet and rotated Joan through the many dimensions of our company world."

A few weeks after their trip, when Joan called Tom from one of their customer sites, Tom immediately asked: "What the hell are you doing that for? We already did that." As Tom envisioned the quick appearances they had made at these sites, he recalls: "We went in, took a look at the business landscape, and said 'Looks fine. Goodbye.'" With the same script in hand, Joan explained the reasoning behind her second visit. "I'm meeting one-on-one with the person who runs the retail stores because I want to show respect and interest in their business, and I want to connect with them differently than I did on the trip with you." In making the time to solidify her alliances, Joan saw a direct connection to the bottom line, which she then shared with Tom: "I think you've done a terrific job of compacting three years worth of learning into ninety days. Thank you for that. Yes, I've seen the facts, but I also need to understand the people who lead these businesses. I want to be able to see our company through the eyes of the person who runs the customer's business."

A week later, Tom picked up his phone to hear a message repeated by several customers: "Joan is spectacular. No one has ever done this before. I really feel like she wants us to do well."

As men like Tom recognize the strength of the female mind at work, they welcome people who see the world in a way they may not. The same traits that some men found irritating or threatening, when seen through a different lens, can evoke admiration and respect.

6

Reality Check

Top-10 Reasons Men Like Working with Women

When Karen Robinson assumed the top administrative post at a well-known investment firm, she faced several immediate challenges: a large department with low morale, a second-in-command lurking in the wings for her to fail, and the perception that fear had forced the firm to put a woman in the job.

After replacing a man with over twenty years of experience, Karen found herself under close scrutiny as one of only a tiny number of women to hold top positions at the firm. "It's a high-visibility job," says Jim Barnes, who heads up the brokerage side of the business. "The scuttlebutt going around was that she was put in the job because of company scandals about gender discrimination. So they wanted a visible female in that role. But she's done an amazing job."

As her first order of business, Karen faced a direct challenge from her most senior report, who, in Jim's opinion, "did everything he could to undermine her because he wanted her job."

Karen, however, held her ground and, according to Jim, changed the atmosphere for the better. "People are happier. There is more business. Things get done." Jim especially admires Karen for her courageous leadership: "She actually stepped up and fired people who weren't doing their jobs." By forcefully altering the status quo, Karen proved her leadership skills under less-than-ideal circumstances.

In Jim's evaluation: "The man she replaced had been here a long time. He seemed to be attentive to his staff, but he was *reactive*, not *proactive.*" Outlining the skills he values in Karen, Jim says: "Clearly, she's a listener, is organized, responsive, and built a strategy. There are about two hundred administrative people in this office and they were really sort of alienated from the brokers. No one really listened to them. She did, and the tone changed for the benefit of the firm."

Despite their implicit confidence in the male establishment, men like Jim also applaud the different sort of power a woman brings to business. We often admire in others those qualities we do not see in ourselves. Jim Barnes went so far as to say that observing Karen and learning to find his "feminine side" enabled him to communicate more openly and honestly with a male business partner at the firm.

Even David Knight, the Wall Street trader who adamantly expressed a yearning for the bygone era of the all-male trading floor, confessed: "The women around here have a tremendous work ethic. In general, they do things smarter than me because they are more organized and think strategically, which is how you succeed in this business."

When I asked men specific questions about their workplace experiences with women, many confessed that they felt simultaneously drawn to and put off by those qualities they see as uniquely female. As readily as they shared experiences about why women at work sometimes drive them crazy, many also admitted: "I like working with women precisely because they're not like me." Jeff Goldberg, a fifty-one-year-old business owner, put it this way: "Women are just more fun to work with than men. They have less of a need to be right and to win." Peter Drake, a biotech investor, echoed this theme: "I like the fact that you don't have the hidden agendas with most women that you do with a lot of guys."

I asked men direct questions, such as: What do you like about working with women? What do you admire most about the women with whom you work? What's the best lesson you've learned from them? Is there anything about working with women that has surprised you?

Three themes resonated throughout the men's responses to these questions. First, they said, women display unique strengths, allowing me to see a perspective I would otherwise have missed. Second, women don't hide behind a game face, and that's a welcome change. Third, women fulfill multiple roles with a grace and ease I truly admire.

Many of the men I interviewed confessed to a dramatic intellectual about-face after they found themselves reporting to a woman. As a rule, men expressed relief on two counts: first, discovering that their fears were largely unfounded, and second, discovering that they actually prefer to work for a woman.

Given the competitive overtones that so often characterize relationships among men at work, many men revealed that they found working for a woman to be a refreshing change. Ray Ingalls, a business manager, comments: "I generally prefer working with women. I'd rather have work relationships that are based, not on competitiveness, but on working in a combined effort toward the same goal." From Ray's perspective, a "somebody-has-to-win, somebody-else-has-to-lose" mentality can stifle his initiative because he fears getting shot down. With a male boss, he observes, "It is often easier and safer just to follow the status quo."

While maintaining the status quo may represent the easier and safer course of action, does doing so really serve the best interests of the business? Even men who could not precisely articulate why and how women are good for business talked about how female colleagues have changed their company's tone for the better.

In CEO Paul Meyer's opinion, women add value not only to the business process but also to the bottom line. "The outcome is better because when we combine a different approach, we're picking up more of the pertinent data." Paul, head of a $50 million company, believes that when men and women join forces, the customer gets better service. "Women have changed the work culture in subtle ways that I can't quite put my finger on," says Paul. "I do know our product line has gotten stronger because women bring different viewpoints."

Like Paul, Joe Leghorn, an attorney, says that even if he does not fully understand all the complexities of the female mind, he recognizes its advantages. In Joe's experience: "Men and women sometimes arrive at the same conclusion using different data sets. By and large, men think in a linear way. Women think relationally. When I'm evaluating a position for which there seems to be no legal precedence, a woman is often able to find another analogous situation that relates to it." Pondering women's strengths in analytic thinking, Joe comments: "I don't know whether it's hard wiring or how women have been trained, but it works."

In other words, even men who cannot immediately articulate what makes women tick acknowledge that they appreciate the undeniable strengths women bring to the office. Drumroll, please. Introducing the top ten reasons men like working with women.

Reason #10
Her Strengths Compensate for My Weaknesses

As college professor Mark Kramer sees it, his female colleagues display their greatest strengths in areas where he does not shine, perhaps explaining his simultaneous aversion to and admiration of traits he deems unique to women. Men like Mark often revealed intensely conflicting reactions about the female mind at work, thereby questioning their own fiercely loyal adherence to standards set by the male code.

As readily as Mark admits to feeling annoyed by what he sees as a woman's over-attention to other people's feelings, he also values a woman's ability to make decisions in a relational context. "I like a certain degree of 'Am I stepping on someone's toes here?' or 'Which approach is going to be more beneficial in the long run?' It's a classic case of women looking at the whole and men looking at the specific task." Despite Mark's earlier assertion that he prefers someone to be "confident and wrong" rather than hesitant and right, Mark concedes that a just-get-it-done approach does not always result in the best decision.

Bruce Kohl, a thirty-two-year-old journalist, agrees with Mark. "I think women are much more attuned to process and to how something 'goes down.' Women are much more attentive to all sides of a problem, not only the business angle, but the ethical side as well." In Bruce's view, many men succumb to the bad effects of tunnel vision as they pursue a single-minded, action-focused course. In contrast, he says, women offer exemplary skills in multidimensional thinking. "I believe women's decisions are more balanced, their communication style more adept, and their analysis more thoughtful than most male counterparts." The potentially lethal combination of power and bravado, Bruce contends, sometimes limits a man's field of vision, particularly with respect to understanding the human and ethical dimensions of decision-making. "Because of the position men hold in the workplace, they don't have to be as circumspect about how they approach things."

The most powerful woman, according to Bruce, exhibits qualities not typically demonstrated by men. In Bruce's experience, the only woman he does not want in the next office is the one who imitates the darker side of the male mind, allowing position and status to cloud her vision. For example, he says: "I've worked with some women, typically over forty and in a career-obsessed mode, who do exactly what men do, which is to storm ahead without really thinking or being attentive to what's going on around them. And that's where we get the whole bitchy woman, dragon-lady stereotype." Behind this stereotype lies an attitude, says Bruce, that conveys an ultimatum of sorts: "Step aside or else. I just have to get ahead. I'm on the run. I just have to break through." The danger lies in the tactics, not in the overall strategy of breaking through: "In order to succeed, some women perceive that it requires the same bull-in-the-china-shop approach that men often use."

In many environments, Bruce believes, women simply must demonstrate a broader range of business skills to meet the higher standards to which they are held. Bruce's assertion poses a slightly different spin on the old nature-versus-nurture debate. How much does culture define behavior, and vice versa. Must women perform more skillfully in order to survive professionally? Would they instinctively adhere to these higher standards, regardless of the circumstances?

In Bruce's evaluation, whatever the answer, the effect on women at work remains the same. Denied the automatic privileges accorded many of their male counterparts, women, he believes, can only succeed in environments designed by men if they demonstrate a keener sense of how their actions affect others.

Bruce has seen men abuse the power embedded in their position and status, and has worked for men who have gotten away with behavior that damaged both morale and results. Bruce comments: "I worked for a man who really was an ogre, difficult and demeaning to people and harmful to the organization as a whole. For him, running over people, sort of like the bulls of Pamplona, was all part of the game. If the tables had been turned and he had been a woman, that behavior would never have been allowed." A woman behaving like this, he proposes, would have instantly gotten herself in trouble and could even lose her job, as colleagues declared, "Gosh, she's out of control and raging against her staff. This can't work."

Like many of the men I interviewed, Bruce believes that gender often determines whether extreme behavior will be sanctioned or penalized. He explains: "Cultural and societal roles around gender in the workplace allow behavior from a man that under no other circumstances should take place." Rob Parks, a forty-year-old banker, agrees, admitting with a chuckle: "Men are sloppier because they think they can get away with it. The average guy thinks he's on a higher plane than the average woman. You may not hear that honestly from people, but that's what men think."

As men admit that their gender allows them to get away with more (more aggression, more insensitivity, more mistakes), they also express admiration for women who perform to higher standards. Working in an intensely competitive investment sphere, Peter Drake believes that women have raised the bar in a way that benefits everyone: "I think women often offer a sense of creativity that men don't have. They look at the world and at problem-solving differently than men do, and I welcome that."

Eric Stephens, vice president in a biotech firm, concludes: "The women in the company carry, on average, more water than the guys. And they are better performers." Describing the performance rankings for his staff of 150, Eric expresses no surprise over the fact that seven out of his top ten performers are women.

Reason #9
She Doesn't Let Her Ego Do the Talking

While Eric felt the need to advise one of the stellar women on his team to add more swagger to her step, other men seemed to rejoice in the fact that rarely do their female colleagues trip over their egos on the way to the top.

Having mentored both male and female lawyers, Joe Leghorn, a senior partner in a Boston law firm, has witnessed greater career success among women. Why? In Joe's view: "Because women don't let egos get in the way. With some men I've mentored, when they reach a certain plateau, their egos blind them. Women generally have a better ability to keep their eyes on the prize." Watching men whose egos, he believes, have arrested their success, Joe concludes: "It's self-destructive behavior. When a young person becomes partner, suddenly they feel they now walk on water. Men are more likely than women to lose perspective with a 'I'm going to do things my way. It's my client, not yours!' attitude."

That same power-blinding stance explains why literary agent Mike Snell says he would much rather negotiate a book contract with a woman. In Mike's view, "The men often feel that 'OK, now it's time to negotiate. I need to be a slick, manipulative son of a bitch.' A female publisher enters the negotiation with an attitude that says: 'Hey, we want to do this book with you. How can we work this out so everybody's happy.'" When it comes to the subject of money, women, he says, will address it straightforwardly: "You want more money? OK, let's talk about it." In contrast, Mike observes: "Men get into gamesmanship." By putting a puffed-up ego ahead of a fair deal, the male publisher ultimately loses to someone who refuses to join his dance of deception.

Gamesmanship that relies too heavily on status and ego carries other liabilities. For some men, suggests Andy Friedlich, a health care consultant, a blinding ego translates into a rigidly hierarchical worldview. "Many males are highly ego-driven, with the attitude 'I just want to deal with the CEO and CFO.' Whereas women will more likely say, 'I also want to deal with the folks in the trenches.'" As someone who prides himself on following the latter approach, Andy now considers it a compliment when another man tells him: "You're too nice of a guy," in speaking of his soft-spoken manner and willingness to listen.

Andy enjoys the fact that his work allows him the freedom to get to know people at all levels of an organization, but he also enjoys what he terms "a secondary reason that is purely selfish from the standpoint of marketing." The business benefit of making a personal connection with people? "You find out facts that you wouldn't normally learn about the organization, as people tell you things they wouldn't dare tell their boss. You hear the real problems management should think about." In Andy's experience, a woman typically rejects the strategy of employing a puffed-up ego and power plays to make her mark as a consultant. Instead, he says: "She conveys 'I am interested in you as a person' rather than 'I just want your data, I'm the expert, and I'm going to tell you what you're doing wrong and how to correct it.'"

Having worked for both men and women, Ray Ingalls, a business manager, detects distinct gender differences in how they each wield power and ego. When reporting to a male supervisor, Ray says: "I felt power being asserted against me in very unsubtle ways. I often felt as though I'd been put in my place. With my female bosses, I've been more inclined to respond to their leadership. Power is used in more indirect ways, more by suggestion rather than a blatant assertion of power." Influence inspires Ray more than control ever would. For him, leadership by example and positive reinforcement always gets better results than fear and intimidation.

Reason #8
She's Much Better At Constructive Feedback

Beware of men who insist they're straight shooters, urges David Kohl, because their actual behavior may demonstrate quite the opposite. David, a thirty-eight-year-old insurance executive, explains why he strongly prefers hearing a critical message from a woman: "When women see a weakness or deficiency, they hit it straight on." According to David, women excel at performance management because they usually take the clear and direct approach: "Here's what the problem is and here are some things we can do to help you work through it." Male bosses, David finds, generally bypass the constructive side of a performance conversation: "Men point out the bad things, but they'll probably tell other people more about it than they will tell you. I'll hear about negatives indirectly."

A hands-off approach may reflect a man's reluctance to become immersed, by association, in someone else's problems, says David: "Because of pride, a man may resist helping someone who is struggling, figuring that 'If I advise the person and he is not successful, then I may have a political problem. If I do nothing, I avoid the problem.'" And David has witnessed examples where this attitude comes back to haunt men whose avoidance of a problem eventually magnifies it into a formal disciplinary process.

For Matthew Arnold, who works for a consulting firm, the difference between how men and women deliver criticism boils down to tone. He compared his female bosses, who delivered critical messages with an aboveboard, yet empathetic ring, with men who maintained emotional distance and hesitated to voice constructive criticism, thereby avoiding confrontation. Matthew much prefers the former: "For male bosses, the message is a lot more cryptic, either by not saying anything or by saying something was OK when it really needed improvement."

In their book *We Have to Talk*, Samuel Shem and Janet Surrey describe why emotional issues often render a man silent: "When asked to go into what he feels or thinks, a man may be overwhelmed with a sense of male relational dread." In her book *Just Like a Woman*, Dianne Hales describes a large-scale study on gender differences in the choice of words. Women use "more words related to emotion (positive and negative); more idea words; more hearing, feeling, and sensing words." Although a women often uses communication as a tool to break down barriers, supporting and confirming her connection with others, a man may use words to confirm his position and fortify emotional distance. "While men use words to preserve independence, women talk to draw others closer," Hales says.

The men I interviewed admit to feeling impatient with a woman they believe uses too many words, but these same men express appreciation for how she packages her message. Marty Bennett, who works for a pharmaceutical company, put it quite simply: "I'd rather hear bad news from a woman. She's much more careful about choosing her words."

For the first time in his career, Marty finds himself working for a woman, and he greatly admires her ability to frame and deliver criticism. "Even when she tells me I'm not doing something right, she always tries to find something good to pull out of it." After he makes a sales pitch, his boss begins their conversation: "So let's talk about how you did. What do you think went over well with the customer? What would you like to work on?" She makes the conversation clear, logical, and task-oriented. "After we've talked a lot about the positive things, she'll talk about the negative and we'll work on the negative a bit. She lets me think about the feedback, but she'll end with 'Overall, Marty you did a really nice job.'" In vivid contrast, a male boss evaluating a less-than-stellar performance will make the conversation short and scathing. As Marty explains, a critique from a male boss will most likely go something like this: "Marty, what were you *thinking* when you said that? You really blew it in there." The effect? "It cuts clear to the bone," Marty says with a sigh.

In Marty's experience, his male bosses rarely dispense positive reinforcement. What little process they apply, he asserts, takes on an unforgiving tone. "Men are quick to find faults, to blow them up, and try to make you learn quickly what you did wrong. And that's it. They don't really care too much about your feelings."

Reason #7
She Sees Shades of Gray Where I See Only Black and White

Steve Grossman, a CEO, awards women high marks for teaching him important lessons about the connection between humanity and leadership: "Your antennae have to be out there enough when you're pushing people too hard or when they have something else going on in their lives and they cannot perform at peak efficiency. Men tend to say; 'Look, just give me the bottom line. Cut to the chase.' Women are more likely to give sensitive issues the time they deserve."

When I asked physician Roger Sims, "What's the best lesson you've learned from a woman in the workplace?", he immediately answered, "How to recognize and express emotion." Roger was referring to the concept of emotional intelligence or the ability to read people with the use of all your senses.

Even men in the most macho of fields, such as brokerage and investment firms, made a strong business case for the ability to understand the finer points of why people behave the way they do. Jim Barnes, who heads a brokerage firm, believes that managing money relies on understanding behavior. "Structuring portfolios is a function of investment psychology and emotion. You're trying to convince people not to do something stupid, so you need to be really attentive to things like family dynamics before you even make a proposal. We watch for situations where subtle criticism from a husband basically puts his wife down in front of us, and it's a power issue. So we look at body language. We try to figure out, 'Is there friction between the two? What is the emotional dynamic between family members?'"

Ed Nelson, a forty-five-year-old investor, believes: "In this business, you have to be good at picking up on the non-spoken feelings and emotions and nuances in a negotiation, the body language, what the person is really trying to tell you and what the person really feels. In my view, the success of a person in this profession is to give the person on the other side of the table what he wants without giving up what you want."

Health care consultant Andy Friedlich believes that women intuitively pay attention to all of their senses, picking up on the subtleties of both verbal and non-verbal communication. "A woman is apt to be much more sensitive to the little nuances that may not be directly spoken. They may be in body language, or, they may be indirectly verbalized if one reads between the lines. Women can cue off of these signals much better than men." Andy adds: "I think a woman almost has the upper hand over a male because of that 'touchy-feely' side that augments the intellectual side and allows her to get much farther than her male counterpart."

As Andy talks about stylistic differences among male and female colleagues, he observes: "Males, with their aggressive nature, tend to take one side of a position and dig their heels in, but unless you understand both sides, you're not going to get the full picture." This, in Andy's opinion, explains why a man and a woman can walk away from the same situation with markedly different evaluations of what took place. What he sees as black and white, she views in shades of gray.

For Andy, a woman's roles outside the office, often as emotional manager for a household, bear a direct correlation to why she sees the business world as a series of relationships. "Traditionally, women have been much better at this. Whether it's because of the way families have been structured, I'm not sure. As mothers, for instance, women have been in a position of having to play intermediary, of having to understand both sides of an issue, and trying to come up with the best remedy for both sides."

Jeff Klein, a high-tech manager, welcomes women on his team, in part because "what women do naturally, men have to work at." He explains: "I hate to generalize, but I have seen first-hand evidence that women are often more creative and better 360-degree thinkers." Trying to explain this gender difference, Jeff comments: "Men tend to direct too much of our logic and reasoning abilities toward rationalizing our actions, whereas women will play with different parts of a problem and approach things from angles in ways that we don't. Women bring multiple perspectives to their analysis." Comparing his analytic style to a female peer's, he sees his process as more solitary and hers as more collaborative. Jeff explains: "I tend to try to think things through myself whereas a woman will immediately go out and do some brainstorming with three to four people she thinks are key and have good ideas. Then she'll come back and synthesize their ideas into a plan." Skills that have taken him years to develop, Jeff says, his female colleague possessed from the start.

David Kohl believes he has learned lessons from a woman he would never pick up from a man. About his current boss, he says: "She is one of the very best sales people around, in part because she's an outstanding listener. She picks up on the nuances of what people say in a positive way. This is not an act for clients. This is who she is twenty-four hours a day." Leading by example rather than by intimidation commands tremendous respect: "Men have more of a tendency to just apply pressure to people. She influences decisions by reading people well and by conveying a positive drive that takes the pressure off and lets people make their own decisions. This is why people not only *like* her, but respect her as well."

Reason #6
She Knows How to Win Friends and Influence People

As someone who buys and sells businesses for a living, Ed Nelson respects colleagues who couple adeptness at reading people with sharp business acumen and great flexibility. Many of his female colleagues, in his view, instinctively know how to win friends and influence people. Citing a woman who took over as president of a newly merged Texas bank, Ed says: "Anne did a phenomenal job of winning the community over. There were three very competitive banks in town. Within the course of eighteen months, one would have thought she ressive personalities. With no perfect road map for building the iness, he says, "that's a trait that is absolutely required."

Reason #5
I Can Let My Guard Down with Her

rsonal trust, the great connector among men, can work in a oman's favor, too, though in a different way. Variations on "she's not e me, so she's not an adversary" resonated throughout stories men ared with me about productive alliances with female colleagues. atthew Arnold, a principal in a consulting firm, summarized what I ard from many men: "I can let my guard down when I talk to her. I n admit my shortcomings to her without being threatened."

Two key reasons emerged for why men often find it less threaten- g to work alongside a woman rather than a male peer. First, the on- oing undercurrent of competition that often prevails among men isappears. Second, absent the fear of repercussions or embarrass- ient, men can safely remove the mask of invulnerability.

As readily as men found the nurturing traits exhibited by women nnoying in one context, they found them supportive in another. Matthew, a father of two, easily commiserates with women at work bout topics rarely discussed, if not forbidden, among his male col- eagues: "I talk to women about issues I could never talk about with a nan in the office: 'Gee, my kids did this at school.' Or 'I'm having problems with one of their teachers. What would you do?'" With his female colleagues, says Matthew, he feels comfortable enough to re- move his mask. Not only does Matthew feel relaxed enough with his female colleagues to share his other life with them, he also feels less cautious about revealing his vulnerabilities on the professional front. While working on a project with one woman, Matthew discovered their shared fear of delivering formal presentations in front of bosses and clients. "It was a situation where we could admit some of our shortcomings to each other in a supportive way," explains Matthew. "And that's something I could never do with most men, unless we are very good friends."

By sharing their trepidation about public speaking, each pumped up the other with friendly, supportive reminders such as "Hey, Matt, don't forget that you know this material better than anyone else."

was mayor of the town. It was the most amazing thing
in my professional life. Her ability to outsmart, out-m
dear the community in a fairly closed, provincial comm
tounding."

Anne, he said, accomplished a daunting goal with a
tive stance and less personal animosity than her male
might have employed. She calibrated just the right bala
self-interest and the needs of her customer. "Anne w
business leaders throughout the community and orch
plan because she was able to gain people's trust. In some
n't happen in the first meeting, or the second or third, bu
over the course of a few years, she had won everybody ov

Ed especially admires Anne's ability to respond effect
ever-changing cast of characters. As one example, he ren
was able to go in and size up Jim, an eighty-five-year-ol
geon, and win him over with a combination of some swe
some charm, but mostly a large dose of 'I know what I'
about so you'd better listen to me.'"

Anne's master plan revolved around a powerful combin
detailed marketing plan, impressive organizational ta
supreme focus. Over a period of eighteen months, Ed co
"She drove the profitability of the bank through the roof,
ended up being banker to probably two-thirds of the town. I
talent of being able to size people up, set an agenda and
place, give people what they want without giving up what *s*
is quite extraordinary."

Anne's ability to react quickly and make good decisions
handy, Ed says, "because people are going to throw curve
you. Some of them are going for your head and you have t
Then you have to pitch back something else." Summarizing
strengths in these areas, Ed comments: "She'd get these brash
guys who would just come in and throw bullets and darts
She'd just throw them right back, but in a nice way. She'd lob i
would perhaps be a better explanation. She could make fun
process or let it roll off her back in a way that was artful an
gant."

Knowing what makes people tick and knowing how to respo
them allowed Anne to excel in an environment loaded with to

Each helped the other feel less tense before presentations. Describing why he would hesitate about engaging in a similar conversation with a male colleague, Matthew admits: "I'm more circumspect about what I view as my weaknesses with men. I tend not to be as competitive with a woman. I feel more at ease because she's less likely to use this information against me, politically."

Some men may describe women, somewhat disparagingly, as "wearing their hearts on their sleeves." Others, like Matthew, greatly value that visible heart.

Reason #4
She's a Great Boss

Although some men expressed annoyance at having to spend more time talking to a woman manager, many expressed gratitude for the fact that female bosses actually do talk to them. David Kohl has worked for both men and women and has seen the difference first-hand: "I expected men to be more honest with me, but in actuality, I find that women are more candid."

Some men admit to the surprising revelation that they strongly prefer to work for a woman. Having worked for a woman who also served as his mentor, Matthew Arnold observes: "To the extent that I've had male mentors, it's very different. I was much more open with her about failures as well as successes. If I made a mistake, she said: 'Put it in the broad perspective. You're doing a great job here and shouldn't worry. It happens to everyone.'" Referring to his boss's management style as one that fostered tremendous loyalty and effort on his part, Matthew says: "I never get those kind of empathizing remarks from a male mentor."

About another senior woman mentor, Matthew remarks, "She has been helpful since the day I joined the firm. As a team, we work very well because I focus on very analytical, quantitative issues. She has more of a qualitative perspective." His mentor, for instance, more adeptly reads people. "She understands what will play well with an audience or a group because of the group demographics, the personalities, knowing what's better left unsaid or perhaps said in a better way. Whether that comes from being a woman, or just being more intuitive, I can't say, but I don't get that from other men."

Before he received his female mentor's advice, Matthew says, he approached clients with a black-and-white "I'm the expert" stance: "Here's what you need to do. This is the right way and there's only one way to do it." His mentor helped him to strengthen his client rapport by acknowledging the power behind a few well-chosen words: "We appreciate the way you've approached this, but if we did it this way instead, here are the benefits."

Ray Ingalls, a business manager, echoes Matthew's theme of women as effective two-way communicators, asserting: "The women I've worked for are much clearer in their expectations of me . . . whereas many of the men I've worked for have an ambiguous idea of what they want done, or maybe they're clear in their own mind, but are just not good at communicating it."

Ray comments: "It's been easier to discuss problems with my female bosses. They were somehow more approachable." He attributes part of the difference to the fact that "there wasn't some kind of competition going on between us." In stark contrast, Ray describes one male boss who asked his opinion about department morale. Believing that his boss wanted an honest response, Ray answered his question truthfully.

His boss's reaction? "He had a defensive answer to everything I said rather than just taking it in and listening. It was as though he really wasn't soliciting my opinion, because he immediately retorted with comments that actually shut down the communication." Ironically, Ray had identified an absence of good communication as the main threat to department morale. Ray said: "I felt I was truly working as a team with my female bosses much more so than with my male bosses. Team building comes more naturally to women because there's less of a need for them to feel competitive with the people around them."

Reason #3
She Brings Vision and Humanity Into the Office

Glenn Sears, a vice president in an intensely competitive Silicon Valley firm, believes that women have more successfully seized the golden career opportunities offered by a young, yet immensely profitable industry. "You know the classic material on the difference between a manager and a leader?" Glenn asks. "Well, I've seen more women in my department take advantage of opportunities to be initiative leaders early in their careers. They've shown themselves to be great team leaders and a lot of people respect them. And that's one reason why many of the younger managers who report to me are women." Outlining the traits common to these women, Glenn says: "They are aggressive, clear-thinking, honest and apolitical, but those are the same qualities I would use to describe some of the men I admire as well."

In his firm, biotech investor Peter Drake sees positive traits unique to the women, who have only recently entered a heavily male professional territory. First of all, he says, women are very loyal. In fact, "they are much more loyal than men." Second, they don't play games when it comes to salary negotiation and compensation. "They are not always fishing for the next best offer. They don't try to hold you up." Third, women seem to focus on what will best serve the organization rather than themselves. "They are much more nurturing and process-oriented as opposed to trying to leverage what they have to get something else." "Women are unbelievably hard working," Peter declares. "You combine all that, hard work, great character, great ethics, a high degree of loyalty. And holy smokes! Sounds pretty spectacular."

Greg Block, a director for the NAFTA Environmental Commission, offers the highest of praise for Carol Browner, his boss's boss, who heads up the Environmental Protection Agency. In his view, her effectiveness derives in large part from the fact that "her message is consistent with her persona." She's believable because she believes her own message. Her image as a person and as a cabinet-level officer do not differ at all.

Greg explains the close connection between Browner's sense of self and her agency's message: "You should care about the environment because this is about your children's future." In Greg's view, "That would be something most men would have difficulty with, not believing or saying, but it would be tougher for them to sell. The public accepts it from Carol because she's a mother, because she spends a lot of time with her children, and because she's not afraid to speak out as a woman in a male-dominated field."

Her style, her image, and her message comprise one complete and consistent package.

Reason #2
She's Multidimensional

Not only does a woman think in three-dimensional terms, but she lives in a three-dimensional world. Consider the picture Ed Nelson, a private equity investor, paints of Cynthia, a colleague who serves as chief counsel for a corporation. Her business strengths range far and wide. First, "She's an incredibly clear thinker. She has an ability to assimilate a host of facts and get to the right conclusion quickly. And she doesn't get bogged down in the detail." Ed recalls, in particular, one "enormously complicated transaction with multiple issues, both economic and tax issues, and some political issues as well."

In Ed's view, if Cynthia had not headed up the negotiations, the deal probably would have fallen through. "She was completely unflappable in the final hours, when one of the four senior partners threatened to go to the beach and leave $50 million on the table. Most people would have gone crazy, just stood up and ranted and raved. I wanted to kill the guy myself, and I remember thinking, 'Then we'll only have three guys to worry about.'" But Cynthia, he says, saved the day and the deal. "She is an exquisite negotiator, not emotional at all, and sifts through the static to get to the core issues."

But a completely separate dimension impressed Ed most: "On top of all that, she's a terrific mother." During one late negotiation, Ed happened to glance at her open bag on the floor between them. "There was a pair of ballet slippers in the bag. She's from San Francisco and we were in New York so I asked, 'What are those doing there?'" Cynthia just smiled, informing Ed: "I need to get my daughter some new ballet slippers and I know of a particularly good place in New York." After sitting next to Cynthia for four days of round-the-clock, grueling negotiations, Ed saw another side of this strong woman. "How can you do this?," he wondered. "How can you possibly even be mindful enough to think about this given all the other stuff in front of us?"

At forty-five, Ed readily admits that striking balance in his own life remains an elusive goal. "It's something that's eating at me badly right now since I was on a plane yesterday for my birthday and my daughters really wanted me home." Struggling to find more family time and worried about what he considers the bad example set by his own father, Ed explains: "I'm hoping that instead of traveling four to five days a week, I can get it down to two, maybe three. I don't want to have the situation my father had, where he ran his own business, was always traveling, and I think his kids passed him by. His kids grew up and he didn't even know it. As a result, I don't have a particularly close relationship with my father and I don't want that to happen with my kids."

Ed admires women at work who seem comfortable in their own skin, comfortable with their multiple roles, and confident about managing those roles, no matter how contradictory. Referring again to Anne, the president of a large Texas bank, Ed says: "I always marveled at two things. One was her energy level. I don't think she ever went to bed. She couldn't have. She has two children, both of whom are the same age as my kids. And she would always be at the class meetings, which I only made half of. She would speak at the school. She was president of the symphony board. And on top of all that, she ran this bank. To this day, I still don't know how she did it."

Reason #1
She's Smarter Than I Am

Interestingly enough, men in the most competitive industries sang the loudest praise for the women with whom they work, perhaps recognizing the special scrutiny and the double standard that have become so thoroughly attached to trailblazing women.

Ed Nelson, the forty-five-year-old private equity investor, comments: "The women I interact with, in order to get to these levels, have to be extraordinary people. They had to be that much brighter, that much more motivated, that much harder working in order to get here. So to a certain extent, I view myself as blessed if I am interacting with a woman because she is likely to be better than most of the guys in the room."

Among the business people he most admires, Paul Meyers cites an investment banker he views as smarter than anyone else in her firm, in large measure because she has comfortably, and quite successfully, merged what are often labeled "masculine" and "feminine" attributes. Her extraordinary talent, he says, stems in part from her keen emotional intuition. "She can be tough, but I admire her intellect and

I like her personally. She's very empathetic to her customers." Bringing the human touch to the highly macho field of investment banking may seem to run counter to its hard-nosed image, but it works, as Paul explains: "When people buy and sell private businesses, it becomes incredibly emotional. You end up with grown men weeping in their office because their 'baby' is going away or the deal is going bad."

Chip Ziering, a founding member of Progress Software, a $200 million company, singles out one woman who served as a company vice president, displaying a style atypical for most company executives: "She was hard-driving, wanted to accomplish things, and had an agenda to get things done." But Chip recalls, "Certain senior executives criticized her for being too emotional, for taking things too personally. And I remember saying to one colleague, 'Well, thank God somebody does.'" In Chip's view, the early strengths of a start-up often turn to weakness when comfort, and even complacency, creep into the culture. In the beginning, he comments, "Everybody cares about the outcome." Then, "Some people just ride the wave," with an attitude that assumes, "It's a job. I can collect my outlandish pay and not rock the boat. Why get emotionally involved?"

As others lapsed into complacency, Chip says, "The woman who was a vice president still got irate when she ran into obstacles for what she wanted to accomplish. It surprised me that the reaction was that she was too emotional because to me that passion was a real plus." As readily as some men assert the advantages of refusing to take things to heart, Chip also sees merit in a passionate and personal connection to a growing business. That's why he so admired and respected his female colleague: "Others characterized her as too emotional, but to me, she was emotional because she cared about the company. So you may want to be emotional about business to the extent that it moves you in directions you want to go, and at the same time moves you past the issues outside your control."

As the head of a $1 billion enterprise, Tom Chase places high value on what he calls a woman's unique ability to think three-dimensionally. One dimension women frequently add to business analysis, one admittedly missing from his own, says Tom, is the ability to put yourself in another person's shoes, considering, "If I were in his place, I would have the following questions about this decision." Tom often tells his female colleagues: "You know, I would have missed that point." Men like Tom define smarter as the ability to see the world through a different and more complex lens, a lens that offers a competitive business advantage.

Code Breakers

Shortly after the publication of a 1996 *Fortune* cover story entitled "Women, Sex, & Power," women's groups buzzed with reactions that ran the gamut from irritated to appalled. Years later, women still groan or shake their heads when someone mentions that piece. Profiling seven executive women who seemed to revel in their "queen-bee" status, the article asserts: "They don't act like men or think like them." No problem with that. But then the author declared: "We also mean sexuality, which these women skillfully exploit." Well, Houston, *now* we have a problem.

Granted, these seven women have made their mark in American business, but other women questioned the assertion that their appearance ("honey-blond" hair, for example, and their "colorful packaging") accounted for their success. With descriptors such as "beguiling," "seductive," "frivolous," "flamboyant flirt," "diva," and "digs in her high heels," the article characterized each executive in highly sexual terms. Would an article on top male executives dwell so much on a man's appearance? Of course not.

Judy Rosener set off a different sort of controversy when she published her 1990 *Harvard Business Review* article entitled "Ways Women Lead." To some critics, simply advancing the notion of a female style of leadership reinforced gender role stereotyping. However, Rosener's analysis struck many women as true. Many female leaders do operate differently, as Rosener asserts: they more naturally "encourage participation, share power and information, enhance other people's self-worth, and get others excited about their work." As we've seen in this chapter, these are the very characteristics the men I interviewed cited as the ones they most valued in women colleagues.

Being a woman need not translate into becoming the office diva; neither should it be assumed that every woman innately possesses the same range of managerial and leadership talents. Many women do bring unique strengths to the business world, but may also face some fundamental barriers that thwart their putting these skills into practice. As Judy Rosener suggests: "Attributes traditionally associated with women (using intuition rather than linear logic, preferring consensus building to competition, encouraging participation rather than giving orders, for example) have been seen as ineffective in our hierarchical, tradition-bound, assimilation-oriented organizations. It is ironic, therefore, that as these attributes become valued in fast-changing, service-oriented, international contexts, we see an effort to divorce them from gender."

Understandably, women may feel pressure to fit in to a work culture designed by the male mind. Yet several of the most senior men I interviewed declared: "Don't you dare fit in. If women don't change the culture, we never will."

Code Breaker #1

Make yourself powerful by following the refrain "to thine own self be true."

As journalist Bruce Kohl points out, a woman's greatest power often derives from qualities not typically demonstrated by men. To women just starting out in a career, Bruce offers this advice: "Do be yourself. Ultimately, you don't get anywhere by modeling the behavior of someone else, or trying to fit a certain mold, or by following the pack. Don't betray yourself to get somewhere because once you're there, you'll find you don't have anything left."

Women don't want anyone to slot them into uncomfortable pigeonholes, like staff and support, as opposed to line management and leadership, roles. But there's nothing wrong with recognizing and applying talents more often possessed by women than by men. Many of the men I interviewed find their female bosses more approachable, better at team-building, and more skilled at 360-degree thinking than many of their male counterparts. Knowing this, a woman can confidently assert her business vision, effectively supervise men and women, serve as their mentors, and build gender-friendly teams.

Code Breaker #2

Be confident about your unique strengths as a woman.

High-profile women now proclaim that they need no longer relinquish their business values to succeed in predominantly male territory. According to a *Fortune* magazine article about Nina DiSesa, who leads McCann-Erickson, the largest advertising agency in the world: "Inside McCann, which recently won the Microsoft account, DiSesa has helped to humanize what had been the roughest culture on Madison Avenue. 'Being a woman in this job is important,' she says. 'I'm dealing with big egos, big personalities. Fragile, high-maintenance people. If I didn't have a strong nurturing component, I couldn't do it.'"

Code Breaker #3

Remember that leading by influence can accomplish more than the exertion of control and heavy-handed power.

Discussing the comfortable merger between her role as a vice president and her role as a caring mother, Connie Moore observes: "If you're doing things right, your life doesn't have to be segregated in a negative sense. You don't have to be *the mom* at home and then *the businessperson* at work. You can very much integrate your personal life and your professional life because so many of the skills transfer from one place to the other." Empathy, tolerance, flexibility, and compassion top the list of those transferable skills.

About her own style, Connie says: "I'm pretty apolitical and pretty unemotional about things. I've seen situations where people seem to get more wrapped up in some of the emotional and political issues, and people tend to think of that as more of a female trait." As for her own view, Connie says: "Whether people like you, whether they have treated you well, whether they were rude, those kinds of things, you just have to cut out all that noise and get right down to 'What is the business issue here?'"

Code Breaker #4

Keep your focus on the job, but don't succumb to the temptation to separate who you are from what you do.

What Connie did not say explicitly, but conveyed quite clearly, was the idea that, yes, she does take seriously her role as a senior-ranking woman in a highly competitive industry, but no, she has not relinquished her sense of who she wants to be as a human being. Who she is as a leader accurately reflects who she is as a person.

Translating her values, the powerful combination of vision and humanity, into business practice, Connie aligns both her intuitive and analytic sides. "I can see things in people that they can't see in themselves, the potential they may not see," she asserts. "If they have values, integrity, and leadership qualities for doing business with maturity and ethics, those qualities will carry them beyond areas where they are deficient in technical knowledge. They can learn those things." And, she emphasizes: "Those are the easy things to learn."

These are the same values I heard espoused by men who I call good men at the top, each of whom demonstrates an openness to perspectives that challenge their own and a willingness to learn even as they occupy the executive suite.

7

Good Men at the Top

Secrets of Strong Leaders

New Year's Eve, 2000, about 10, Christine Murray's phone rang. Clicking it on, she heard her brother Ryan's voice wishing her a happy new year. Where was Ryan? Sitting behind his desk at a community bank in western Massachusetts. With concern about Y2K problems not yet behind him, Ryan told Christine: "You know, I add absolutely *no* value being here tonight, given my level of computer expertise, but I wouldn't feel right about calling my people in on a holiday while I was out partying." At age forty-two, Ryan Murray has acquired a certain amount of wisdom, including the wisdom to treat people the way he himself wants to be treated, the wisdom to know that even if the Y2K bug did indeed crash the bank's computers on Monday, January 3, his loyal staff would pull together as a team and solve the problem.

Small gesture. Powerful message.

As scores of the senior executives I interviewed talked about organizational vision and business strategy, they also described the symbolic messages, large and small, conveyed in the daily signals they send to the people who work for them. One theme resonated throughout their comments: Organizations thrive when people thrive. Frank Andryauskas, formerly chief information officer for Staples and now a partner at an Internet start-up, offers this view: "The critical resource, the limited resource in this economy, is people. And if you can retain the best people, then you're the outstanding leader."

The notion that an organization's tone cascades from the top brings with it the formidable expectation that you should lead by example. Bob Gault, a partner at the Boston law firm Mintz, Levin, talks about the consistent philosophical legacy passed down from one generation of lawyers to the next. Bob describes the firm, founded by men who had experienced the sting of discrimination and who wanted to send a clear signal about their personal values and beliefs: "This firm was founded in the early 1930s by a group of Jewish lawyers in this Yankee town. They, of course, knew what discrimination was all about and set up a culture that won't tolerate any discriminatory conduct or attitudes. People who joined the firm over the years, including our chairman (who happens not to be Jewish) have brought that same kind of ethos and perpetuated it."

With great pride, Bob explains how the tone from the top, when truly integrated into a culture, withstands the test of several generations: "When Richard Mintz, our most senior partner, speaks, he constantly reminds us about remembering what our core values are and about the need to treat all people with respect. We call him the 'conscience' of the firm."

Given such clarity of conscience in the organization, Bob can run the risk of standing firm against a client whose work ethic conflicts with the firm's values. "If a client ever told us that they did not want a woman on the case, my response would be 'If you're working with me and I've assigned a woman to the case, you're going to work with that person or you can go to another law firm.'" He emphasizes: "I would not give into that kind of pressure at all. Now, if they don't get along with the person for some other reason, then maybe we need to reassign the case. But I would never give in to a client's preferences based upon race, gender, ethnicity, or sexual preference." After a pause, Bob adds: "But you see, I'm in a firm where I have that luxury. So it's not just me being brave out there and risking business. I know that that's what my firm would want me to do." Actions do speak louder than words, and when words from the top back up the actions, the message comes through loud and clear.

A *Business Week* cover story profiling Ken Chenault, president and chief operating officer of American Express, described Ken's personality as "mercifully free of the rough edges that usually accompany vaulting ambition" and underscored the integrity with which he leads his life, inside and outside of the executive suite. The message? Ken stands out because of his unusual combination of decency and ambition. A nice guy has risen to the top ranks of traditional corporate America.

Sadly, the expectations we hold for business leaders do not automatically include a prerequisite of decency, humanity, strong character, and treating people well, traits too readily sacrificed for the sake of the bottom line.

Tom Chase, the CEO of a $1 billion company, refers with great pride to the lessons he learns every day from his wife, a specialist in child development: "It is unbelievably relevant to trying to manage an organization and a group of people, things like learning styles and how people listen and interpret communication." With his wife's help, Tom says, he has learned to find his empathic side and to put as much emphasis on Tom the person as on Tom the CEO. "My wife is committed to me becoming a human being. And that's a lifelong task," he says, chuckling, "but she works very patiently at trying to help me become a three-dimensional person." Being human, suggests Tom, need not undermine power. In fact, he believes, being human can make you truly powerful. "Every time I make progress in that direction, it turns out to be a good thing for the company and its shareholders."

Tom Chase, like other good men at the top, has mastered the secrets of leadership, secrets from which anyone can learn. Many women already know these secrets—and prefer to align themselves with organizations where they govern behavior in the workplace. Many of the men I interviewed voiced intolerant views about the women with whom they work. In vivid contrast, the men in this chapter offer perspectives I admire.

Secrets of Strong Leadership

"Is the character of leaders revealed or stated?" asks Steve Grossman, a CEO. In posing this rhetorical question, Steve raises the issue of how the person behind the title translates humane, visionary leadership into practice that benefits both people and business.

How do men like Steve Grossman and Tom Chase incorporate who they are as people into how they lead their organizations? Their strategies for leading by example rely on the basics, including a style and demeanor that convey dignity and respect and a passionate commitment to aligning their vision with their values. Consider these twelve lessons from those I consider good men at the top.

One: Share Your Life Lessons

Glenn Sears, vice president for a Silicon Valley high-tech firm, answers Steve's question without hesitation. You cannot, he insists, separate leadership and personal character. He explains: "I've had both wonderful managers and horrible managers, and I've learned a lot from both experiences. Some of them, I wouldn't want to repeat." In fact, he says, jokingly, "I don't know that I could survive repeating some of them, but you learn a tremendous amount about the person you want to be when you work for somebody who is a person you do not want to be."

About his own approach to leadership, Glenn says: "A lot of the people who work for me are very young, right out of school. They have relatively few life experiences from which to draw. So I could just tell them what to do: 'I know what to do because I'm your boss, so go ahead and do it this way.' Or, I can tell them a story about why I think this is the best option for them to try. That kind of discussion helps them understand some of the life lessons I've learned and how they can apply them to what they are doing."

Sharing his hard-won life lessons, Glenn reveals his personal values and beliefs, including the view that leadership extends beyond his commitment to achieving strong numbers for a highly profitable company. As an example, he describes a rehabilitation program from which he hires employees to work in his warehouse. "We work with the Veterans Administration, the counselors, and the therapists to help these men develop their job skills and become professionals once again," he says. "A lot of them were homeless. Some haven't had contact with their families or children for years, but they're getting their lives back together. And we're very proud in this department to be participating in this program."

Two: Maintain Humility

On the subject of building a reputation, Glenn Sears observes: "There are two schools of thought in high tech about building a reputation.

One is to be highly visible at every opportunity to produce a blinding flash of light. The other is to build your reputation over time by letting other people promote you. If you have a lot of people in the organization talking positively about your department, then you build a strong reputation and you're afforded opportunities for career growth. Little successes over time build a stronger foundation than a few quick flashes of success."

The advice of Ryan Murray, the banker? Lead by example in every action you take, from the mundane to the visionary. Shed hubris on your way into the corner office. "You can't have an inflated ego in community banking," Ryan says. "I have a senior position, but if I walk by a bunch of cartons that need to be moved, I pick them up and move them. That's one thing that can either build or destroy team players. Some people think 'Oh no, that's not my job. The guy in shipping does that.'"

Both Ryan and Steve Grossman alluded to a humility born from the fact that seniority does not equal infallibility, it just affords you more opportunities to keep learning. Even CEOs make mistakes, comments Steve, and they should always be the first to admit them. Owning full responsibility for errors in judgment allows him to return to work each day with a clean slate. "I've made very few enemies in my life because when I make a mistake, I am the first person to step up to the plate, publicly or privately, and say 'I did wrong. I'm sorry. It was thoughtless of me. It was inconsiderate of me. This decision was too hasty.'" When he does so, Steve says, people respect that. Rather than seeing him as weak, they express their relief that he is, like them, only human. "When you say you're sorry," Steve emphasizes, "it disarms most people. When you're genuine about it, which obviously you have to be, even a person who is irritated at you is forced to say 'You know? It takes a big person to say that.'" For both Steve and Ryan, small gestures of humility go a long way toward increasing the power of their position beyond the symbolic.

Three: Treat People with Dignity

It's so basic, asserts Steve Grossman: What you give to people comes back to you multifold. When you treat people with respect, declares Steve, you motivate them; when you do not, you encourage them to sabotage you whenever you falter. "When you need people to come through, they will do anything for you because they care about you as a person. They want you to succeed and they want to be part of that success."

The best-kept secrets of good men at the top for getting people to support their business vision are graciousness and generosity of spirit. Even as I interviewed them for this book, the CEOs to whom I spoke conveyed these qualities.

Without knowing if he could squeeze me into his schedule, I called Steve Grossman the day before he was to be honored for his work on the Democratic National Committee, in front of 700 people, including the president of the United States. Graciously, Steve returned my call that evening, from his car phone, agreeing to an interview and offering me several openings on his calendar.

"To the best of my knowledge, I return every single phone call, I mean *every single one,*" Steve states. "To stockbrokers, sales people, to people I've never heard of, because as a business owner, I'm a salesman myself. And why should I expect people to return my calls if I don't return theirs? You never know who's at the end of the phone. I don't care how late I have to stay, or how many calls I have to make, or how late it is at night, I am constantly returning phone calls."

Despite calendars scheduled to the nanosecond, each of these men, once our interview began, conveyed an impressive ability to focus clearly and explicitly on my questions. One CEO conducted our interview in a four-part series during his drive home, each time remembering precisely where we had left off, gracefully moving from one task to the next, never wasting a minute of my time or his.

The CEOs I interviewed shared several traits: grace under pressure, razor-sharp focus, and the ability to communicate ideas with convincing passion. One executive conducted our interview in the conference room of the company he was about to acquire, between his morning run and a meeting with his lawyers. Another calmly answered my interview questions as he anticipated a call from his wife, who was about to go into labor.

According to Steve Grossman, his formula for running a company and for working in politics relies on one basic tenet: treat people with dignity. Noticing how even the smallest gesture of thanks, such as leaving a congratulatory voice mail for a project well done, brings enormous appreciation, Steve purposefully reminds himself to make these human touches part of his daily routine. Bearing in mind the example set by his father, who worked in the business he now runs, Steve tries to lead according to the following principles:

- Say yes to people as often as you can.
- Be gracious to everybody.
- Treat each person as if they are of infinite worth.
- Say you're sorry when you've made a mistake.
- Thank people every day.

Invariably, the best qualities of human behavior—honesty, dignity, and just plain old politeness—go a long way toward gaining the affection, attention, and all-out effort of those around you.

Four: Let Humor Lighten the Load

Successful leaders set a positive tone for conducting business with just the right combination of humanity, drive, optimism, and confidence, all flavored with a healthy dose of humor.

"If you ever allow your sense of humor to disappear, you're lost," advises Steve Grossman. Calling upon humor, particularly during tough times, serves Steve well. "It doesn't mean cracking jokes at inopportune or inappropriate times," he says. "But you need to be able to punctuate a very difficult, or sad, or tense moment with a little lightheartedness that relaxes people." That lightheartedness brings tangible benefits. "People who are relaxed and comfortable, even in crisis environments, are going to make better decisions."

Getting people to feel good about working for you, suggests Ryan Murray, requires the ability to laugh at yourself every once in a while. According to Ryan: "You've got to get people to lighten up and be able to laugh at themselves. If people take life too seriously, they'll always be stressed out and that hurts business and morale. When you do something stupid, you don't want to make a big announcement, but don't be ashamed to say 'Yeah, that was pretty dumb, huh?'" But, Ryan emphasizes: "You *cannot* use humor to offend."

Five: Always Hire People Smarter Than You

It may take confidence to laugh at yourself when you've made a stupid move, but it takes even more to admit that you don't have all the answers.

Although Dan Harris expresses tremendous admiration for a woman who serves as president of one of his companies, he believes that a lack of confidence has held her back. "She is very nervous about her position as a female executive. She will not hire people who are smarter and more knowledgeable than she is. I keep reminding her 'That's the real reason *I* have been successful.'" Don't be afraid to select and groom a person who can succeed you, he advises. In Dan's view, you can leave your company no greater legacy than someone you believe can run it better than you did.

As head of a large division, Glenn Sears agrees with Dan. "A lot of managers feel threatened by people around them who are exceptionally talented," observes Glenn. "That may just be human nature, but you have to get over it if you want to be successful." For his part, Glenn says: "I always tell my people, I'm only here as a successful manager if they are successful. Nothing makes me happier than to see them do well." A strong believer in practicing what he preaches, he adds: "There is one young guy who works for me who is just brilliant. I've been very aggressive about getting him in front of my boss, who is the CFO, and letting him work on as many high-profile projects as he will undertake."

On one hand, Glenn sees a certain risk in showcasing the best talent on his staff. "The downside to doing this is that this person is going to be offered a lot more opportunities to leave the department because of this visibility." But Glenn knows that establishing a reputation as someone who develops others yields significant rewards, especially when it encourages new talent to come knocking at his door. "In the long run, it's the right thing to do for everybody," concludes Glenn. "When people observe my behavior, they'll say, 'He's someone who is not afraid to help people develop' and then good people will gravitate toward my department."

Six: Surround Yourself with People Who Keep You on Your Toes

As strong leaders develop others, they make certain that their closest advisors also function as their toughest critics. Having taken deliberate steps to surround themselves with people who will always tell them the truth and feel free to deliver bad news, the CEOs I interviewed also recruit board members who constantly challenge them.

Asking for and digesting brutally frank criticism, asserts Paul Meyers, requires a certain mental fortitude and a little humility. "At the top, you have to be able to take a certain amount of abuse and then be willing to be self-reflective and admit 'Boy, I really screwed that up, and here's what I need to think about so I don't do it again.' And most people, men and women, have trouble doing that."

Earlier in his career, Eric Stephens, now an executive vice president at a biotech firm, worked for a CEO who took him under his wing. "He made it clear that he saw something in me. And he gave me challenges when I was barely ready for them." Vividly recalling some of the more grueling aspects of his boss's tutelage, Eric now reflects on his mentor's profound impact on his career. "My boss would take me out to dinner where we would sit for four or five hours. Basically, you'd be dying at the end of it because it felt as invasive as the worst type of prostate exam."

The first part of the conversation focused on a new career opportunity, recalls Eric. Then came the reality check. "The CEO would spend the next hour telling me all the ways I could fail, pointing out how it could become a major turning point, a highly negative one, for my career. And talk about a detailed examination of all your character defects and all your talent flaws!" Despite the mix of fear and admiration he held for his boss, Eric found himself, upon reflection, invigorated by these intensive one-on-ones. "You realize that if someone cares that much about you, you have to rise to the challenge."

More typically, Eric has experienced the cursory three-minute performance review. In contrast to performance conversations with his mentor based on a career plan and new challenges, most reviews run along these lines: "Yeah, yeah. You did a great job. Here's your compensation."

Seven: Exercise Restraint

How do good men at the top deal with lackluster performers? Ryan Murray tries to show the utmost respect because he believes restraint always works better than anger, accusation, or avoidance.

"I've had both men and women come back to me a day after a critical performance review and say, 'Listen, I'm really having a problem with what we went over. Can we talk about it in further detail?'" Admittedly, Ryan says, his first instinct, when he sees such a person waiting outside his door is to run for cover or to put the person off with a plausible excuse. "But it's my responsibility to be open-minded and not look up when they show up at the door, and say 'Oh shoot, here we go again.'"

According to Ryan, true leadership requires treating the weak link on his staff with the same respect he accords a star. When someone submits a weak proposal or bad idea, rather than simply dismissing it, Ryan will elaborate on his response, hoping to heighten the other person's awareness. "If someone has put the time into a proposal, regardless of how stupid it may be, they obviously believe in it. If I want them to continue to work well with me, and for them to feel a level of respect from me, I owe them an explanation other than just 'No way.'"

Turning down an unworkable proposal without putting the person down, advises Ryan, need involve little more than a few well-chosen words: "These are the reasons it doesn't make sense for us to consider this at this time. Let's look at this other set of factors." In Ryan's view: "You owe people certain things as their manager. You owe people communication. They may not like what they hear, but at least if you stay open-minded and have a matter-of-fact conversation with them, they don't start working in fear."

The worst message you can send from the top? Fear me because I hold the power to make or break you. "Don't spark up the keyboard just because I'm walking by," Ryan tells his staff. In too many organizations, he observes: "When the chief honcho comes walking through, suddenly everybody stops talking or people feel they have to look busy. Well, looking busy doesn't get the job done!"

Eight: Draw a Clear Line Between Business and Personal Issues

Ryan and many other successful men revealed that, yes, they do carefully consider the image they wish to project, especially when they feel least powerful or confident. In their experience, people remember more about how a man handles the bad days than he does the good.

Steve Grossman explains: "I try to keep the personal out of it. I don't yell at people. I don't swear at people. I don't threaten people. But people know when I'm deadly serious about something."

Not drawing a clear line between business and personal issues, suggests Glenn Sears, can both impair your ability to get things done and corrode morale. Explaining his company's performance management philosophy, he says: "We try very hard not to make it personal. When employees aren't working out, we've found that when we're direct, we give good feedback, we're honest and straightforward, we end the relationship with few repercussions. But when we drag it out and aren't straightforward about the process, the person gets both upset and confused."

Eliminating the personal, he says, does not mean you can't care about the individual. When dealing with someone he must fire, Glenn tries to incorporate dignity and face-saving into the process, with a tone that conveys: It's not that you're a jerk, it's not that you're incompetent. It's just that this isn't a good fit.

In attorney Bob Gault's opinion, what people say about an organization after they leave it most accurately reflects the company's culture. At his law firm, he explains: "Each year, we hold alumni parties and scores of people come back. Of those, some were asked to leave the firm. If the people you fire (I hate to use the word) feel comfortable coming back, you know you did something right."

What's the magic secret? Compassion. Why does a company care about employees who end up leaving? Pragmatism. Addressing the compassionate side of the equation, Bob says: "Our attitude has always been that just because someone didn't work out here doesn't mean they are bad people. Maybe they just weren't cut out for this. When people leave here, 99 percent of the time, it's on good terms."

On the pragmatic side, allowing people to walk out the front door with dignity, fostering some measure of loyalty even among those who leave, benefits the business. People who leave the right way will not say or do things that might injure the company or its reputation.

Nine: Learn from the Good, the Bad, and the Ugly

Each senior executive I interviewed described experiencing some degree of failure along the way. What happens when you stumble? How should you respond when you make a big mistake?

As a member of the senior staff at a Silicon Valley firm, Connie Moore attends the Thursday morning meetings run by the CEO. Recalling a presentation made by one of her peers, Connie remarks: "It did *not* go well. In fact, it went very poorly. The CEO lambasted him, saying 'This is the stupidest thing I've ever heard of! How could you even profess to knowing what you're talking about?'"

As Connie recalls, the ten other senior managers walked out of the room in stunned silence, not knowing quite what to say to Bob, the man who had stumbled so badly. When Connie walked into her office the next day, she noticed an e-mail from Bob, addressed to everyone who had attended the meeting: "This was not my finest hour and I regret you had to witness it. However, I gained some good information yesterday. Here are the steps I'm going to take, the programs I'm going to initiate, and the strategy I'll use for turning this around."

Impressed by Bob's upbeat, proactive, and decisive response to a humiliating day, Connie sent a return e-mail: "I'm proud to be your peer. You've taken a very difficult situation and turned it around to extract the maximum lesson from it and move on. I admire that." Having been advised by her mentor never to kick a person who has fallen down, Connie also learned a lesson from Bob, who revealed his best colors when tested by adversity. Don't waste valuable time wallowing in self-pity when you should be developing Plan B.

The ultimate Plan B depends on taking a long-term view, suggests Steve Grossman, particularly when you face high-risk situations where you may hope for the best, but must prepare for the worst. Focusing on the personal vision he has defined for himself, says Steve, allows him to accept challenges that others would avoid. Talking about what he calls "the darkest days of 1997," Steve told me about taking over a functionally bankrupt Democratic Party, as head of the Democratic National Committee. Steve accepted the challenge of turning the organization around, keeping in mind the words a friend had written on a three-by-five card he had handed to his daughter as she headed off to college: "Work hard, have fun, don't panic."

Focusing on his ultimate goal of restoring the party's power rather than simply fixing the immediate financial problems, Steve reminded himself that even if he did not succeed in this one mission, that need not compromise his personal vision. He set three goals for himself: "When I return to Boston, I want to come back with three things intact: my good name and reputation, my sense of humor, and my dignity." Steve adds with a smile: "I think I did."

Ten: Sponsor Spectacular Risks

Success sometimes walks a fine line. Vision, at times, defies logic. Risk-taking, many business leaders said, often requires them to stand alone, relying solely on the strength of their convictions. Although they deliberately seek wise counsel, these leaders also maintain a keen sense for when they should ignore well-intentioned advice. Here's where the powerful combination of confidence and instinct comes into play.

Dan Harris, who has run several $300 million companies, says that many of his best business decisions have defied the conventional wisdom. Recently, while evaluating a new business, people told Dan: "How can you be so dumb as to go into the travel business at the moment? If you pick up any business magazine in the world, they will tell you how terrible it is." Having successfully ignored similar advice about his last acquisition, Dan says: "I believe this may be the *best* time to go into the business. I believe in my ability to change things. I have clear objectives for what I want to get out of it. And I rely on instincts where I see things as positives other people would see as exactly the opposite."

As I chatted with Tom Chase about strategies for moving his organization and his leadership to an even higher level of success, I asked him where he finds the confidence to take that risk. He answered: "I don't have an exact answer to that. It comes from within. It's almost like a salmon swimming upstream. It's kind of illogical, but it works." Justifying the logic behind a seemingly illogical approach, Tom went on to explain: "One of our directors told me there's no such thing as the right answer. You have to have an instinct, and then you have to go for it. And you go for it until you find out that you're wrong." He adds: "I'm still in the go-for-it mode."

As a follow-up question, I asked Tom: "Do you ever have to deal with the fear factor? Are there things you worry about?" Without hesitation, Tom replied: "Me personally? Constantly. It's hard to keep growing with a company. I worry a lot about trying to get to the next level. Because I'm trying to create an environment where spectacular failure is rewarded and applauded." How does Tom define "spectacular failure"? A bad result does not derail your confidence. It's not about being right or wrong, but about remaining true to what you believe, despite the ultimate outcome. "It's when you believe something is right, you enlist the best people for effort, and it's done carefully, thoughtfully, and cross-functionally, but it still doesn't work. That's spectacular failure."

Tom willingly sponsors a reasonable risk of failure: "I tell people explicitly, 'It's OK to be wrong.'" In his view, initiative and out-of-the-box thinking always encourage risks. Welcoming fear of the unknown rather than fighting it, observes Tom, means exploring uncharted, and sometimes rough, terrain. To encourage high-risk thinking, Tom follows the leadership-by-example tenet: "I try to model the behavior that I ask for and that puts huge pressure on me." Concerning the philosophy that drives his behavior, Tom says: "We have a model here that says the Godfather was wrong when he said 'nothing personal, just business.' We tend to make it very personal. I want to respect the people I work with, I want to trust them, I want to like them, and I want to value them."

What does he mean by "making it personal?" Tom emphasizes one key point: "Working through difficult issues with people you like is a lot more fun than working through easy issues with people you don't." He continues: "I want to like everybody I work with and that's something that screens reasonably easily in an interview. We conduct team interviews, so people go through a pretty rigorous process. We don't want Stepford Wives; we want this place to be very diverse in terms of its style and its range of personality and experience, but not in terms of its range of values."

Eleven: Welcome Women at the Top

According to both Tom Chase and Steve Grossman, the presence of executive women has prompted them to think differently, thereby enhancing their own skills. Steve talked about going into business with his two sisters, hiring a woman president for one of his divisions, and naming women to top slots at the Democratic National Committee. Then he got to the point: "If you're gathering from this conversation that I like to work with women, the answer is yes. I find the women with whom I'm in business as well as in politics fun to be around, totally dedicated, and highly skilled."

Steve particularly values the lessons he has learned from observing his two sisters, with whom he runs his $20-million business. His sisters, he says, have helped him achieve a balance between paying too much attention to every little nuance and picking up on subtle clues that may signal a serious concern for an employee. "You just have to be willing to look around you and extend your eyes, your ears, and your antennae out to people. Which doesn't mean you have to look at people and constantly ask 'What's wrong?' But it's pretty obvious when somebody's being petty versus when they have something serious going on in their lives."

Working closely with women has also taught Steve the virtue of patience in a manager. "Just because I learn a certain way doesn't mean its OK to be impatient with people who don't have the same learning style. Men, in general, tend to get too impatient with people, and that causes stress on both sides." In addition, Steve observes: "Women tend to have empathetic qualities, in greater abundance than men, that are very critical in highly charged organizations when people's emotions run high."

Steve describes his hiring of Linda Martyn to head his Connecticut company as "one of the smartest decisions we ever made." During negotiations to acquire this company, Steve and his father closed the deal only after the seller agreed to one key condition. "Linda Martyn [the outgoing president's right hand person] has to come on board and be part of this deal. Without Linda, there is no deal." As president, Linda went on to grow the business from $800,000 in sales to $10 million.

What did Steve see in Linda that inspired his faith in her? "She is goal-oriented, always." As president of his Connecticut branch, observes Steve, Linda has never exhibited the "I'm-going-to-show-you-who's-boss" mentality. She didn't need to, Steve explains: "We gave her the ball. She knew she had it. Everybody else knew she had it. We clearly defined who the leader was." As a result, Linda wasted no valuable time and effort trying to prove herself all over again. Not only does Steve hire women into senior positions, he also supports them.

Steve sees in Linda leadership traits that, he proposes, more men could emulate. "Linda is willing to spend more time with employees.

Because she is willing to be a good listener and offer non-judgmental advice, she creates very strong, close, personal relationships with people, but never inappropriately so. People always know she is the president of the company."

Twelve: Don't Make "Progressive" a Dirty Word

On the subject of ensuring equal footing for women at work, Bob Gault, the Mintz, Levin law partner, feels quite strongly: "It has to come from the top. If there's no buy-in from the top, you don't have it." What does he mean by "buy-in" from the top? Quite simply, says Bob, you make your support a visible management practice.

Without a moment's hesitation, Bob begins: "The head of our litigation department is a woman who works part-time. And if that isn't an endorsement that part-time work is consistent with being a professional." The firm, he says, has embraced progressive policies: "We have quite a few gay people in this office, and we make the same kind of policies available to them that we do to heterosexual couples."

Base your actions on respect, Bob stresses: "We are very quick to react if we encounter issues of sexual harassment or any kind of harassment here. We send a strong message to everybody concerned indicating that kind of behavior is not tolerated. It comes out in the way we deal with these issues and it is reinforced in the spoken word from the very top." In addition, he says, the firm also transmits its values through demonstrated commitment to the local community. "We've also been named in professional journals as one of the leaders in doing pro bono work. That's something else that makes our associates happy and makes this an attractive place for them to work."

As the father of three school-age children, Bob appreciates the tough choices between family and career that all parents face. In Bob's view, what makes Mintz, Levin stand out from the pack is addressing head-on the questions employees in other organizations would hesitate to ask. For example, "I have a personal family crisis and need to be away for eight weeks. May I take a leave of absence?" At his firm, "If I walked into the chairman's or president's office, the answer would be 'Go deal with it. We'll take care of things here. Don't worry about it.'" Despite the Family and Medical Leave Act, employees in many environments worry that they will jeopardize their careers if they take a parental leave of absence.

"These are human beings," asserts bank vice president Ryan Murray. "And this is the way life really works." With that declaration, Ryan goes on to explain his openness to flexible work options. Has Ryan taken specific steps to reduce potential resentment from staff not on a flexible schedule? "I haven't had to," says Ryan, "because in this culture we have clear expectations about performance that are a separate issue from a person's schedule." He makes occasional flexibility available to all staff because, as he says: "We all have things that come up in life that have an impact at the workplace. What may be someone's child needing to be picked up at school this week could be my dentist appointment or car problem next week."

Paul Meyers also feels quite strongly about workplace flexibility at his company: "It just makes good business sense." While some executives worry about non-traditional work options promoting chaos, he applauds them for sponsoring productivity in the highly competitive wholesale industry. He also admits that he has taken full advantage of the fact that a local competitor, notorious for its insensitive treatment of women, offers absolutely no flexibility in employee schedules.

The secret to the success behind flexibility at his company, suggests Steve Grossman, the CEO, comes not so much from the arrangement itself as from the way managers greet requests for flexibility. "We exhibit a willingness to provide time off without penalty. That is the key reason why people so seldom leave our company." As we chat, Steve comments: "I'm looking at a great example right now, a senior telemarketer who works a reduced schedule. With two young children, she asked, 'Ideally, I'd like to leave every day at 3:30. Can I do that? Will it work?'" Steve made the accommodation by offering her slightly lower compensation and a shorter lunch break. "She's been a consummate success. She leaves every day at 3:30 and works very hard when she's here." Keeping a good person on board with a bit of flexibility has also rewarded the business, explains Steve: "She's generated over $1 million in business, on the telephone."

In his own life, Steve has also faced challenges sorting out priorities. His departure from the Democratic National Committee made headlines, in large part, because he left to spend more time with his nine-year-old son and his father, whose health was failing. Like Steve, Tom Chase also considers the sacrifices he has made spending so much time away from his family. "I'd like to take a summer off, which in one sense is inconceivable," he remarks. "This is a billion-dollar public company, and I'm the CEO. Take the whole summer off? Yes, that would be a leadership model of enormous consequences."

As he contemplates the possibility of a ninety-day professional sabbatical, Tom says: "I can imagine coming back fired up and ready to attack the world. And I could also imagine how the team would feel. I remember the first time my predecessor traveled to Asia for two weeks. For the two weeks he was out of the building the senior managers met as a team every single day and reviewed the open list of issues. When the CEO returned, there was a notebook waiting on his desk listing every issue he'd left us, and every one of them was addressed. And I'm certain that if he'd been around, we'd never come close to making those accomplishments."

Secure enough in his own position to examine where he hopes to grow as a leader, Tom concedes: "If you look at my day, I do lots of things that other people can do, and I have to stop that." In considering the sabbatical, Tom says: "It will certainly be good for me, but I want it to be better for the company than it is for me." A sabbatical might enhance his leadership, Tom believes: "What do I do that holds things back? Who would emerge as the team's leaders while I was gone? It wouldn't necessarily be the usual cast of characters. Imagine how good they'd feel. It would be great to ask them to step up to the plate."

Contemplating the tone he sets at the top, Tom comments: "We used to be a very charisma-based, follow-me leadership environment where there was a powerful premium placed on being right, being the smartest, the glibbest, being the most powerful. And I am very anxious to undo that. That doesn't mean I want to be stupid or powerless or inarticulate as an individual, but I don't want to convey an 'I'm right, you're wrong' attitude either. I want it to be about 'This is the best solution for us,' and I am very anxious to create an environment where people are glad to follow that lead."

Humane leadership takes more time, effort, and sensitivity than controlling leadership, says Tom. Being courageous can make you feel lonely, but it can reap huge rewards for individuals and the organizations. Tom makes the business case for his version of leadership:

"Give me a full human against a half human any time, and we should be able to win; we should be able to advance our agenda." Rather than signaling an absence of competitive spirit, Tom finds that this vision fuels a deeper passion to win.

Code Breakers

Each of the CEOs I interviewed agreed on two points. First, good leadership is a gender-blind concept. Second, lessons from the top apply to every stage of a career.

How did Connie Moore make the transition from manager to leader?

A friendly shove into the pool before you know how to swim marked a turning point in Connie's career. "My boss, who was also a mentor, pushed me just the way he would push a man," recalls Connie, now a vice president at a Silicon Valley firm. "He recognized capabilities within me before I even knew that I had them." Her boss, envisioning opportunities too remote for Connie's career radar screen to detect, would announce: "I'm going to promote you to this, first as a manager, and then as a director." She responded confidently: "Thank you very much, Jerry. This will be a great opportunity to learn. I've always had an interest in these areas." But her inner voice was screaming: "Jerry, what are you, crazy? I don't know anything about this!" Still, as calm returned after the storm, she thought: "He could see something in me I couldn't."

Code Breaker #1

Learn something new every day.

Connect with people who can accelerate your learning curve. It's the old "you-don't-ask, you-don't-get" principle. Seek the counsel of people you admire and respect, recommends systems administrator Carl Sullivan. Don't think, "Well, they would never talk to me," or "Why would they want to help me?" In his own experience, Carl has found: "People may be surprised and delighted to hear that you think they have something worth learning."

While the myth of the lifelong mentor may have died, Mary Rowe, an ombudsperson at the Massachusetts Institute of Technology, believes that, over the course of their careers, most people will relate to multiple mentors, each serving different purposes. You don't even have to like your mentor, she suggests. You just have to open yourself up to learn from the person.

While it may seem amateurish to stroll into an office and ask for mentoring, many people welcome a request for their advice: "Here's a project I'd like to undertake. Can we sit down and discuss it?" Women, of course, also face an issue less likely to arise in a same-sex mentor relationship. A man and a woman who work closely together may worry about appearances of impropriety if others see them too often dining together or meeting privately.

One woman, reporting to a president who believes in her potential, became aware of the gossip and rumors circulating about their frequent meetings. Choosing a direct approach with her boss and mentor, she told him: "Look, people are talking about the fact that we're together a lot. I just want to say that, like you, I know this is about business and nothing more." Even though she knew their close working relationship was totally professional, saying the words out loud took the pressure off responding to the rumors. She and her boss agreed to a contingency plan: "Let's talk about this again if rumors become too big of a problem."

Code Breaker #2

Forge alliances with key players according to a well-conceived business plan.

As she talks about access to key players and key information, Connie Moore explains: "I'm pretty aggressive about identifying people who I think have background information or who can influence the decision that I'm driving." Before she even considers contacting a key player, Connie prepares carefully. "I succinctly identify why I'm contacting them, what I need from them, how much time I think it's going to take." As for the "don'ts" Connie advises: "We've all gotten e-mail messages that ramble on page after page with every detail, every contact, everything anybody said about it, the whole bit." Instead, ensure that your message will be read. "The first paragraph should be an executive summary, 'Here's why I'm contacting you and here's the compelling issue.'" Connie emphasizes, "At most, this should take three sentences. Ideally, the whole e-mail should fit in one screen. 'We have a customer problem; $20 million is on the line unless we resolve this issue by the end of the month. I need a contact person in your group to work with us on this.'"

Does her gender figure into the confidence she feels communicating and networking? "I don't think this is a male/female thing, but I've found this an interesting barometer of talent: People who cannot learn to communicate succinctly, effectively, and with an economy of words, either written or spoken, will never rise up. They're trapped in their thinking, 'I have to know everything. I have to give every detail.' And that's not the reality."

Code Breaker #3

Lead by example to strengthen your leadership and your organization.

In Connie's view, a good leader invests heavily in coaching staff on how to focus on the business issues that matter. As an example, Connie recalls her response to comments made by an all-male software team: "How will this new woman you hired ever keep up? She's got four kids." Refusing to let that stereotype rattle her, Connie sticks to business issues, encouraging her staff to drop preconceptions that might cloud their judgment. She responded to the software team calmly, but forcefully: "Hey guys, the real question is, can this person conduct business and do her job? Talk to me if someone is deficient and I'll deal with that. Let's try to maximize everybody's effectiveness and try to focus on getting the next product out."

Nevertheless, Connie realistically recognizes how closely women in a male industry are watched and has advised other working mothers to avoid signals a man might misinterpret. For instance, "Be careful about the way you describe your day and the fact that your life is scheduled down to the second." A man might read stress or potential burn-out into a statement that simply reflects a normal day.

Code Breaker #4

As you face the dilemmas all leaders encounter, consider doing what may at first feel counterintuitive.

Err on the side of generosity, advises Connie. Treating people with dignity, at all levels of the organization, always makes good business sense. It can also mean the difference between who will and who will not rush to your aid when you really need help. "I try to be even-handed, to be an unemotional business person, even to people I might not like," Connie explains. As an example, she says: "There is a senior person, in a very visible position, who has been extremely hurtful to many people and because of his lack of attention to issues, he's had a very negative impact on the stock." When this manager failed to follow through on something crucial to her area, Connie admits: "It was real easy to feel like, 'OK, I want to jump on the disparaging bandwagon and try to get the guy fired.'" When Connie spoke to her boss and mentor about her colleague's obstructionist behavior, he agreed, then advised her: "Everything you're saying is absolutely true. However, the fact is, the guy *is* in the position and the best thing we can all do is to try and make him successful." In other words, until the CEO took action, Connie needed to support even the weak link on the executive team. "I've learned to take my worst enemies and to whatever extent I can, not to avoid them, but to try to work proactively with them to turn things around or to make them successful."

Code Breaker #5

Rely on your personal values and align them with your role as a leader.

Connie comments: "I feel as much male as female in a business sense. For someone to be successful, first and foremost they have to know themselves. They have to be aggressive in growing the areas where they are weak. They have to know what their values are, what integrity means to them, and how they want those values to guide them in business."

If you want to understand and evaluate a work culture, study the person at the top. The values that person holds and exhibits in words and deeds tremendously affect the organization. Rather than imitating the worst models for leadership, we can follow our own instincts, take valuable lessons from good women and men at the top, and raise the bar for what we expect from all business associates.

As business leaders open the gender lens on the culture of work, they make themselves more powerful as they elevate standards for themselves and for the organization.

8

Conclusion

Opening the Gender Lens

Frank Andryauskas, former CIO of Staples and now a partner in an Internet start-up, describes power as a double-edged sword, with an intimidating and excluding blade on one side, an inspiring and including blade on the other. With respect to gender, Frank describes a corporate board meeting at which a leader welcomed male input but ignored anything a woman said: "It was obvious to me that when a male executive said something, even if the point was dismissed at the time, it would rattle around with some credibility in the back of the chairman's mind. Whereas, if a woman offered a new approach, his instinct was not to let it cloud his thinking. It just wasn't within his window of thinking." The reason? According to Frank: "It was a prejudice that he was unconsciously demonstrating. And it was remarkable how all the executives on that team were clones of the chairman."

In other words, the man at the top held power so closely that he heard ideas only from people who look and act and think like him. Since Frank believes that such controlling, exclusionary leadership limits perspective and causes you to miss great ideas, he has embraced a markedly different philosophy for his own company. "Leveraging for strengths and compensating for weaknesses, I look for people who offer skills in areas I don't," Frank says. "I want to build better teams at work, integrating the best from what is typically considered the masculine and feminine side."

Even as a CEO, Tom Chase never paid much attention to his company's unwritten rules of work until he heard his senior team termed "a school of sharks." That revelation served as a wake-up call to examine the company culture and the reasons so few women entered senior management. As Tom explains: "We're tough, and we're strong, and we have a lot to do. This is the kind of company where there are urgent issues every two seconds, so people really go for it, people really work hard. And that's great. Usually we tear up the enemy with this approach, but every once in a while, one of us gets in a feeding frenzy of trying to get the job done. Then we act like sharks, sort of mindlessly tear each other apart." He adds: "We forget that what we're biting right now is the arm of our colleague."

Tired of swimming in shark-infested waters, Tom wants to steer the group away from the "every-man-for-himself" standard. Even good men at the top struggle with creating an organization where the best talent rises, regardless of gender. As much of a commitment as Tom Chase has made to changing his company's culture, he admits that he does not always get things right the first time.

Among the goals Tom articulated to his board was his desire to create more diversity in the management team. "I didn't mean just by checking a box on the EEOC form, but by forcing different styles into the way we do things and hopefully by encouraging people to listen to ideas differently." This concept met with skepticism, chiefly from members of his senior staff. "This is not the way the game is played by a lot of these guys on the team," concludes Tom. They think: "Why do we need to talk about this stuff and why do we need to change?" Tom shares their frustration in some ways. In many situations, he understands the allure of a "just do it" approach: "Don't think. There's no need for reflection here. Cut your losses and move on."

To reduce the frustration he feels, Tom redefines his challenge this way: "There's real conflict between the urgent and the important. In our company, everything is always urgent. The urgent always overwhelms the important. And the important rarely gets worked on." Taking a hard line with staff who insist they can't afford to take time to deal with issues he deems important, such as encouraging a broader range of management styles, Tom tells them: "Work with me to figure out this problem together."

Tom shared his resolution for inclusiveness with Joan Clarke, the first woman to join his inner circle. In response, Joan adopted this philosophical view, perhaps as a way of maintaining some emotional distance on the challenges she would face: "This company *does* have a really strong culture. There are good things about that, and limiting things about that." When Tom asked, "Is this a male/female issue?", Joan answered: "To some extent, but it's more an inside/outside problem. For anyone from the outside to succeed here, it's important for that person to be conscious of how the game is played. For a woman, it's even more important because there aren't thirty examples of powerful, successful women who have already made it here." With respect to being an outsider, Joan explained to Tom: "It doesn't mean I should compromise my principles; it doesn't mean I should become somebody I'm not. It just means this place has a very strong culture. The more I know, the better off we'll both be."

Exploring the insider code she needed to crack, Joan told Tom: "You guys speak in shorthand. You have conversations that reflect the fact that you've worked together for years. If you don't understand the code, you can be locked out of the discussion." Tom agrees: "If you have to push yourself into a conversation, it's not all that comfortable if you're an outsider trying to find his/her way the first time."

Don't congratulate yourself just because you brought the first woman into senior management, cautions Tom, if you then expect her to fend for herself. In his experience, the message "sink or swim" does not work. Acknowledging someone might misconstrue his approach as special treatment, Tom says that addressing how you bring an outsider into a culture rigid in traditions and rituals sets the stage for many more, and more different, managers to succeed in the organization.

Mike Snell, literary agent, believes: "The history of gender skirmishes has been a history about power." Bruce Kohl, a journalist, asserts, "I don't think men realize the power they have. One of the first steps to being a responsible, open man in the workplace is to think about the invisible power that you hold, that you didn't ask for, but that society has given you. How does it impact the way I interact with others? What do I need to learn about what other people are experiencing? How do I handle this power?" After Bruce poses these questions, he confirms what he instinctively practices: "I have great, warm relationships with women at work who are very funny, powerful, and dynamic. I think it's because they feel I'm open to their ideas. I listen to them and I respect them."

Humbled by the reality that his status in the workplace derives, in part, from gender alone, Bruce cautions against using power as an intimidating force. "I'm aware of the power that, as a man, I bring to the workplace. I don't flaunt it, and I don't manipulate it the way many men do." Organizations created by the male mind, he believes, quite naturally reflect the comfort, confidence, and control that dominate the male code. Bruce notes the rarely questioned behavior that often excludes women from full participation in the heart of an organization. It may not always follow the stereotypic cigar-smoking, whiskey-drinking scenario, Bruce says, but it still happens. "It can be in a hallway conversation that only lasts thirty seconds, or running into a male colleague in the elevator, where a decision is made before the meeting is even held. It's much more insidious and much more subtle."

Frank Andryauskas gets to the heart of the matter: "Organizations that have succeeded according to masculine characteristics, left unto themselves, are not going to change." Perhaps not, but surely the old barriers to women will fall by the wayside when the old guard retires. Maybe, maybe not. As John Lucas, a thirty-three-year-old marketing director, asserts: "I find that the people who tend to think like me, for the most part, tend to be men. There are a few women who think like me, but they're the exception, not the rule."

John's statement explains why a man will not usually make the first move to revise the unwritten rules of work that reinforce the male code. "Why rock the boat? The status quo works just fine for me." Feelings of comfort, confidence, and control always stall change.

As psychologist Leslie Brody points out, likeness often engenders unquestioned acceptance and unconditional trust while difference causes just the opposite. Men naturally feel more secure in the office, declares Ray Ingalls, a twenty-nine-year-old business manager, because they gain comfort and control from two sources. "Let's say you're sitting in a meeting and four of the five other people in the room are like you in that they're men. That adds to a sense of security. In addition, even if you *did* feel uncomfortable, you were taught that men don't show it." In other words, men benefit both from the likeness factor and from the mask of invulnerability, conditions that feed off one another.

Tom Chase agrees. "Like any other culture, this organization has a point of view. I'd be foolish not to at least understand what the ground looks like." He has learned from Joan Clarke's assessment of the challenge before her: "This is still a boys' club, which is to say, most of the managers here are still guys. They make the rules for how this place works. I may not play by those rules, but it would be a mistake not to know what they are."

Understanding that point of view need not oblige conformity to the male code, however. In his 1950 article "The Nature of Femininity," psychologist Bernard Robbins proposes that "for women to become pale images of men would prove nothing other than the assumption that masculinity per se is superior and is, therefore, to be copied." This proposition rings true today for women who work in organizations that support the notion of male dominance in both subtle and not-so-subtle ways. Men-only symbols, ranging from the elk head mounted on the wall to the golf bag leaning in the corner, represent symbols of the club. And these symbols can exclude those who do not honor them from opportunities to shape their organizations.

Knowledge may equal power, but knowledge alone does not drive radical change. As Jean Baker Miller contends in *Toward a New Psychology of Women*, women's strengths "will remain 'unreal' and unrealized, if women do not have the power to put them into effective operation. To do so, they will have to acquire economic, political, and social power and authority." In other words, those exceptional talents men identified in their Top Ten list will remain largely untapped in many organizations until a certain power shift occurs.

Genetics

Healthy companies and healthy people share many traits. "It's genetics in large measure," asserts Frank Andryauskas. "Take a careful look at a company's gene pool. If women don't occupy line positions close to the top, something is probably wrong. Senior women are out there. If the board remains all-male or has, for years, had one token woman, something is amiss." In Frank's estimation, organizations that adhere to insider-only values get stuck in rigid expectations that limit roles and performance, especially when those values pivot on gender.

A 1965 *Harvard Business Review* article asked "Are Women Executives People?" When Margaret Hennig and Anne Jardim wrote *The*

Managerial Woman in 1976, they concluded: "As outsiders to the system, women have often tried to ensure their own survival by creating a job situation in which they could be wholly and solely dependent on themselves." Yet this strategy poses an inherent problem: "The outcomes of this strategy conflict directly with the requirements of a management position. . . . The leadership of other people demands an ability to depend on and trust in them." In other words, hard work and talent alone will not carry us to the top. To get there, successful women, just like successful men, need access to the informal systems and unspoken expectations that so greatly affect all careers.

The frustrating theme of women as outsiders, excluded from the shadow organization behind the visible organization, continues to plague working women. Describing his own status as an outsider, a gay man in a culture defined according to a traditional male image, Ray Ingalls comments: "It's difficult for someone like me to be involved with them because I'm not necessarily like them. I can certainly understand why it would be difficult for a woman to try to tap into that without having to try to change her identity."

As an example, Ray describes how exclusionary male networks often reinvent themselves in new forums, in new traditions that confirm a woman's status as intruder: "I've been on men-only e-mail lists with jokes women would find very offensive. It's a covert way of continuing a bad dialogue about women."

While some men chalk such covert behavior up to a backlash against political correctness gone awry, journalist Bruce Kohl offers a different perspective: "The broader issue is respect, and if you're really respecting your coworkers, those are things that would never cross your mind because you are treating them the way you treat people outside the workplace for whom you have the highest regard." Bruce feels little sympathy for male colleagues who whine about the burden of working alongside women: "It's a cop-out, an attitude that says 'My hands are tied because I'm being asked to act responsibly.'"

Among the men I interviewed, some actually still view women as a workplace experiment, expressing confusion and even fear about their women colleagues. One senior executive, age forty-four, admits that women have eroded his comfort zone, saying: "I've given a lot of thought to these issues because I want to be a participant in this experiment, but it is very difficult for me to make business decisions that I have to worry about getting sued for. I've *already* been sued for age discrimination by women."

This executive also shared his assumptions about women's career and life choices: "I have a talented woman who works for me now and is getting married. She's a strategic asset, but she's probably either going to quit or get pregnant. What do I do with her?" Explaining the source of his concern, he continued: "She'll become less effective. You can't have a baby and be an analyst." Essentially, he considers families a career burden, one that women alone should carry. For this executive, whose own wife left the workforce to be at home with their children, his vision for women who want to merge multiple roles is acutely distorted.

Voicing a similar perspective, Harry Mills, a forty-eight-year-old investment banker, told me that he will share exactly the same career advice with his daughter and his two sons, with one caveat for her: "Realize that you do not have an unlimited set of options." Continuing this line of thought, Harry declared: "My daughter is capable of doing just about anything she wants to do. The difference is in regard to children and what she's going to do. She's the type of person who will have children, but she's not a person who's going to want to have a nanny raise the kids."

In Harry's view, the real reason so few women enter investment banking boils down to biology and family. In his opinion: "To me, the most significant question for women coming out of college is: What are you going to do about your family? Because we're not yet at a point where the males traditionally stay home with the kids. And that's a huge difference because our society has not set up the obvious things, like day-care centers in the investment bank itself. But the harder point is, our society has not transcended the socialization that convinces mothers that they are bad mothers if they don't stay home with their kids."

Does Harry maintain these definitive expectations for his own family? Yes. Can he leave them at home? Probably not. How will he view a talented woman at work, whose life choices may differ from what he expects from his daughter? Confusion, at best. Fortunately, not all men adhere to such a double standard based on gender alone.

Context and Comfort

What goes on in the minds of men who practice what they preach when it comes to working with women?

As we opened our conversation, Bob Gault described a current managerial challenge in his law practice: "I have a small department of fifteen lawyers and right now I have two lawyers out on leave. And they're both men." Talking about how his role as a manager and his organization's culture have changed, he says: "A couple of years ago, you would have thought I would be juggling maternity leaves, but here I am handling the impact of three- and four-month paternity leaves." And who picks up the billable hours while the two men take their leaves? "I pick up some of it myself," explains Bob. "And I'll probably hire another lawyer since I see our business as expanding, and we'll need another lawyer by the time they come back."

Bob purposefully sends signals that define his organization's tone. "The people in my department know they can speak up. There isn't one person who won't tell me whatever's on their mind. And they know they can do that." Having trained himself to seek insight from unexpected sources in unexpected places, Bob reflects: "I know women bring unique traits to the table, although they're hard to identify specifically. I'm a fifty-five-year-old man, and I grew up with certain notions. I need to be careful that I'm well-grounded with today's realities, that I'm connecting with a woman's point of view and sometimes a younger point of view. I look for any kind of insight I can get."

"Men don't have any monopoly on wisdom," declares Bob. With a hearty laugh, he adds: "The women in our firm never get talked over. We have very assertive women here and that's one reason we like them and we hire them. Just like the men, they have to be assertive to have their voices heard." As someone who welcomes differences in the workplace, Bob believes: "The people who are valuable to me, not only in terms of policy issues, but in how I run a case, are the ones who challenge my way of thinking and argue it out with me. Two women come to mind who will thrash things out with me and keep telling me I'm wrong, wrong, wrong. Colleagues who prevent me from making a mistake are the people I value most."

Peter Drake, the forty-six-year-old biotech investor, agrees with Bob: "I lead by sharing honestly both my strengths as well as my shortcomings, because I'm trying to create an environment where people recognize that we're all fallible, but we're trying to drive the process together." In other words, an open mind sponsors an open culture.

Makes sense. Seems pretty simple and straightforward. Why, then, do some men and some organizations find this wide-open territory so unsettling?

Invisible Power

In her 1973 book *Psychoanalysis and Woman,* Jean Baker Miller offers a perspective about gender and power that makes the case for challenging a business culture hostile to women. As Miller explains: "Women have developed thus far within a milieu that fosters and reflects a distorted conception about their essential nature. This occurs not to an obvious 'minority group,' but to one of the two main bodies of all humankind . . . it has been weighted toward a profound underestimation of women's attributes, since their strengths go unrecognized."

What fuels this distorted view? Invisible power. The power of whose rules prevail, the threat of sharing, or perhaps relinquishing power. Fear is about power; exclusion is about power.

First, the traditional business environment tends to reinforce more comfort and control for men. When talking about fit with the male code, business manager Ray Ingalls remarks: "I've seen more men being humorous in the workplace, in meetings for example. It makes sense to me that the more secure you feel, the more relaxed you feel about bringing humor into something. It's really contextual."

Second, a double standard limits the range of workplace styles deemed acceptable for a woman. Harry Mills, forty-eight, admits: "I try to catch myself when I rely on male stereotypes. If men are honest about it, most see a very aggressive man and say, 'Gee, he's kind of a jerk, but at least he went for the jugular trying to get the information.' And my first reaction to a woman who does that is, 'Gee, what a bitch!'" And then "When I find myself guilty of thinking 'This is a male strategy rather than a female strategy.' I hope I realize, 'Wait a minute, what I'm seeing is just a style issue.'" Even a woman who chooses to play by the male rules of the game and who feels perfectly comfortable employing an aggressive, hard-hitting approach may not find herself welcomed into the fold. According to Frank Andryauskas, a man expects another man to meet him with force, but he may not accept similar behavior from a woman.

Third, gender-based display rules sometimes constrain the roles women will consider and practice. Attorney Joe Leghorn offers strong words of caution against defaulting into gender-based expectations that reduce our effectiveness. To his female colleagues, he says: "Don't defer to men. Don't stifle your instincts. You're as good, if not better, than any man around." Joe specifically cautions the women he mentors against the "kept-women syndrome where you are content taking a subordinate role within the organization in terms of what you do and how much you are paid simply to avoid going out and developing your own client base." Yet Joe understands why some women fall into the trap. Barry Walker, also an attorney, believes: "Men are more comfortable taking a risk because they're already there. They have less to lose if someone turns them down and a buddy to call when they need help."

Fourth, fear clouds the lens with which some men view women. Joe Leghorn quickly acknowledges that his female colleagues face subtle barriers that men do not: "There are still a large number of men who are threatened by women. 'I'm not going to be beaten by a girl.' It goes back to the grade-school mentality. Some men feel a certain discomfort with not knowing how to deal with women as equals."

Fifth, no two people interpret the same event exactly the same way. Anyone can misjudge a woman's behavior as readily as a man's, suggests negotiation expert Richard Shell, particularly when it comes to gender-based communication cues and rituals. Observe a woman's place at the conference table, he suggests: "Women may be just as competitive, the underlying effect might be just as competitive, but their communication process *looks* less competitive. When you see women negotiating with other women, they look a little more relaxed. They look a little more attentive with each other, as if they are really listening instead of making up what they're going to say next. They may or may not, in fact, be doing that."

Deborah Kolb, also a negotiation expert, attributes differences in negotiation style to differences in the exercise of power. "Power is often conceived as the ability to exert control over others through the use of strength, authority, or expertise to obtain an outcome on one's own terms . . . Power gained at the expense of others may feel alien to some women . . . Because women may feel that assertiveness can lead away from connection, they tend to emphasize the needs of others so as to allow them to feel powerful."

The real question becomes: Through the lens of whose culture do we make these judgments about power, competence, and acceptance that determine the daily practice in the places we work?

The Lens of a Different Culture

According to Jean Baker Miller, author of *Toward a New Psychology of Women*, people often mislabel certain stereotypically female characteristics because they do not traditionally think of them as a source of power. As a result, she asserts, strengths "have been called 'weaknesses' and even women, themselves, have so interpreted them."

Perceptions and misperceptions about what constitutes strong or weak often spring from gender-based assumptions. As an example, says Frank Andryauskas: "Collaboration has been seen as a weakness in many organizations, even in those that espouse a team image." Under the old rules of the game, a hard-charging approach propelled a career forward, but men who rely on the kamikaze tactic may find themselves caught off guard. Frank observes: "Heads-down bullheaded men are finding themselves displaced in collaborative environments. 'Wait a minute! People used to like it when I charged ahead. Now they're saying I'm not a team player.'"

Attorney Joe Leghorn agrees with Frank. In situations that require conflict resolution, Joe feels the need to remind his male colleagues: "Don't be so macho." When that doesn't work, Joe makes his point in a way that usually grabs a man's attention: "Why don't you try to think like a woman on this one?" Joe's real message? "We're not going to move forward without consensus. You've got to achieve consensus instead of just banging your foot on the floor and your fist on the desk."

Keeping it competitive keeps it simple and maintains emotional distance. Explaining the persistent overlay of sports on the work culture, Frank Andryauskas comments: "The sports metaphor appeals to people with strong masculine traits because it simplifies the various battles and struggles that go on in the workplace. The purpose of sports is very, very focused. You know what you have to achieve. You don't have to care too much about the other person."

Ray Ingalls, a business manager, draws upon the concept of work styles to describe the differences he sees between male and female behavior at work. "Is it really more productive when men are aggressive in trying to force their ideas in the workplace?" he wonders. "Or is it better for the company when people work on consensus building instead? Women are in a much better place in the modern workplace because they are able to build good personal relationships more easily. There seems to be less of a need for them to feel competitive with the people around them. Because we're constantly working on teams, it's easier for women in some ways."

In one meeting, Ray recalls, "The roomful of men had such strong and unwavering opinions that no one budged. Everyone just kept repeating his position. They were competing on the level of who had the best idea and, since no one would take a look at anyone else's position, the meeting was really fruitless."

Making the case for a less competitive model, Ray suggests: "A consensus strategy builds up each member of the team without pushing anyone down through an aggressive stance. You don't have to be dominant over people in order to get something done. It's hard for men to follow this model because of how they're acculturated, not being able to show weakness, for example. It inhibits men when you're trying to build a strong team and a team member can't display weakness or uncertainty about something because he's afraid of feeling weak."

Again, it depends on who defines strong and weak. Since many men limit their definitions to those found in the male code, why should they even consider a different point of view? In "Masculinity-Femininity," Lester Gelb offers one possible answer: "Men often lose opportunity for full human existence by being socially coerced into the mythical masculine stereotype for fear of not being 'manly.' They are deprived of the full freedom to express their feelings. . . ."

The Bottom of the Ninth

Psychological theories about men's development have consistently suggested that as men grow older they think more and more like women. In *The Psychology of Supervising the Working Woman,* Donald A. Laird proposed, in 1942, an idea backed by many psychologists today: "Age works like education. The more of it, the more feminine men become. But age does not have as feminizing an effect as education . . . Most men do change more or less toward the feminine side as they grow older." Some of the men I interviewed agree, particularly when they explore the meaning of success.

What motivates men to get up and go to work in the morning? How do they define success?

Investment banker Harry Mills defines success according to a highly competitive model, explaining: "Our society is reward-driven from day one. When you're a little kid, you get a report card. When you get your first job, you get your bonus. And that bonus, or that grade, isn't as important as what the other person got. Competition is the way you measure success."

Though he admits to a highly competitive spirit, Paul Meyers attributes a lot of his success to a burning passion for his work. "You can feel a sickness when you walk into some companies. In our organization, there's an energizing sense of momentum. 'Wow, we're really on to something here.'" For his part, Paul laughingly admits: "I get almost evangelical. I talk about this place with my arms flailing. I'm animated and I'm passionate. When I talk about being evangelical, I think about the old Chinese saying that 'A fish rots from its head.' So if I'm not passionate about the work, I can't expect anybody else to be."

In an article about his career in investment banking, Peter Drake wrote: "I still go to sleep tired every night and wake up scared every morning. But I live in and thrive on the brokerage business." He credits a mentor for having taught him the cornerstones to a rewarding profession: "to work and think independently; to be curious and creative; to write succinctly and to communicate clearly with strong and persuasive selling skills; to take risks and to be scared; and above all, to challenge the wisdom of the status quo."

In Peter's experience, our personal and our professional roles can nourish and inspire one another. "As a research director, I can't be dictating to people. Because then I end up with a bunch of robots. If I didn't have four kids, I don't think I would be as effective in this job." The communication skills that serve him well as a parent work just as well in the fast-paced, high-stakes investment arena, Peter says: "I lead by example. I'm spot-on honest. I don't let things linger. I use rewards and punishments. I push, I cajole, I comfort, I encourage. Creating and setting appropriate expectations, all these things I learned at home."

Having discovered that his "feminine side" helped cement a long-term and highly successful business partnership, senior vice president Jim Barnes, at fifty, feels good about how the skills and values he brings to work coincide with how he leads his personal life. "What really keeps us in business is the people. The investment stuff is boring as all get out. It's easy to do. Anybody can do it. But the hard part is the people. That's the challenge. That's what's interesting. It's always like a puzzle, a nineteen-dimensional puzzle. We've learned those lessons from our clients, from one another, and especially from our wives. And hopefully, it's been beneficial for all of us."

A man's true acceptance of his female colleagues may propel him ahead of the learning curve when it comes to discovering his feminine side. Steve Grossman, fifty-four, praises, in particular, his two sisters for serving as role models both in business and in life outside the office. Acknowledging that elder parent care often falls on a woman's shoulders, Steve says: "The sensitivity, the love, the care, and patience that my sisters exhibit toward our father is a good model for me. I need to do more of that, which is one of the reasons I just came from having lunch with my father." Don't use a desk buried in paperwork as an excuse for not spending more time with family, he advises: "Did that forty-five minutes I spent with my father at lunch today put me behind? Yes, it put me behind. Would I exchange that forty-five minutes for any other forty-five minutes in my day? Absolutely not."(Shortly after this interview took place, Steve's father passed away.)

Fiercely determined to look back at this period in his life with pride, Steve explains: "I didn't want to look back and say, I might have been a good son at some point, but in the bottom of the ninth inning, I let the ball go through my legs."

The Measure of a Man

Aligning the feminine and masculine side that exists within each of us often begins at home, in the way our parents raise us as children and in the behaviors and values we pass on to our own children. Inspired by the example set by his father, Matthew Arnold, the thirty-four-year-old consultant, recalls: "My dad was my role model. He was always home for dinner. He spent a lot of time with me stamp collecting, building models, playing baseball, and other times I remember him coming to my school." His second greatest influence? His wife. "She has always wanted a career," Matthew says, "And that's great. There's no reason why I can't cook and do the laundry and dishes. We can both teach the kids to read, so we're teaching them lessons about values in an equal way."

When I raised the topic of life balance, Matthew immediately interjected, "I don't have any!" As an involved father of two toddlers, Matthew calculates that he has undoubtedly sacrificed some career momentum for the sake of his family life. "It's hard to know for sure," he admits. "I may not have risen as fast as if I'd spent more hours at the office, or if I had a single focus perhaps, or if I had a stay-at-home wife and never had to worry much about family life, but I'm very happy with the way things have turned out. So I don't have regrets."

On the subject of whether he feels working-parent guilt, Matthew answers: "Sure I do. There is a tremendous amount of time during the day each week that they're in someone else's care. We've made our choices, and we just hope and pray it doesn't screw them up in some way." He continues: "I feel guilty at least once a day, but I like to think that we're sending our children a message about work ethic and the value of an education, leading to the value of a career. Hopefully, they'll see work as something outside the family that is also important to their parents."

Selling your soul to the corporation, at the expense of an involved family life, does not appeal to many of the men I interviewed. Just back from a business trip, Frank Andryauskas scheduled our interview around weekend activities with his three children, first checking with his wife for any possible conflicts. Pondering his multiple roles, Frank said: "The balance I've achieved is basically compartmentalization. I say 'These are the hours I'm working' and 'This is my time to be home.'" Unfortunately, Frank adds, technology has eroded the distinct boundaries he has always drawn around each aspect of his life. "It's become more difficult with computers, the Internet, and e-mail that can all be accessed through the home." Still, Frank says, when he picks up a football with his son, he kisses his workday goodbye.

Do men really compartmentalize their work and home roles more easily than women? Management consultant Pat Heim believes they do: "My personal opinion is that some of this behavior is hard-wired. Men tend to live linear lives, 'I'm only doing one thing at a time.' Women tend to do multiple things simultaneously." Explaining the differences, she says: "Men put their lives in boxes. They've got their work box. They've got their home box. They've got their fishing box. And they don't mix up their boxes. So when a man goes home, he's in a new box. A woman's got all of her boxes open all the time."

However, many of the men I talked to expressed a desire to rearrange their "boxes" in terms of priority. Offering his perspective on success, Wharton professor Richard Shell comments: "I think of my home life as being the reason I'm working, so I don't have a whole lot of trouble making family my priority. It's not the other way around. In other words, I don't view my home life as supporting my professional life. My wife and I have always both worked."

What does this mean for the roles Richard and his wife share in the home? "We divide almost everything in the household fifty-fifty, so I do the dishes one night, she does them the next. I help our youngest child with homework one night, and she does the next. I take Saturday for child care and she takes Sunday. I do the grocery shopping this week and she takes over the next." What happens in the Shell household when business travel or evening meetings challenge their carefully crafted schedule? They negotiate, explains Richard: "I'll trade you this afternoon for two nights during the week." Richard emphasizes that they try to remind one another that they should allot some of this "free" time to personal needs, such as exercising or having coffee with a friend.

Investment banker Harry Mills, a father of three children, two in college and one in elementary school, treats his youngest child differently than he did his older two. His profession no longer represents his primary identity. Harry explains it this way: "The older I've gotten, and, frankly, the more successful I've gotten, the more ready I am to focus on family. Now, I will, without any hesitation, go to every one of my son's soccer games and tennis matches, just take off at three in the afternoon." Since Harry has achieved seniority in the office, that perhaps explains his ability to reset his priorities without fear of repercussions. But surely, a revised view of work/life balance figures into the equation as well.

The definition of success, of course, varies from individual to individual. In 1869, a pamphlet entitled *Think and Act: A Series of Articles Pertaining to Men and Women, Work and Wages* offered this perspective: "How often is man represented as the head, woman as the heart! We advocate a union of the head and heart, in both man and woman—a happy blending of the two."

For one CEO, Tom Chase, that idea makes a lot of sense. As Tom weighs the advice he will share with his two sons, he says: "I'm going to encourage my children to listen to their hearts. I want my boys to push for something because it's from their heart, not what's in their head. I've spent a lot of my life trying to figure out what was in my heart. That's what makes the day-to-day rewarding, satisfying, and powerful."

Code Breakers

Connie Moore takes very seriously the fiscal responsibility involved in heading up a 250-person department at a Silicon Valley firm. She also places a wider lens on her role, one that relates very little to gender. "I don't feel that the way I do business really has much of a signature of male or female. 'How do I do the right thing?' is not really a matter of male or female. It's a matter of trying to conduct good business with morality and ethics. It is really through our actions, through our passions, and through our drive that we define ourselves and hopefully bring honor and excellence to our business, our careers, our families, and to ourselves."

With graceful confidence, Connie has pledged to honor business values based on her mind, her heart, and her passion for her work. A good business mind does not require the presence of the Y chromosome. A woman wants to crack the male code in order to achieve equality, not sameness. She would never eliminate the compelling differences between men and women, but she would always open up the workplace culture, creating opportunities to put her unique strengths into practice.

Women want to feel comfortable choosing from a wide range of styles and strategies, following a vision that allows them to feel good about themselves when they peer into the mirror at the end of the day. Jean Baker Miller says it best in *Toward a New Psychology of Women*: ". . . when women begin to perceive forms of strength based on their own life experiences, rather than believing they should have the qualities they attribute to men, they often find new definitions of strength."

Power, not gender alone, determines equal footing. Power sponsors control, and control strengthens position. Given such a long history as majority players, some men may view the sharing of power in the workplace as a personal threat, even if on a subconscious level. Particularly in industries that remain heavily male, men may not appreciate the support they enjoy from organizations whose design reflects a traditional male code.

Real power comes from the confidence we feel in being true to ourselves. As we look through our own gender lens with a clearer understanding of why men think and act the way they do, we can build on this knowledge to assert our own business vision, opening the organizational lens and drawing on a broader range of talent and ideas.

Must a woman play by the traditional male rules of the game in order to succeed? Absolutely not. Instead, she can gain power by deploying the unique strengths of the female mind at work.

Code Breaker #1

Assert your strengths via a compelling business case.

No revolution can succeed until it captures the hearts and minds of those who most resist, or fail to recognize, the need for change. When it comes to working productively with men, making a strong business case reduces the chance that gender will enter the process. Talked over at a meeting? Reassert your position by stating: "Let me put these numbers on the white board to show you why this proposal makes sense." Ignored by a boss? Volunteer for the high-risk, high-visibility assignment. Tackle the job everyone in the office wants done, but no one dares attempt. No feedback on your work? Do your own benchmarking. Set goals with your boss and ask for continual feedback.

Code Breaker #2

Take pride in your life choices.

You can also make a strong business case for whatever you choose to accomplish in your life. For example, if you choose motherhood, focus on the business case to counteract dangerous misconceptions about mothers in the workplace. To a boss who exclaims: "You're pregnant! How could you do this to me!", respond with the right words, perhaps saying, "You know, I love my job here. Can we talk about my proposal for covering my maternity leave, for handling my clients, and for returning to work." Just the facts. Business continues.

Code Breaker #3

Leverage your strengths and strengthen weaknesses.

Mike Snell, literary agent, proposes: "Learning how a man thinks doesn't mean a woman must think like a man, but she can find useful business tools that she can incorporate into her repertoire of skills. And men feel the same. If I look at a dozen ways a woman thinks, I'll find a few things in there I really ought to be concentrating on developing in myself. That doesn't mean that, at the end, women and men become indistinguishable."

Keep an open mind and sponsor an open culture. To do that, suggests Mike, men and women should consider the next phase in gender politics, what he calls the synthesis stage. A healthy, as opposed to divisive, tension between women and men at work makes life more interesting. "It's not an either/or proposition. It's 'and.' More men and women have evolved to the point where they see that it doesn't make sense to draw a line so clearly between black and white. There's a hell of a lot of gray out there. We all experience the gray and wrestle with the gray."

As law partner Bob Gault recommends, seek unexpected insight from unexpected places. Another man I interviewed, referring to his perspective as a gay man, said: "As an outsider, I listen a lot. I listen to all sides and try to figure out what's motivating a behavior, instead of just reacting to the behavior."

Code Breaker #4

Build your internal customer base.

Encourage non-exclusionary alliances. Be a role model for both men and women. Does that mean you can't schedule regular lunches with a woman friend? Of course not. But also make time to meet informally with your business colleagues. Paul Meyers offers this suggestion: Break bread with the men. Citing his own example for getting to know people one-on-one, Paul says: "I don't go out for beers after work, but we have a cafeteria in the company, and I make darn sure I sit with different people throughout the week. Good executives break bread with other people because there is something special about that. For me, that's being a good manager, plus it builds that internal customer base which makes you a better manager. You don't want to see your colleagues only at meetings."

Stressing the importance of building professional networks, Patricia Hunt Dirlam, a management trainer, observes: "Not only do rainmakers keep in touch, but they call for non-billable and non-business reasons. They become a resource to all who know them." Passing on a client referral, sharing professional journal articles, or inviting a colleague to a professional seminar offer gender-blind strategies for building alliances.

Code Breaker #5

Find your own patch of grass.

If you dislike the tone from the top, vote with your feet whenever you can, choosing where you will work and with whom. Some men you encounter may not yet know the value of forging productive alliances with female peers, so borrow the best from the male code: Don't take it personally. Follow the advice offered by Margaret Hennig and Anne Jardim in *The Managerial Woman*: "Remember that most men's defenses tend to work on a basis of denial: you win some, you lose some, you don't ever really lose everything." If you decide to brave all-male terrain, know what you're getting yourself into, prepare yourself for challenges, but never opt out of a field you love. Consider Glenn Sears's example of gleaning his best leadership lessons from his worst bosses, because he set his mind on projecting a dramatically different tone as he rose through the ranks.

In response to *Fortune*'s annual most-powerful women list, one reader wrote: "You don't change the world if you play by the rules. And the rules in corporate America are established and vigorously enforced by men. So women have two choices: They can stay in familiar territory, play with the guys, and be bound by their rules, or they can find their own patch of grass and create their own rules."

That patch of grass can flourish within a company, in a department or division, or in a business you start for yourself.

Code Breaker #6

Act like a winner.

Convey confidence from the first hello, the first day on the job. Brian O'Neil, now a vice president in a start-up, has spent most of his career in traditional organizations and recommends: "From the first hello with your boss, you should be thinking about the raise you want six months or a year from now."

Seek guidance and feedback from bosses and mentors, but create new opportunities yourself. John Lucas, marketing director for a *Fortune* 500 company, describes what worked for him: "The way I've gotten my last three jobs has been to find new things to work on and propose to the company that I should be working on them. The response has always been: 'Sure, go ahead and work on that.' It doesn't infringe on anybody's territory. It's all new territory."

The challenge of any new venture entails risk. When he first became CEO, Paul Meyers received this advice from a friend: "You know, there's nothing wrong with being afraid. In fact, you'd be an idiot not to be scared. The difference between people who are great successes and those who are not, is in having the courage to execute. So it's OK to be afraid. You just need to summon the courage to execute."

Code Breaker #7

Open the lens and open the culture.

When women and men accept the challenge to make organizations more diverse, they open up the possibilities for collaborative success, employing peoples' differences to engender trust and acceptance. Honest disagreement about a business plan can strengthen the plan. As we explore conflicting options, we often identify new ones that will work even better. Organizations consist, after all, of human beings struggling to work effectively with other human beings.

As we look through the male lens on work, we discover more questions than answers, particularly about how we will raise our daughters and our sons, and the legacy we want to leave for them. Understanding the strengths and the limitations of the male mind at work, we can also examine our own. Human beings are complex and paradoxical creatures, and many aspects of our behavior will continue to dance on a double-edged sword.

We may never fully understand the male mind at work, but that is not the ultimate goal. Our ultimate goal is to reach for our full potential as human beings. As we strive to reach that goal, we can find inspiration in one essential truth: Our strengths often emanate from our differences.

NOTES

Chapter 1

11 William Pollack, *Real Boys: Rescuing Our Sons from the Myths of Boyhood* (New York: Owl Books, Henry Holt and Company, Inc., 1998), p. 188.

11 Samuel Shem, M.D. and Janet Surrey, Ph.D., *We Have to Talk: Healing Dialogues Between Women and Men* (New York: Basic Books, 1998), p. 53.

11 Deborah Tannen, Ph.D., *You Just Don't Understand: Women and Men in Conversation* (New York: Ballantine Books, 1990), pp. 273–274.

14 Pollack, p. 16.

17 Pollack, p. 24.

22 Leslie Brody, *Gender, Emotion, and the Family* (Cambridge, Massachusetts: Harvard University Press, 1999), p. 235.

24 William Betcher, Ph.D., M.D. and William Pollack, Ph.D., *In a Time of Fallen Heroes: The Re-Creation of Masculinity* (New York: Macmillan Publishing Company, 1993), p. 153.

25 Brody, p. 228.

27 Carol Hymowitz, "Men and Women Fall Back into Kids' Roles at Corporate Meetings," *The Wall Street Journal*, December 15, 1998, B1.

Chapter 2

37 Betcher and Pollack, p. 173.

40 Betcher and Pollack, p. 171.

40 Margaret Hennig and Anne Jardim, *The Managerial Woman* (New York: Pocket Books, 1976), p. 71.

41 Hennig and Jardim, p. 41.

41 Betcher and Pollack, p. 138.

44 Betcher and Pollack, p. 184.

46 Hennig and Jardim, p. 41.

46 Pollack, p. 188.

47 Sylvia Senter, Ph.D., *Women at Work* (New York: Coward, McCann, and Geohegan, 1982), p. 26.

47 Mariah Burton Nelson, *Are We Winning Yet?: How Women are Changing Sports and Sports are Changing Women* (New York: Random House, 1991), p. 9.

47 Martha Brandt, "It Went Down to the Wire. . . and Thrilled Us All," *Newsweek* (July 19, 1999), p. 51.

49 Pollack, p. 23

50 Betcher and Pollack, p. 37.

60 Wilbur L. Brower, Ph.D. , *A Little Book of Big Principles: Values and Virtues for a More Successful Life* (Edgewood, Maryland: Duncan & Duncan, 1998), p. 16.

64 Patricia Sellers, "These Women Rule," *Fortune*, October 25, 1999, p. 120.

64 "Letters," *Newsweek*, August 9, 1999, p. 15.

Chapter 3

73 Margaret Cussler, *The Woman Executive* (New York: Harcourt, Brace & Company, 1958), p. 3.

74 *Women in Corporate Leadership: Progress and Prospects* (New York: Catalyst, 1996, p. 15.

76 Rosabeth Moss Kanter, *Men and Women of the Corporation* (New York: Basic Books, 1977), p. 216.

77 Ann M. Morrison, Randall P. White, Ellen Van Velsor, and the Center for Creative Leadership, *Breaking the Glass Ceiling: Can Women Reach the Top of America's Largest Corporations?* Updated Edition (Reading, MA: Addison-Wesley Publishing Company, 1992), pp. 54–55.

79 Shem and Surrey, p. 63.

85 Pollack, p. 24.

86 Senter, p. 27.

87 Hennig and Jardim, p. 96.

92 Radcliffe Public Policy Institute, *Women and Public Discourse, Guest Lecture, Professor Deborah Tannen* (Cambridge, MA: Radcliffe College, 1995), p. 4.

94 Tannen, p. 225.

95 Hennig and Jardim, p. 198.

Chapter 4

100 Pollack, p. 281.

118 Tannen, p. 232.

121 G. Richard Shell, *Bargaining for Advantage* (New York: Viking, 1999), p. 15.

Chapter 5

128 Dale Carnegie, *How to Win Friends and Influence People* (New York: Simon and Shuster, 1936), p. 151.

132 Tannen, p. 150.

134 Tannen, p. 150.

135 Anthony Bianco, "The Prophet of Wall Street," *Newsweek*, June 1, 1998, p. 127.

136 Radcliffe Public Policy Institute, p. 5.

137 Radcliffe Public Policy Institute, p. 8.

137 Regina Barreca, *They Used to Call Me Snow White. . . But I Drifted* (New York: Viking, 1991), p. 136.

138 Barreca, pp. 71–72.

139 Susan Stewart, "Laughing Matters," *Parenting*, November 1998, p. 169.

139 Stewart, p. 168.

139 Barreca, p. 134.

Chapter 6

167 Shem and Surrey, p. 17.

167 Dianne Hales, *Just Like a Woman: How Gender Science is Redefining What Makes Us Female* (New York: Bantam Books, 1999), p. 269.

179 Patricia Sellers, "Women, Sex & Power," *Fortune*, August 5, 1996, p. 44.

179 Sellers, "Women, Sex & Power," p. 42+.

179 Judy B. Rosener, *Harvard Business Review*, November-December, 1990, p. 120.

180 "Debate: Readers and authors face off over HBR's last issue," *Harvard Business Review*, January-February, 1991, p. 153.

181 Sellers, "These Women Rule," p. 120.

Chapter 7

184 Anthony Bianco, "The Rise of a Star," *Business Week*, December 21, 1998, p. 63.

Chapter 8

209 Lester A Gelb, "Masculinity-Femininity: A Study in Imposed Inequality," *Psychoanalysis And Women*, edited by Jean Baker Miller, M.D. (Baltimore, Marlyand: Penguin Books, 1973), p. 366.

209 Jean Baker Miller, *Toward a New Psychology of Women* (Boston: Beacon Press, 1976), p. 36.

210 Hennig and Jardim, pp. 195–196.

213 Jean Baker Miller, *Psychoanalysis and Women*, p. 385.

215 Deborah M. Kolb, "Her Place at the Table: Gender and Negotiation," *Women, Men and Gender: Ongoing Debates*, edited by Mary Roth Walsh (New Haven: Yale University Press, 1997), p. 140.

215 Jean Baker Miller, *Toward a New Psychology of Women*, p. 27.

216 Lester Gelb, p. 368.

217 Donald A. Laird, *The Psychology of Supervising the Working Woman* (New York: McGraw-Hill Book Company, 1942), p. 170.

217 Peter Drake, Ph.D., "Investment Banking: Dreams and Reality," *Alternative Careers in Science: Leaving the Ivory Tower*, edited by Cynthia Robbins-Roth (San Diego: Academic Press, 1998), p. 91.

222 Miller, p. 36.

224 Patricia Hunt Dirlam, "Networking, Rainmaking Go Hand-in-Hand," *Massachusetts Lawyers Weekly*, May 24, 1999, B5.

224 Hennig and Jardim, p. 202.

224 "Letters to Fortune," *Fortune*, November 9, 1998, p. 26.

INDEX